QUOTATIONS
FOR PUBLIC SPEAKERS

"I have gathered a posie of other men's flowers, and nothing but the thread that binds them is mine own."

—Michel de Montaigne

QUOTATIONS FOR PUBLIC SPEAKERS

A HISTORICAL, LITERARY, AND POLITICAL ANTHOLOGY

EDITED BY
U.S. SENATOR ROBERT G. TORRICELLI

RUTGERS UNIVERSITY PRESS
NEW BRUNSWICK, NEW JERSEY

LIBRARY OF CONGRESS CATALOGING-IN-PUBLICATION DATA

Quotations for public speakers : a historical, literary, and political anthology / edited by Robert G. Torricelli.

p. cm.

Includes bibliographical references and index.

ISBN 0-8135-2889-5 (alk. paper)

1. Public speaking. 2. Quotations, English. I. Torricelli, Robert G.

PN4193.I5 Q68 2000

808.5'1—dc21

00-039030

British Cataloging-in-Publication data for this book is available from the British Library

Manufactured in the United States of America

To Susan King Holloway
for every reason that matters

Contents

Introduction

During the first months of 1978, I was hired by Vice President Walter Mondale. I joined the White House staff with all the excitement that one would expect from a twenty-six-year-old recent law school graduate. It wasn't long before I had my first genuinely sobering experience.

The Vice President was scheduled to campaign for Congressman Paul Simon of Illinois. All of the speechwriters were busy and I was expected to draft a few pithy and interesting remarks. Some basic ideas arrived in a simple memo attached to an old black loose-leaf notebook.

Quotations for Public Speakers is what evolved from that notebook. Walter Mondale had borrowed it from Hubert Humphrey and made some additions of his own. It has traveled with me ever since. Often it would rest in the leather pouch behind the seat of my campaign car. Sometimes it traveled the country in my briefcase. It has a new home in my desk on the Senate floor.

Each time that I heard an interesting quotation or read a special passage in a book, I wrote a note in the margin. Political observations were complemented by historical references, lines of poetry, and excerpts from novels. Through the years, these notes amounted to several thousand entries.

The sources are as broad as the language itself. The only common thread is the potential to add power to the spoken word. These are not quotations for a term paper or essay. A quotation for a speech is different. The words must be direct and clear enough to be understood immediately. The ear must grasp its meaning because the eye cannot return to consider it again. The source must add a credibility that reinforces the speaker. The words should stir an emotion or touch some latent truth within the audience.

These are some of the most powerful words that I have encountered during my public life. They offer the public speaker a starting point. Added to the filter of my own experience must be a careful accounting of the timing, tone, and appropriateness of invoking the name and words of another individual. The most important consideration is the speaker's own level of comfort. Both the person quoted and the thought borrowed should be a natural extension. Simply because a Shakespearean character used a phrase that parallels the situation in a locker room at half-time doesn't make it the right reference for a coach. General Patton might have inspired the troops with powerful language, but his words might not create the right imagery for motivating the school board.

Use a quotation to introduce or reinforce a central theme. The right words from a chosen source can bring intensity to your argument. Deliver a quotation in the context of when or why it was first used. Such references not only convey familiarity but offer continuity. Adjust the tone or rhythm of your remarks to bring proper emphasis to the quotation that you have chosen.

This anthology includes over 2,300 references from 840 writers, poets, and politicians. Find a few of your own favorites. Let them become the beginning of your own collection. Call upon them like old friends when a personal or business situation requires an ally in the language. I'm certain that Hubert Humphrey and Walter Mondale would be proud to have you use the margins and add to our collection.

Robert G. Torricelli
United States Senator
Washington, D.C.

Acknowledgments

The genealogy of this book begins with Andrew Dubill. Even before the idea of publication was broached, Andrew threw himself unabashedly into the task of creating an invaluable speechwriting resource. It is due to the quality of his efforts that this published work even exists.

Rabbi Menachem Genack of the Orthodox Union contributed boundless time and energy to this project, devoting himself wholeheartedly to making my vision of the book a reality. The rabbi and his daughter Rachel served as invaluable sources of advice. Their constant infusion of new material, whether gleaned from the rabbi's religious and historical expertise or his prodigious memory, added substance and vitality to the final product.

Heartfelt thanks certainly go to Vice President Walter Mondale, his speechwriter Martin Kaplan, Senator Hubert Humphrey, and the many other members of their staffs for the countless hours they spent collecting many of the quotations that eventually became this book. I am also extremely grateful to Senators Tom Daschle, Robert Byrd, Jack Reed, and Evan Bayh, whose input and submissions were invaluable in our efforts to create an indispensable resource.

Overseeing the many arms of the project was Scott Mulhauser, whose vigilance provided impetus and inspiration to all. He adopted the project and made it a team effort—truly understanding the conceptual basis of the book and devoting his free time to bringing it to completion. Embodying the perfect mix of humor, patience, and perseverance, Scott unified the efforts of everyone involved. Under his guidance, the book tripled in length and improved exponentially in quality.

Michael Lambert and Dana Mulhauser spent countless hours devising categories and divining the origins of obscure quotes. Fired by their keen historical acumen, on many summer days they ventured bravely from their air-conditioned downtown office to the dark recesses of the Library of Congress, where they sought out hundreds of quotes and built new sections of the book. The pride that they took in their work invigorated all of us.

We are deeply grateful to Sarah Lightdale and Ben Neville for coming in early and staying late to enter, edit, format, verify, and forever search for new quotations. Sara Persky, Zach Sheinberg, and a veritable squadron of others also spent substantial time unearthing quotes and pertinent information. As the book neared completion, they were joined by Adam Overett and Dave Steib, who helped to refine this project. Their collective attention to detail and hunger for perfection were what finally allowed the "Great Book of Quotations" to shed its Kinko's binding and don a more flattering hard cover.

I certainly owe a debt of gratitude to Lona Valmoro, whose understanding and flexibility permitted me to orchestrate an undertaking of such daunting size. Andrew Carroll, whose work with me on *In Our Own Words* provided a substantial basis of material for this book, once again lent his support. Professor Louis Feldman spent considerable time and effort in contributing to the depth and accuracy of the Latin section. Bryan Banks spent ample time on the book as well—tweaking and reformatting until everything was synchronized. I would like to thank Shoshanna Poloner and Miriam Posner, who graciously volunteered their time to both reformat the text and input new quotations into the manuscript.

The project would also not have reached its conclusion without Brett Kitt. Brett spent hours on all aspects of the book and truly prepared it for publication. He amalgamated everyone's previous work, added yards of his own research, and tied up every loose end to see this through to completion. A master of proofreading, Brett went through these pages, catching each and every question and answering it resolutely. The book is on shelves today thanks to Brett.

Finally, these acknowledgments would not be complete without thanking Marlie Wasserman and the staff of Rutgers University Press. Their guidance, patience, and confidence in this anthology were certainly integral to its success.

QUOTATIONS
FOR PUBLIC SPEAKERS

I ACTION

"Action is character."

—***F. Scott Fitzgerald,*** *The Last Tycoon,* 1941

"Aggressive fighting for the right is the greatest sport in the world."

—***Theodore Roosevelt***

"As I grow older, I pay less attention to what men say. I just watch what they do."

—***Andrew Carnegie***

"Avoiding danger is no safer in the long run than outright exposure. Life is either a daring adventure or nothing."

—***Helen Keller,*** *The Open Door,* 1957

Between the idea
And the reality
Between the motion
And the act
Falls the shadow.

—***T. S. Eliot,*** "The Hollow Men," 1925

"Delay is preferable to error."

—***Thomas Jefferson,*** letter to George Washington, May 16, 1792

"Deliberation is the function of the many; action is the function of one."

—***Charles de Gaulle,*** *War Memoirs,* 1960

"The difficult we do immediately; the impossible takes a little longer."

—***U.S. Army slogan***

"Do not put off until tomorrow what can be put off until the day-after-tomorrow just as well."

—***Mark Twain***

"Don't take the fence down, until you know why it was put up."

—***Robert Frost***

"Dost thou love life? Then do not squander time; for that's the stuff life is made of."

—***Aristotle***

"Dream as if you'll live forever. Live as if you'll die today."

—***James Dean***

"Even when I had nothing to do I always vaguely felt that I had no time to waste."

—***Napoleon Bonaparte,*** upon his defeat at Waterloo, 1815

"An event had happened, upon which it is difficult to speak, and impossible to be silent."

—***Edmund Burke,*** *Speeches . . . in the Trial of Warren Hastings,* May 5, 1789

"Experience is the child of Thought, and Thought is the child of Action."

—***Benjamin Disraeli,*** *Vivian Grey,* 1826

"Four things come not back—the spoken word, the sped arrow, time past, and the neglected opportunity."

—***Abbas Ibn Al-Ahnaf,*** *Aphorisms*

"The great end of life is not knowledge, but action."

—***Thomas Henry Huxley,*** *Technical Education,* 1877

"Happiness lies not in the mere possession of money. It lies in the joy of achievement, in the thrill of creative effort."

—***Franklin Delano Roosevelt,*** First Inaugural Address, March 4, 1933

"Here I stand. I can do no other."

—***Martin Luther,*** speech to the Diet of Worms, 1521

"Human life nearly resembles iron. When you use it, it wears out. When you don't, rust consumes it."

—***Cato the Elder***

"If I rest, I rust."

—***Martin Luther***

"If you will it, it is no dream."

—***Theodor Herzl,*** at the First Zionist Congress, Basel, Switzerland, 1897

"I have set before you life and death, blessing and cursing: therefore, choose life!"

—***Deuteronomy 30:19***

"In actual life every great enterprise begins with and takes its first forward step in faith."

—***Frederich von Schlegel***

"Indifference . . . is not only a sin, it is a punishment."

—***Elie Wiesel,*** on a visit to the White House, April 12, 1999

"In this theater of man's life, it is reserved only for God and for angels to be lookers-on."

—***Francis Bacon***

"It doesn't matter how small the beginning may seem to be; what is once done well is done forever."

—***Henry David Thoreau***

"It is better to light one candle than to curse the darkness."

—***Chinese proverb***

"It is hard to fail, but it is worse never to have tried to succeed."

—***Theodore Roosevelt,*** speech at the Hamilton Club, Chicago, April 10, 1899

"It is necessary only for the good man to do nothing for evil to triumph."

—***Edmund Burke***

"I was seldom able to see an opportunity until it had ceased to be one."

—***Mark Twain***

I would rather be ashes than dust,
I would rather my spark should burn out in a brilliant blaze,
Than it should be stifled dry rot.
I would rather be a superb meteor,
Than a sleepy and permanent planet.

—***Jack London***

"Life is doing things, not making things."

—***Aristotle***

"Life is one long process of getting tired."

—***Samuel Butler,*** *Notebooks,* 1912

"Never mistake motion for action."

—***Ernest Hemingway***

"Nothing will ever be attempted if all possible objections must be first overcome."

—***Samuel Johnson,*** *Rasselas,* 1759

"An ounce of sweat will save a gallon of blood."

—***Gen. George S. Patton,*** rallying American troops in Britain, June 1944

"People today distinguish between knowledge and action and pursue them separately, believing that one must know before he can act. Consequently, to the last day of life, they will never act and also will never know."

—***Wang Yang-ming,*** *Instructions for Practical Living,* a Confucian text

"A person may cause evil to others not only by his action but by his inaction, and in either case he is justly accountable to them for the injury."

—***John Stuart Mill***

"Procrastination is the thief of time."

—***Edward Young,*** *Night Thoughts,* 1742–1746

"The proper function of a man is to live, not exist. I shall not waste my days trying to prolong them. I shall use my time."

—***Jack London***

"Rhetoric is a poor substitute for action, and we have trusted only to rhetoric. If we are really to be a great nation, we must not merely talk; we must act big."

—***Theodore Roosevelt,*** speech at the Hamilton Club, Chicago, April 10, 1899

"So little done, so much to do."

—***Cecil Rhodes,*** on the day of his death, 1902

"Somewhere deep down we know that in the final analysis we *do* decide things and that even our decisions to let someone else decide are really *our* decisions, however pusillanimous."

—***Harvey Cox,*** *On Not Leaving It to the Snake,* 1967

"They never fail who die in a great cause."

—***George Gordon, Lord Byron,*** *Marino Faliero,* 1821

"Think like a man of action, act like a man of thought."

—***Henri Bergson***

"To be busy is man's only happiness."

—***Mark Twain***

"The value of life lies not in the length of days, but in the use we make of them."

—***Michel de Montaigne,*** *Essays,* 1580–1588

"Vision without action is a daydream. Action without vision is a nightmare."

—***Japanese proverb***

"We are that which we repeatedly do. Excellence, therefore, is not an act but a habit."

—***Aristotle***

"We know which a person thinks not when he tells us what he thinks, but by his actions."

—***Isaac Bashevis Singer***

"Wherever there's a fight so hungry people can eat, I'll be there. Wherever there's a cop beatin' up a guy, I'll be there. I'll be in the way guys yell when they're mad. I'll be in the way kids laugh when they're hungry an' they know supper's ready. An' when the people are eatin' the stuff they raise, livin' in the homes they build—I'll be there, too."

—***Henry Fonda as Tom Joad,*** in the 1940 film version of John Steinbeck's *The Grapes of Wrath*

"While women weep, as they do now, I will fight. While men go to prison, in and out, in and out, as they do now, I will fight. While there is a drunkard left, while there is a poor lost girl upon the streets, while there remains one dark soul without the light of God, I'll fight. I'll fight to the very end."

—***William Booth.*** Inscribed at the entrance of the Salvation Army's office in New York City

"Who can protest and does not is an accomplice in the act."

—***The Talmud***

"The world is divided into people who do things and people who get the credit. Try, if you can, to belong to the first class. There's far less competition."

—***Dwight Morrow***

"You've got to be very careful if you don't know where you are going, because you might not get there."

—***Yogi Berra***

2 AGE AND AGING

"Age is nothing but experience and some of us are more experienced than others."

—***Andy Rooney,*** at age seventy-four

"At 50, everyone has the face he deserves."

—***George Orwell,*** last words written in his notes

"At twenty years of age the will reigns; at thirty the wit; at forty the judgement."

—***Benjamin Franklin***

"By my rambling digressions I perceive myself to be growing old."

—***Benjamin Franklin,*** *Autobiography,* 1798

"The first half of life consists of the capacity to enjoy without the chance; the last half consists of the chance without the capacity."

—***Mark Twain***

"Great artists say that the most beautiful thing in the world is a little baby. Well, the next most beautiful thing is an old lady, for every wrinkle is a picture."

—***Will Rogers***

"Growing old is no more than a bad habit which a busy man has no time to form."

—***André Maurois,*** *The Art of Living,* 1940

"If wrinkles must be written on our brows, let them not be written upon the heart. The spirit should never grow old."

—***James A. Garfield***

"I'll never make the mistake of being seventy again."

—***Casey Stengel***

"I'm at an age when my back goes out more than I do."

—***Phyllis Diller,*** *The Joys of Aging and How to Avoid Them,* 1981

"I'm having a glorious old age. One of my greatest delights is that I have outlived most of my opposition."

—***Maggie Kuhn,*** speech to Vermont state legislature, 1991

"It gives me great pleasure to converse with the aged. They have been over the road that all of us must travel, and know where it is rough and difficult and where it is level and easy."

—***Plato,*** *The Republic*

"It takes some little time to accept and realize the fact that while you have been growing old, your friends have not been standing still in the matter."

—***Mark Twain,*** *Life on the Mississippi,* 1883

"I was brought up to respect my elders and now I don't have to respect *anybody.*"

—***George Burns,*** at age eighty-seven

"I will not make age an issue. . . . I am not going to exploit for political purposes my opponent's youth and inexperience."

—***Ronald Reagan,*** presidential incumbent at age seventy-three, in televised debate with opponent Walter F. Mondale, 1984

"Just old age. It's the only disease, Mr. Thompson, that you don't look forward to being cured of."

—***Everett Sloane as Mr. Bernstein*** in the film *Citizen Kane,* screenplay by Herman J. Mankiewicz and Orson Welles, 1941

"Life would be infinitely happier if we could only be born at the age of eighty and gradually approach eighteen."

—***Mark Twain***

"A man is not old until regrets take the place of dreams."

—***John Barrymore,*** quoted in *Good Night, Sweet Prince,* by Gene Fowler, 1944

"A man over ninety is a great comfort to all his elderly neighbors: he is a picket-guard at the extreme outpost; and the young folks of sixty and seventy feel that the enemy must get by him before he can come near their camp."

—***Oliver Wendell Holmes,*** *The Guardian Angel,* 1867

"The man who is a pessimist before forty-eight knows too much; if he is an optimist after it, he knows too little."

—***Mark Twain***

"The man who views the world at fifty the same as he did at twenty has wasted thirty years of his life."

—***Muhammad Ali,*** interview, 1975

"My experience is that as soon as people are old enough to know better, they don't know anything at all."

—***Oscar Wilde,*** *Lady Windermere's Fan,* 1892

"Nothing so dates a man as to decry the younger generation."

—***Adlai Stevenson,*** speech at the University of Wisconsin, Madison, 1952

"Old age isn't so bad when you consider the alternative."

—***Maurice Chevalier***

"The old believe everything, the middle-aged suspect everything, and the young know everything."

—***Oscar Wilde***

"The older I get . . . the more I become aware that I have more yesterdays than tomorrows."

—***Bill Clinton,*** commencement speech at Princeton University, June 4, 1996

"The older I grow, the more apt I am to doubt my own judgement of others."

—***Benjamin Franklin,*** 1787

"Old men are twice children."

—***Aristophanes,*** *The Clouds*

"One should never trust a woman who tells her real age. A woman who would tell one that, would tell one anything."

—***Oscar Wilde,*** *A Woman of No Importance,* 1893

"Perhaps one has to be very old before one learns how to be amused rather than shocked."

—***Pearl S. Buck,*** *China, Past and Present,* 1972

"The person who has lived the most is not the one with the most years but the one with the richest experiences."

—***Jean Jacques Rousseau,*** *Emile,* 1762

"That is the great fallacy, the wisdom of old men. They do not grow wise. They grow careful."

—***Ernest Hemingway,*** *A Farewell to Arms,* 1929

"This increase in the life span and in the number of our senior citizens presents this Nation with increased opportunities: the opportunity to draw upon their skill and sagacity—and the opportunity to provide the respect and recognition they have earned. It is not enough for a great nation merely to have added new years to life—our objective must also be to add new life to those years."

—***John F. Kennedy,*** special message to the Congress on the needs of the nation's senior citizens, 1963

"When our vices quit us we flatter ourselves that it is we who quit them."

—***François, duc de La Rochefoucauld,*** *Maxims,* 1665

"Wrinkles should merely indicate where smiles have been."

—***Mark Twain***

"Yet somehow our society must make it right and possible for old people not to fear the young or be deserted by them, for the test of a civilization is in the way that it cares for its helpless members."

—***Pearl S. Buck,*** *My Several Worlds,* 1954

You and I are old; old age hath yet his honor and his toil.
Death closes all; but something ere the end,
Some work of noble note, may yet be done,
Not unbecoming men that strove with Gods.
The lights begin to twinkle from the rocks;
The long day wanes; the slow moon climbs; the deep
Moans round with many voices. Come, my friends,
'Tis not too late to seek a newer world.

—***Alfred, Lord Tennyson,*** "Ulysses," 1842

"You realize that the time you have is limited, and you want to live like a laser beam instead of a shotgun."

—***Bill Clinton***

"Youth is a blunder, manhood a struggle, old age a regret."

—***Benjamin Disraeli***

3 AMERICA

"All America is thrown into one mass. Where are your landmarks—your boundaries of colonies? They are all thrown down. The distinctions between Virginians, Pennsylvanians, New Yorkers, and New Englanders are no more. I am not a Virginian, but an American."

—***Patrick Henry,*** speech to the Continental Congress, Philadelphia, September 5, 1774

"All of us, from the wealthiest and most powerful of men, to the weakest and hungriest of children, share one precious possession: the name *American.*"

—***Robert F. Kennedy,*** speech to the Citizens Union, New York, December 14, 1967

"America has a unique record. We never lost a war and we never won a conference in our lives."

—***Will Rogers,*** radio broadcast, April 6, 1930

"America is a vast conspiracy to make you happy."

—***John Updike,*** *Problems,* 1980

"America is much more than a geographical fact. It is a political and moral fact—the first community in which men set out in principle to institutionalize freedom, responsible government, and human equality."

—***Adlai Stevenson***

"America is not a mere body of traders; it is a body of free men. Our greatness—built upon freedom—is moral, not material. We have a great ardor for gain; but we have a deep passion for the rights of man."

—***Woodrow Wilson,*** speech, New York, December 6, 1911

"America is not like a blanket—one piece of unbroken cloth, the same color, the same texture, the same size. America is more like a quilt—many patches, many pieces, many colors, many sizes, all woven and held together by a common thread."

—***Jesse Jackson,*** address to the Democratic National Convention, July 17, 1984

"America is the only nation in history which miraculously has gone from barbarism to degeneracy without the usual interval of civilization."

—***Georges Clemenceau,*** quoted in the *Saturday Review,* December 1, 1945

"[America] is the well-wisher to the freedom and independence of all. She is the champion and vindicator only of her own. She will recommend the general cause, by the countenance of her voice, and the benignant sympathy of her example."

—***John Quincy Adams,*** *An Address . . . Celebrating the Anniversary of Independence, at the City of Washington on the Fourth of July, 1821*

"The American Journey has not ended. America is never accomplished. America is always still to build; for men, as long as they are truly men, will dream of man's fulfillment."

—***Archibald MacLeish,*** speech at the Economic Club of New York, November 13, 1961

"As long as men are not free—in their lives and their opinions, their speech and their knowledge—that long will be the American Revolution not be finished."

—***Robert F. Kennedy,*** commencement address, Queens College, New York, June 15, 1965

"The business of America is not business. Neither is it war. The business of America is justice and securing the blessings of liberty."

—***George Will***

"But where, say some, is the King of America? I'll tell you, Friend, he reigns above."

—***Thomas Paine,*** *Common Sense,* 1776

"The commitment I seek is not to outworn views but to old values that will never wear out. Programs may sometimes become obsolete, but the ideal of fairness always endures. Circumstances may change, but the work of compassion must continue. It is surely correct that we cannot solve problems by throwing money at them; but it is also true that we dare not throw our national problems into a scrap heap of inattention and indifference. The poor may be out of political fashion, but they are not without human needs. The middle class may be angry, but they have not lost the dream that all Americans can advance together."

—*Edward Kennedy,* address to the Democratic National Convention, August 12, 1980

"Either the United States will destroy ignorance or ignorance will destroy the United States."

—*W.E.B. Du Bois,* speech at Harpers Ferry, Virginia, August 1906

"An Englishman is a person who does things because they have been done before. An American is a person who does things because they haven't been done before."

—*Mark Twain*

"The faithful marble may preserve their image; the engraven brass may proclaim their worth; but the humblest sod of Independent America, with nothing but the dew-drops of the morning to gild it, is a prouder mausoleum than kings or conquerors can boast. The country is their monument. Its independence is their epitaph."

—*Edward Everett,* memorial address honoring John Adams and Thomas Jefferson (who died the same day, July 4, 1826), Charlestown, Massachusetts, August 1, 1826

"Fellow-citizens, we cannot escape history."

—*Abraham Lincoln,* First State of the Union Address, December 1, 1862

"For more than three centuries, the word 'American' designated a man who was defined not by what he had done, but what he would do."

—*Octavio Paz*

"For the American people are a very generous people and will forgive almost any weakness, with the possible exception of stupidity."

—*Will Rogers*

"For we must consider that we shall be as a city upon a hill. The eyes of all people are upon us."

—*John Winthrop,* evoking Matthew 5:14 in "A Modell of Christian Charity," a sermon delivered aboard the *Arabella* on the way to America, 1630

"The genius of the United States is not best or most in its executives or legislatures nor in its ambassadors or authors, or colleges or churches or parlors, nor even in its newspapers or inventors—but always most in the common people, south, north, west, east, in all its states, through all its mighty amplitude."

—***Walt Whitman,*** Preface to *Leaves of Grass,* 1855

"God has special providence for mad dogs, Englishmen in the noonday sun, and the United States of America."

—***Otto von Bismarck***

"God preserve the United States. We know the race is not to the swift nor the battle to the strong. Do you not think an Angel rides in the whirlwind and directs this storm?"

—***John Page,*** letter to Thomas Jefferson, two weeks after the signing of the Declaration of Independence, July 18, 1776

"I anticipate the day when to command respect in the remotest regions it will be sufficient to say, 'I am an American.'"

—***Gouverneur Morris,*** address to the U.S. Senate, 1800

"I have no misgivings about or lack of confidence in, the cause in which I am engaged, and my courage does not halt or falter. I know how strongly American civilization now leans on the triumph of the Government, and how great a debt we owe to those who went before us through the blood and sufferings of the Revolution. And I am willing—perfectly willing—to lay down all my joys in this life, to help maintain this Government, and to pay that debt."

—***Sullivan Ballou,*** major, Second Rhode Island Volunteers, last letter to his wife, Sarah, prior to the First Battle of Bull Run, July 14, 1861

"I look forward to an America which commands respect throughout the world, not only for its strength, but for its civilization as well. And I look forward to a world which will be safe not only for democracy and diversity but also for personal distinction."

—***John F. Kennedy,*** speech at Amherst College, October 26, 1963

"In America, Surrealism is invisible for all is larger than life."

—***Salvador Dali***

"In no other country in the world is aspiration so definite a part of life as it is in America. The most precious gift God has given to this land is not its great riches of soil and forest and land but the divine discontent planted deeply in the hearts of the American people."

—***William Allen White***

"In the Old World, the first things you see as you approach a great city are steeples; here you see, first, centers of intelligence."

—***Thomas Henry Huxley***

"I sought for the greatness and genius of America in her commodious harbors and her ample rivers—and it was not there, in her fertile fields and boundless forests—and it was not there, in her rich mines and vast world commerce—and it was not there, in her democratic Congress and her matchless Constitution—and it was not there. Not until I went to the churches of America and heard her pulpits aflame with righteousness did I understand the secret of her genius and power. America is great because she is good, and if America ever ceases to be good, America will cease to be great."

—***Alexis de Tocqueville,*** *Democracy in America,* 1835–1840

"It was already a region accustomed to dealing in millions—'the land of the endless noughts.'"

—***Paul Johnson,*** on the prosperity of the colonies
in *A History of the American People,* 1997

"No nation ever had two better friends than we have. You know who they are. Well, they are the Atlantic and the Pacific Ocean."

—***Will Rogers***

"Our gross national product does not allow for the health of our children, the quality of their education, or the joy of their play. It does not include the beauty of our poetry or the strength of our marriages, the intelligence of our public debate or the integrity of our public officials. It measures neither our wit nor our courage, neither our wisdom nor our learning, neither our compassion nor our devotion to our country; it measures everything, in short, except that which makes life worthwhile. And it can tell us everything about America except why we are proud that we are Americans."

—***Robert F. Kennedy,*** "Recapturing America's Moral Vision,"
speech at the University of Kansas, Lawrence,
March 18, 1968

"Ours is the only country deliberately founded on a good idea."

—***John Gunther,*** *Inside U.S.A.,* 1947

"A place of full tables and open doors."

—***Anonymous visitor*** to the United States

"The principle of free governments adheres to the American soil. It is imbedded in it—immovable as its mountains."

—***Daniel Webster,*** at the dedication of the Bunker Hill Monument, Charlestown, Massachusetts, June 17, 1825

"There are no people in the world who are so slow to develop hostile feelings against a foreign country as the Americans and there are no people who, once estranged, are more difficult to win back."

—***Winston Churchill***

"There is no room in this country for hyphenated Americanism."

—***Theodore Roosevelt,*** speech, October 12, 1915

"There's the one thing no nation can ever accuse us of and that is secret diplomacy. Our foreign dealings are an open book, generally a check book."

—***Will Rogers***

"The trouble with this country is that there are too many people going around saying, 'the trouble with this country is——.'"

—***Sinclair Lewis,*** *Dodsworth,* 1929

"They [the Americans] have all a lively faith in the perfectability of man, they judge that the diffusion of knowledge must necessarily be advantageous, and the consequences of ignorance fatal; they all consider society as a body in a state of improvement, humanity as a changing scene, in which nothing is, or ought to be, permanent; and they admit that what appears to them today to be good, may be superseded by something better tomorrow."

—***Alexis de Tocqueville,*** *Democracy in America,* 1835–1840

"This country will not be a really good place for any of us to live in if it is not a really good place for all of us to live in."

—***Theodore Roosevelt***

Thou, too, sail on, O ship of State!
Sail, on, O UNION, strong and great!
Humanity with all its fears,
With all the hopes of future years,
Is hanging breathless on thy fate!

—***Henry Wadsworth Longfellow,*** "The Building of the Ship," 1849

"['Tis] not the affair of a City, a County, a Province, or a Kingdom; but of a *Continent*—of one-eighth part of the habitable Globe. 'Tis not the concern of a day, a year, or an age; posterity is virtually involved in the contest, and will be more or less affected even to the end of time, by the proceedings now. The cause of America is . . . the cause of all mankind."

—***Thomas Paine,*** *Common Sense,* 1776

"The vigor of our history comes, largely, from the fact that, as a comparatively young nation we have gone fearlessly ahead doing things that were never done before."

—***Franklin Delano Roosevelt***

"We Americans today are fortunate that our statues of Lincoln have marble eyes; were they human eyes, I fear we would wilt before their gaze."

—***Karl Vollmer***

"We are not a narrow tribe of men. . . . No: our blood is as the flood of the Amazon, made up of a thousand noble currents all pouring into one. We are not a nation, so much as a world."

—***Herman Melville,*** *Redburn,* 1849

"We are the only hope of mankind. Dare we reject it and break the hearts of the world?"

—***Woodrow Wilson,*** arguing for U.S. participation in the League of Nations, July 10, 1919

"We become not a melting pot but a beautiful mosaic. Different people, different beliefs, different yearnings, different hopes, different dreams."

—***Jimmy Carter,*** speech, Pittsburgh, Pennsylvania, October 27, 1976

"We can get hot and bothered quicker over nothing, and cool off faster than any nation in the world."

—***Will Rogers***

"When our nation was founded, there was a holy Roman Emperor, Venice was a Republic, France was ruled by the King, China and Japan by an Emperor, Russia by a Czar, and Great Britain had only the barest beginnings of a democracy. All of these proud regimes and scores of others have long since passed into history, and among the world's powers, the only government that stands essentially unchanged is the Federal Union put together in the 1780s by thirteen states on the east coast of North America."

—***Walter F. Mondale***

"Whoever is fighting for liberty is defending America."

—*William Allen White*

"The wrecks of the past were America's warnings."

—*George Bancroft*

4 THE ARTS

"The aim of art is to represent not the outward appearance of things, but their inward significance."

—***Aristotle***

"The aim of every artist is to arrest motion, which is life, by artificial means and hold it fixed so that a hundred years later, when a stranger looks at it, it moves again since it is life."

—***William Faulkner,*** interview, 1958

"All art consists in bringing something into existence."

—***Aristotle,*** *Nicomachean Ethics*

"All art is a revolt, a protest against extinction, a rebellious act against death and man's tragic mortality."

—***André Malraux,*** *Voices of Silence,* 1956

"All art is but imitation of nature."

—***Seneca,*** *Epistulae Morales*

"Architects cannot teach nature anything."

—***Mark Twain***

"Art does not exist only to entertain, but also to challenge one to think, to provoke, even to disturb, in a constant search for truth."

—***Barbra Streisand,*** speech to the JFK School of Government, Harvard, in defense of the National Endowment for the Arts, February 3, 1995

"Art is a collaboration between God and the artist, and the less the artist does the better."

—***André Gide***

"Art is an extension of language—an expression of sensations too subtle for words."

—***Robert Henri,*** *The Art Spirit,* 1923

"Art is a revolt against fate."

—***André Malraux,*** *Voices of Silence,* 1951

"Art is either a revolutionist or a plagiarist."

—***Paul Gauguin***

"Art is essentially the affirmation, the blessing, and the deification of existence."

—***Friedrich Nietzsche,*** *The Will to Power,* 1888

"Art is meant to disturb. Science reassures."

—***Georges Braque,*** *Pensées sur l'art,* 1948

"Art is too serious to be taken seriously."

—***Ad Reinhardt***

"The artist is not a special kind of man, but every man is a special kind of artist."

—***Ananda Coomaraswamy,*** *Transformation of Nature in Art,* 1934

"An artist is primarily one who has faith in himself. He does not respond to the normal stimuli: he is neither a drudge nor a parasite. He lives to express himself and in so doing enriches the world."

—***Henry Miller,*** "Dr. Souchon: Surgeon-Painter," *The Air-Conditioned Nightmare,* 1945

"The artist's morality lies in the force and truth of his description."

—***Jules Barbey d'Aurevilly,*** Introduction to *Une Vieille Maîtresse,* 1851

"An authentic work of art must start an argument between the artist and his audience."

—***Rebecca West,*** *The Count and the Castle,* 1957

"Bad art is a great deal worse than no art at all."

—***Oscar Wilde,*** "House Decoration," lecture, 1882

"Being an artist means ceasing to take seriously that very serious person we are when we are not an artist."

—***José Ortega y Gasset,*** *The Dehumanization of Art,* 1925

"A book should serve as an axe to the ice inside us."

—***Franz Kafka***

"By artist I mean of course everyone who has tried to create something which was not here before him, with no other tools and material than the uncommerciable ones of the human spirit."

—***William Faulkner,*** speech, New York City, January 25, 1955

"Can't act. Can't sing. Slightly bald. Can dance a little."

—***Report on Fred Astaire's first screen test***

"A doctor can bury his mistakes, but an architect can only advise his clients to plant vines."

—***Frank Lloyd Wright***

"Drawing is the art of taking a line for a walk."

—***Paul Klee***

"Every artist dips his brush in his own soul, and paints his own nature into his pictures."

—***Henry Ward Beecher***

"Every child is an artist. The problem is how to remain an artist once he grows up."

—***Pablo Picasso***

"Every great work of art has two faces, one toward its own time and one toward the future, toward eternity."

—***Daniel Barenboim***

"Every master knows that the material teaches the artist."

—***Ilya Ehrenburg,*** "What I Have Learned,"
Saturday Review, 1967

"Fine art is that in which the hand, the head, and the heart go together."

—***John Ruskin,*** "The Two Paths," *Art and Life,* 1886

"He is the true enchanter whose spell operates, not upon the senses, but upon the imagination and the heart."

—***Washington Irving,*** "Stratford on Avon," *The Sketch Book of Geoffrey Crayon, Gent.,* 1819–1820

"If art is to nourish the roots of our culture, society must set the artist free to follow his vision wherever it takes him."

—***John F. Kennedy,*** speech at Amherst College, October 26, 1963

"If you ask me what I can do in this world, I, an artist, will answer you: I am here to live out loud."

—***Émile Zola,*** *Mes Haines,* 1866

"If you gotta ask what jazz is, you'll never know."

—***Louis Armstrong***

"If you want to know what actually is occurring inside, underneath, at the center, at any given moment, art is a truer guide than politics more often than not."

—***Wyndham Lewis,*** *Time and Western Man,* 1927

"If you would have me weep, you must first of all feel grief yourself."

—***Horace,*** *Ars Poetica*

"I have been told that Wagner's music is better than it sounds."

—***Mark Twain***

"I know with certainty that a man's work is nothing but the long journey to recover, through the detours of art, the two or three simple and great images which first gained access to his heart."

—***Albert Camus***

"I look forward to an America which will not be afraid of grace and beauty."

—***John F. Kennedy,*** speech at Amherst College, October 26, 1963

"In art, as in love, instinct is enough."

—***Anatole France,*** *Le Jardin d'épicure,* 1895

"I saw the angel in the marble and carved until I set him free."

—***Michelangelo***

"It is art that *makes* life, makes interest, makes importance . . . and I know of no substitute whatever for the force and beauty of its process."

—***Henry James,*** letter to H. G. Wells, 1915

It is the glory and good of art
That art remains the one way possible
Of speaking truth,—to mouths like mine, at least.

—***Robert Browning,*** *The Ring and the Book,* 1868

"Life beats down and crushes the soul, and art reminds you that you have one."

—***Stella Adler***

"Life is very nice, but it lacks form. It's the aim of art to give it some."

—***Jean Anouilh,*** *The Rehearsal,* 1950

"Literature is the immortal part of history; it is the best and most enduring part of personality. But book-friends have this advantage over living friends; you can enjoy the most truly aristocratic society in the world whenever you want it. The great dead are beyond our physical reach, and the great living are usually almost as inaccessible; as for our personal friends and acquaintances, we cannot always see them. Perchance they are asleep, or away on a journey. But in a private library, you can at any moment converse with Socrates or Shakespeare or Carlyle or Dumas or Dickens or Shaw or Barrie or Galsworthy."

—***William Lyon Phelps,*** April 6, 1933

"A man paints with his brains and not with his hands."

—***Michelangelo***

"Most works of art, like most wines, ought to be consumed in the district of their fabrication."

—***Rebecca West,*** "Journey's End Again," *Ending in Earnest,* 1931

"Music is the best means we have of digesting time."

—***W. H. Auden,*** "In Praise of Limestone," 1948

"Music played at weddings always reminds me of the music played for soldiers before they go into battle."

—***Heinrich Heine***

"One of my chief regrets during my years in the theater is that I couldn't sit in the audience and watch me."

—***John Barrymore***

"Painting is a blind man's profession. He paints not what he sees, but what he feels, what he tells himself about what he has seen."

—***Pablo Picasso***

"Poetry is a way of taking life by the throat."

—***Robert Frost***

"Poetry is man's rebellion against being what he is."

—***James Branch Cabell,*** *Jurgen,* 1919

"The poet's voice need not merely be the record of man. It can be one of the props, the pillars to help him endure and prevail."

—***William Faulkner,*** accepting the Nobel Prize for literature, Stockholm, Sweden, December 10, 1950

"Some editors are failed writers, but so are most writers."

—***T. S. Eliot***

"There are painters who transform the sun into a yellow spot, but there are others who, thanks to their art and intelligence, transform a yellow spot into the sun."

—***Pablo Picasso***

"There are two golden rules for an orchestra: start together and finish together. The public doesn't give a damn what goes on in between."

—***Thomas Beecham***

"There is a great deal to be said for the Arts. For one thing they offer the only career in which commercial failure is not necessarily discreditable."

—***Evelyn Waugh,*** *A Little Order: Careers for Our Sons: Literature,* 1977

"There is no better deliverance from the world than through art; and a man can form no surer bond with it than through art."

—***Johann Wolfgang von Goethe,*** *Elective Affinities,* 1809

"This is not a novel to be tossed aside lightly. It should be thrown with great force."

—***Dorothy Parker,*** book review

"Trees have roots; men have legs; as a poet I have wings."

—***Arthur Schnitzler,*** explaining his opposition to Theodor Herzl's desire to transplant the best of European culture to Palestine

"The unwanted cockroach in the kitchen of a frontier society."

—***John Sloan,*** on the American artist

"We all know that Art is not truth. Art is a lie that makes us realize truth."

—***Pablo Picasso***

"We must never forget that art is not a form of propaganda; it is a form of truth."

—***John F. Kennedy,*** speech at Amherst College, October 26, 1963

"When I want to read a novel, I write one."

—***Benjamin Disraeli***

"When power leads man toward arrogance, poetry reminds him of his limitations. When power narrows the areas of man's concern, poetry reminds him of the richness and diversity of his existence. When power corrupts, poetry cleanses. For art establishes the basic human truth which must serve as the touchstone of our judgment. . . . If sometimes our great artists have been the most critical of our society, it is because their sincerity and their concern for justice, which must motivate any true artist, makes them aware that our Nation falls short of its highest potential."

—***John F. Kennedy,*** speech at Amherst College, October 26, 1963

"Without art, the crudeness of reality would make the world unbearable."

—***George Bernard Shaw,*** *Back to Methuselah,* 1921

"The work of art is a part of nature seen through a temperament."

—***André Gide,*** "The Limits of Art," *Pretexts,* 1903

"You must treat a work of art like a great man: stand before it and wait patiently till it deigns to speak."

—***Arthur Schopenhauer***

5 CHARACTER AND ETHICS

"Aim above morality. Be not simply good; be good for something."

—***Henry David Thoreau,*** *Walden,* 1854

"Alike for the Nation and the individual, the one indispensable requisite is character."

—***Theodore Roosevelt***

"Always do right. This will gratify some people, and astonish the rest."

—***Mark Twain***

The art of our necessities is strange,
That can make vile things precious.

—***William Shakespeare,*** *King Lear,* 1608, scene 9

The best lack all conviction, while the worst
Are full of passionate intensity.

—***William Butler Yeats,*** "The Second Coming," 1922

"Conscience: the inner voice that warns us that someone may be looking."

—***H. L. Mencken***

"The difference between perseverance and obstinacy is that one comes from a strong will; and the other from a strong won't."

—***Henry Ward Beecher,*** *Seven Lectures to a Young Man,* 1844

"Difficulties are things that show what men are."

—***Epictetus***

"Drug use is wrong because it is immoral, and it is immoral because it enslaves the mind and destroys the soul."

—***John Q. Wilson***

"Every difference of opinion is not a difference of principle."

—***Thomas Jefferson,*** First Inaugural Address, 1801

"Few things are harder to put up with than the annoyance of a good example."

—***Mark Twain,*** *The Tragedy of Pudd'nhead Wilson,* 1893

"A foolish consistency is the hobgoblin of little minds, adored by little statesmen and philosophers and divines. With consistency a great soul has simply nothing to do."

—***Ralph Waldo Emerson,*** "Self-Reliance," *Essays,* 1841

For one that has been esteemed, disgrace
Is worse than death.

—***Bhagavad Gita 2:34***

"For what is a man profited, if he shall gain the whole world, and lose his own soul?"

—***Matthew 16:26***

"The foundation stone of national life is, and ever must be, the high individual character of the average citizen."

—***Theodore Roosevelt,*** speech decrying "muckrakers," April 14, 1906

"The gentleman understands what is moral. The small man understands what is profitable."

—***Confucius,*** *The Analects*

"Get your principles straight; the rest is a matter of detail."

—***Napoleon Bonaparte***

"Good nature and good sense must ever join; to err is human; to forgive, divine."

—***Alexander Pope,*** *An Essay on Criticism,* 1711

"The greatest of all warriors in the siege of Troy had not the preeminence because nature had given him strength and he carried the largest bow, but because self-discipline had taught him how to bend it."

—***Daniel Webster***

Have more than thou showest,
Speak less than thou knowest,
Lend less than thou owest.

—***William Shakespeare,*** *King Lear,* 1608, scene 4

"He conquered by weapons, but was conquered by his vices."

—***Seneca,*** on Hannibal

"He has all the virtues I dislike and none of the vices I admire."

—***Winston Churchill*** on Sir Stafford Cripps

"He that is good for making excuses is seldom good for anything else."

—***Benjamin Franklin***

"His heart was as great as the world, but there was no room in it to hold the memory of a wrong."

—***Ralph Waldo Emerson,*** "Greatness," *Letters and Social Aims,* 1883

His life was gentle and the elements
So mixed in him that Nature might stand up
And say to all the world: "This was a man!"

—***William Shakespeare,*** Mark Antony on the death of Brutus, *Julius Caesar,* act 5, scene 5

"How easy it is for generous sentiments, high courtesy, and chivalrous courage to lose their influence beneath the chilling blight of selfishness, and to exhibit to the world a man who was great in all the minor attributes of character, but who was found wanting when it became necessary to prove how much principle is superior to policy."

—***James Fenimore Cooper,*** *The Last of the Mohicans,* 1826

How oft the sight of means to do ill deeds
Make deeds ill done!

—***William Shakespeare,*** *King John,* act 4, scene 2

How poor are they that have not patience!
What wound did ever heal but by degrees?

—***William Shakespeare,*** *Othello,* act 2, scene 3

"I am a man of fixed and unbending principles, the first of which is to be flexible at all times."

—***Everett McKinley Dirksen***

"I am being frank about myself in the book. I tell of my first mistake on page 850."

—***Henry Kissinger,*** referring to the second volume of his memoirs, *Years of Upheaval*

"I am not bound to win, but I am bound to be true. I am not bound to succeed, but I am bound to live up to what light I have."

—***Abraham Lincoln,*** in response to critics of his unwavering support for the Union

"I can resist everything except temptation."

—***Oscar Wilde,*** *Lady Windermere's Fan,* 1893

"I count him braver who overcomes his desires than him who conquers his enemies; for the hardest victory is over self."

—***Aristotle***

"I do not criticize persons, but only a state of affairs. It is they, however, who will have to answer for deficiencies at the bar of history."

—***B. H. Liddell Hart***

"If someone can enjoy marching to music in rank and file, I can feel only contempt for him; he has received his large brain by mistake, a spinal cord would have been enough."

—***Albert Einstein,*** *Out of My Later Years,* 1936

"If you aren't fired with enthusiasm, you'll be fired with enthusiasm."

—***Vince Lombardi***

"If you don't stand for something, you'll fall for anything."

—***Maya Angelou***

"If you hate a person, you hate something in him that is part of yourself. What isn't part of ourselves doesn't disturb us."

—***Hermann Hesse,*** *Demian,* 1919

"If you pick up a starving dog and make him prosperous, he will not bite you. This is the principal difference between a dog and a man."

—***Mark Twain,*** *The Tragedy of Pudd'nhead Wilson,* 1893

"If you want to know how a man stands, go among the people who are in his same business."

—***Will Rogers***

"I have never believed there was one code of morality for a public and another for a private man."

—***Thomas Jefferson***

"It is wonderful how well men can keep secrets they have not been told."

—***Winston Churchill***

"Labor to keep alive in your breast that little spark of celestial fire,—conscience."

—***George Washington***

"Let us be thankful for the fools. But for them the rest of us could not succeed."

—***Mark Twain,*** *Following the Equator,* 1898

"The lighthouse in a sea of absurdity."

—***Friedrich Nietzsche*** on Victor Hugo, *The Twilight of the Idols,* 1889

"The louder he talked of his honor the faster we counted our spoons."

—***Ralph Waldo Emerson,*** "Worship," *Essays,* 1841

"The man of wisdom is never of two minds; the man of benevolence never worries; the man of courage is never afraid."

—***Confucius,*** *The Analects*

"Man will do many things to get himself loved; he will do all things to get himself envied."

—***Mark Twain,*** *Following the Equator,* 1898

"The measure of a man's real character is what he would do if he knew he would never be found out."

—***Thomas Babington, Lord Macaulay***

"Misery acquaints a man with strange bed-fellows."

—***William Shakespeare,*** *The Tempest,* act 2, scene 2

"The most dangerous criminal may be the man gifted with reason, but with no morals."

—***Martin Luther King, Jr.,*** "The Purpose of Education," *Maroon Tiger,* January–February 1947

"My heart has always been the master of my judgment."

—***Alexander Hamilton***

"My idea of an agreeable person is a person who agrees with me."

—***Benjamin Disraeli,*** *Lothair,* 1870

"Never allow perfection to become the enemy of the good."

—***Walter F. Mondale***

"Never give in, never give in, never, never, never, never—in nothing, great or small, large or petty—never give in except to convictions of honor and good sense."

—***Winston Churchill,*** address at Harrow School, October 29, 1941

"No one can make you feel inferior without your consent."

—***Eleanor Roosevelt,*** *This Is My Story,* 1937

"No people were ever yet benefited by riches if their prosperity corrupted their virtue. It is more important that we should show ourselves honest, brave, truthful, and intelligent than we should own all the railways and grain elevators in the world. We have fallen heirs to the most glorious heritage a people ever received and each of us must do his part if we wish to show that this nation is worthy of its good fortune."

—***Theodore Roosevelt***

"Nothing is gained, everything is lost, by subordinating principle to expediency."

—***William Lloyd Garrison***

"Nothing is lost save honor."

—***Jim Fisk,*** on the mass sale of his gold holdings, which caused a decline in the worldwide price of gold

"Nothing is worthwhile that is not hard. You do not improve your muscle by doing the easy thing; you improve it by doing the hard thing, and you get your zest by doing a thing that is difficult, not a thing that is easy."

—***Woodrow Wilson,*** commencement address at the Naval Academy at Annapolis, June 5, 1914

"Nothing so needs reforming as other people's habits."

—***Mark Twain***

"Only the shallow know themselves."

—***Oscar Wilde,*** "Phrases and Philosophies for the Use of the Young," 1891

"On the whole it is better to deserve honors and not have them than have them and not deserve them."

—***Mark Twain***

"Rowing to his object with muffled oars."

—***John Randolph,*** on Martin Van Buren's concealment of his quest for the presidency

"Sir, I had rather be right than be President."

—***Henry Clay,*** 1850

"There is no man so good, who, were he to submit all his thoughts to the laws, would not deserve hanging ten times in his life."

—***Michel de Montaigne***

"They are not all saints who use holy water."

—***English proverb***

"Though personally opposed to war with Spain, [McKinley] was unpracticed in the art of living up to his convictions."

—***Barbara Tuchman,*** *The Proud Tower,* 1966

"To know what is right and not to do it is the worst cowardice."

—***Confucius***

"Too often the strong, silent man is silent because he has nothing to say."

—***Winston Churchill***

"Watch your thoughts; they become words. Watch your words; they become actions. Watch your actions; they become habits. Watch your habits; they become your character. Watch your character; it becomes your destiny."

—***Frank Outlaw***

"When a fellow says it hain't the money but the principle o' the thing, it's th' money."

—***Kin Hubbard,*** *Hoss Sense and Nonsense,* 1926

When that the poor have cried, Caesar hath wept:
Ambition should be made of sterner stuff.

—***William Shakespeare,*** *Julius Caesar,* act 3, scene 2

"Where there is patience and humility there is neither anger nor worry."

—***Francis of Assisi***

Who can be wise, amazed, temperate, and furious,
Loyal and neutral, in a moment? No man.

—***William Shakespeare,*** Macbeth justifying his murder of two guards suspected of murdering the king, *Macbeth,* act 2, scene 3

"You can easily judge the character of people by how they treat those who can do nothing for them."

—***Anonymous***

"You shall judge a man by his foes as well as his friends."

—***Joseph Conrad,*** *Lord Jim,* 1900

6 COMPETITION AND SPORTS

"Adversity causes some men to break; others to break records."

—***William A. Ward***

"Americans love a winner. Americans will not tolerate a loser. Americans despise cowards. Americans play to win all the time."

—***Gen. George S. Patton***

"The athlete approaches the end of his playing days the way old people approach death. But the athlete differs from the old person in that he must continue living. Behind all the years of practice and all the hours of glory waits that inexorable terror of living without the game."

—***Bill Bradley***

"Baseball is a game of race, creed, and color. The race is to first base. The creed is the rules of the game. The color? Well, the home team wears white uniforms, and the visiting team wears gray."

—***Joe Garagiola,*** *Baseball Is a Funny Game,* 1960

"Boxing is egalitarian. In the ring, rank, age, color, and wealth are irrelevant. When you are circling your opponent, probing his strengths and weaknesses, you are not thinking about his color or social status."

—***Nelson Mandela,*** *Long Walk to Freedom,* 1995

"Do not tell fish stories where the people know you; but particularly, don't tell them where they know the fish."

—***Mark Twain***

"Every great hitter works on the theory that the pitcher is more afraid of him than he is of the pitcher."

—*Ty Cobb*

"Fall seven times, stand up eight."

—*Japanese proverb*

"Football incorporates the two worst elements of American society: violence punctuated by committee meetings."

—*George Will*

"Go out there and win one for the Gipper."

—*Knute Rockne*

"Golf is a good walk spoiled."

—*Mark Twain*

"If a horse can't eat it, I don't want to play on it."

—***Dick Allen,*** on the introduction of artificial turf onto the baseball field

If all the year were playing holidays,
To sport would be as tedious as to work.

—***William Shakespeare,*** *King Henry IV, Part I,* act 1, scene 2

"I firmly believe that any man's finest hour is that moment when he has worked his heart out in a good cause and lies exhausted on the field of battle, victorious."

—*Vince Lombardi*

"I'm no different from anybody else with two arms, two legs, and forty-two hundred hits."

—*Pete Rose*

"I'm not sure [whether] I'd rather be managing or testing bulletproof vests."

—*Joe Torre*

"In life as in a football game, the principle to follow is: Hit the line hard."

—***Theodore Roosevelt,*** *The Strenuous Life: The American Boy,* 1900

"In the end the great truth will have been learned, that the quest is greater than what is sought, the effort finer than the prize, or rather that the effort is the prize, the victory cheap and hollow were it not for the rigor of the game."

—*Benjamin Cardozo*

"It ain't over till it's over."

—*Yogi Berra*

"It's necessary to relax your muscles when you can. Relaxing your brain is fatal."

—*Stirling Moss*

"It's not the size of the dog in the fight, but the size of the fight in the dog."

—*Archie Griffin*

"I wish to preach, not the doctrine of ignoble ease, but the doctrine of the strenuous life."

—*Theodore Roosevelt,* speech at the Hamilton Club, Chicago, April 10, 1899

"Nice guys finish last."

—*Leo Durocher*

"Nobody roots for Goliath."

—*Wilt Chamberlain*

> Oh, somewhere in this favored land the sun is shining bright;
> The band is playing somewhere, and somewhere hearts are light,
> And somewhere men are laughing, and little children shout;
> But there is no joy in Mudville—mighty Casey has struck out.

—*Ernest Lawrence Thayer,* "Casey at the Bat," 1888

"Pro football is like nuclear warfare. There are no winners, only survivors."

—*Frank Gifford*

"Say it ain't so, Joe. Say it ain't so."

—*Anonymous young baseball fan* to "Shoeless" Joe Jackson, distraught over the "Black Sox" conspiracy to throw the World Series in 1919

"Show me a good and gracious loser and I'll show you a failure."

—*Knute Rockne*

"There was larceny in his heart, but his legs were honest."

—*"Bugs" Baer,* on a baseball player caught while trying to steal second base

"The three toughest jobs in the world are: President of the United States, Mayor of New York City, and head football coach at Notre Dame."

—*Beano Cook*

"Today I consider myself the luckiest man on the face of the earth."

—*Lou Gehrig,* upon his retirement from baseball due to complications caused by the disease that would later bear his name

"To say that politics is not a part of sports is not being realistic. When I run, I am more than a runner. I am a diplomat, an ambassador for my country."

—*Filbert Bayi*

"We all played poorly. It wasn't just one guy's fault. It was a real team effort."

—*Arnette Hallman*

"The will to win is important, but the will to prepare is vital."

—*Joe Paterno*

"Winning isn't everything, but wanting to win is."

—*Vince Lombardi*

7 COURAGE

"All the men who signed the Declaration of Independence died in bed."

—***W. R. Brock,*** *The Character of American History,* 1960

"Any dangerous spot is tenable if brave men will make it so."

—***John F. Kennedy***

"Caution, caution, sir! It is nothing but the word of cowardice."

—***John Brown***

"Courage is not simply one of the virtues, but the form of every virtue at the testing point."

—***C. S. Lewis***

"Courage to oppose a popular mania, above all to go against party, is not so common a political virtue that we can afford not to pay our tribute to the man who exhibits it."

—***Thomas B. Reed***

> Cowards die many times before their deaths;
> The valiant never taste of death but once.

—***William Shakespeare,*** *Julius Caesar,* act 2, scene 2

"Dad always used to say the only causes worth fighting for were lost causes."

—***James Stewart as Jefferson Smith*** in *Mr. Smith Goes to Washington,* screenplay by Sidney Buchman, 1939

"The desire for safety stands against every great and noble enterprise."

—***Marcus Claudius Tacitus***

"The dogmas of the quiet past are inadequate to the stormy present. The occasion is piled high with difficulty, and we might rise to the occasion. As our case is new, so we must think anew and act anew. We must disenthrall ourselves, and then we shall save our country."

—***Abraham Lincoln,*** Annual Message to Congress, December 1, 1862

"Each of us carries his own mirror in which is reflected hope—or determined desperation—courage or cowardice."

—***Bernard Baruch,*** speech to the United Nations Atomic Energy Commission on Atomic Control, 1946

"Far better it is to dare mighty things, to win glorious triumphs, even though checkered by failure, than to take rank with those poor spirits who neither enjoy much nor suffer much because they live in the gray twilight that knows not victory or defeat."

—***Theodore Roosevelt,*** speech at the Hamilton Club, Chicago, April 10, 1899

"Few men are willing to brave the disapproval of their fellows, the censure of their colleagues, the wrath of their society. Moral courage is a rarer commodity than bravery in battle or great intelligence. Yet it is the one essential, vital quality of those who seek to change a world which yields most painfully to change."

—***Ernest Hemingway,*** *A Farewell to Arms,* 1929

"The hottest places in Hell are reserved for those who in time of moral crisis preserve their neutrality."

—***Dante Alighieri***

"If you are a minority of one, the truth is the truth."

—***Ben Kingsley as Mohandas K. Gandhi*** in the film *Gandhi,* 1982

"If you have no confidence in self, you are twice defeated in the race of life. With confidence, you have won even before you started."

—***Marcus Garvey***

"I have not yet begun to fight."

—***John Paul Jones,*** during a battle with the heavily armed H.M.S. *Serapis,* September 23, 1779

"I'm very brave generally . . . only today I happen to have a headache."

—***Lewis Carroll,*** *Through the Looking Glass,* 1871

"In a calm sea every man is a pilot."

—*Spanish proverb*

"In Germany they came first for the Communists, and I didn't speak up because I wasn't a Communist. Then they came for the Jews, and I didn't speak up because I wasn't a Jew. Then they came for the trade unionists, and I didn't speak up because I wasn't a trade unionist. Then they came for the Catholics, and I didn't speak up because I was a Protestant. Then they came for me, and by that time no one was left to speak up."

—*Martin Niemoeller*

"It is a far, far better thing that I do, than I have ever done."

—*Charles Dickens, A Tale of Two Cities,* 1859,
spoken by Sydney Carton as he goes to the guillotine
in place of another man

"It is a tragedy we live in a world where physical courage is so common, and moral courage is so rare."

—*Claude Monet*

"It is from numberless diverse acts of courage and belief that human history is shaped. Each time a man stands up for an ideal, or acts to improve the lot of others, or strikes out against injustice, he sends a tiny ripple of hope, and crossing each other from a million different centers of energy and daring those ripples build a current which can sweep down the mightiest walls of oppression and resistance."

—*Robert F. Kennedy,* "Day of Affirmation" address,
University of Cape Town, South Africa, June 6, 1966

"It is not death that a man should fear, but he should fear never beginning to live."

—*Marcus Aurelius*

"It is often easier to fight for principles than to live up to them."

—*Adlai Stevenson,* address to the American Legion
Convention, Madison Square Garden, New York,
August 27, 1952

"Keep your fears to yourself, but share your courage with others."

—*Robert Louis Stevenson*

"Let me assert my firm belief that the only thing we have to fear is fear itself—nameless, unreasoning, unjustified terror which paralyzes needed efforts to convert retreat into advance."

—*Franklin Delano Roosevelt,* First Inaugural Address,
March 4, 1933

"Life for him was an adventure; perilous indeed, but men are not made for safe havens."

—***Edith Hamilton*** on the Greek author Aeschylus

"Life shrinks or expands in proportion to one's courage."

—***Anaïs Nin***

"Man cannot discover new oceans unless he has the courage to lose sight of the shore."

—***André Gide***

"One man with courage makes a majority."

—***Andrew Jackson***

"Only those who risk going too far can possibly find out how far one can go."

—***T. S. Eliot***

"Play for more than you can afford to lose and you will learn the game."

—***Winston Churchill***

"Rebellion to tyrants is obedience to God."

—***Henry Stephens Randall,*** an epitaph proposed for his subject, *Life of Thomas Jefferson,* 1858

"Resolved, never to do any thing, which I should be afraid to do, if it were the last hour of my life."

—***Jonathan Edwards,*** *Resolutions,* July 30, 1722

"The stories of past courage can define that ingredient—they can teach, they can offer hope, they can provide inspiration. But they cannot supply courage itself. For this each man must look into his own soul."

—***John F. Kennedy,*** *Profiles in Courage,* 1956

"Strengthen ye the weak hands, and make firm the tottering knees. Say to them that are of a fearful heart: 'Be strong, fear not.'"

—***Isaiah 35:3–4***

"The strongest, most generous, and proudest of all virtues is true courage."

—***Michel de Montaigne***

> That which has made them drunk hath made me bold.
> What hath quench'd them hath given me fire.

—***William Shakespeare,*** *Macbeth,* act 2, scene 2

"There are truths which are not for all men, nor for all times."

—***Voltaire,*** letter to Cardinal de Bernis, April 23, 1761

"These are the times that try men's souls. The summer soldier and the sunshine patriot will, in this crisis, shrink from the service of their country; but he that stands it *now,* deserves the love and thanks of man and woman."

—***Thomas Paine,*** *The American Crisis,* December 1776

> Tho' much is taken, much abides; and tho'
> We are not now that strength which in old days
> Moved earth and heaven; that which we are, we are—
> One equal temper of heroic hearts,
> Made weak by time and fate, but strong in will
> To strive, to seek, to find, and not to yield.

—***Alfred, Lord Tennyson,*** "Ulysses," 1842

"Though I walk through the valley of the shadow of death, I will fear no evil, for Thou art with me."

—***Psalm 23:4***

"Thus choosing to die resisting, rather than to live submitting, they fled only from dishonor."

—***Thucydides,*** *History of the Peloponnesian War,* 403 B.C.

"To avoid criticism, do nothing, say nothing, be nothing."

—***Elbert Hubbard***

"To conquer we have need to dare, to dare again, always to dare."

—***Georges Jacques Danton***

"Toughness doesn't have to come in a pinstripe suit."

—***Dianne Feinstein***

"The ultimate measure of a man is not where he stands in the moments of comfort and convenience, but where he stands at times of challenge and controversy."

—***Martin Luther King, Jr.,*** *The Strength to Love,* 1963

"Victory has a hundred fathers and defeat is an orphan."

—***Galeazzo Ciano***

"We also know that only those who dare to fail greatly can ever achieve greatly."

—***Herodotus***

"We will either find a way or make one."

—***Hannibal***

"Without belittling the courage with which men have died, we should not forget those acts of courage with which men . . . have lived. The courage of life is often a less dramatic spectacle than the courage of a final moment; but it is no less a magnificent mixture of triumph and tragedy."

—***John F. Kennedy,*** *Profiles in Courage,* 1956

"The world breaks everyone and afterward many are strong at the broken places."

—***Ernest Hemingway,*** *A Farewell to Arms,* 1929

"You gain strength, courage, and confidence by every experience in which you really stop to look fear in the face. You must do the thing which you think you cannot do."

—***Eleanor Roosevelt,*** *You Learn by Living,* 1960

8 CRISIS AND CONFLICT

"Against the assault of laughter nothing can stand."

—*Mark Twain*

"All treaties between great states cease to be binding when they come in conflict with the struggle for existence."

—*Otto von Bismarck*

"Diplomacy and defense are not substitutes for one another. Either alone will fail."

—*John F. Kennedy,* campaign speech, September 6, 1960

"The enemy is anybody who's going to get you killed, no matter which side he's on."

—*Joseph Heller, Catch-22,* 1961

"Great crises produce great men, and great deeds of courage."

—*John F. Kennedy*

"How many a dispute could have been deflated into a single paragraph if the disputants had dared to define their terms."

—*Aristotle*

"If a lot of cures are suggested for a disease, it means that the disease is incurable."

—*Anton Chekhov, The Cherry Orchard,* 1904

"If Mr. Gladstone fell into the Thames, that would be a misfortune; if someone pulled him out, that would be a calamity."

—*Benjamin Disraeli,* when asked to define the difference between a misfortune and a calamity

"If the only tool you have is a hammer, you tend to see every problem as a nail."

—***Abraham Maslow***

"In a false quarrel there is no true valor."

—***William Shakespeare,*** *Much Ado about Nothing,* act 5, scene 1

"It is not the mountain we conquer but ourselves."

—***Edmund Hillary***

"It was the best of times, it was the worst of times."

—***Charles Dickens,*** *A Tale of Two Cities,* 1859

I was angry with my friend;
I told my wrath, my wrath did end.
I was angry with my foe;
I told it not, my wrath did grow.

—***William Blake,*** "The Marriage of Heaven and Hell," 1790

"Keep your friends close, but your enemies closer."

—***Al Pacino as Michael Corleone*** in Mario Puzo's
The Godfather, Part II, 1974

"Let us never negotiate out of fear but let us never fear to negotiate."

—***John F. Kennedy,*** Inaugural Address, January 20, 1961

"Love your enemies; for they shall tell you all your faults."

—***Benjamin Franklin***

"Men and nations behave wisely once they have exhausted all other alternatives."

—***Abba Eban***

"Nothing makes a man broad-minded like adversity."

—***Will Rogers***

"Problems are only opportunities in work clothes."

—***Henry J. Kaiser***

"Sirs, the vessel of our State, after being tossed on wild waves, hath once more been safely steadied by the gods."

—***Sophocles,*** *Antigone*

"Sweet are the uses of adversity."

—***William Shakespeare,*** *As You Like It,* act 2, scene 1

"Tempt not a desperate man."

—***William Shakespeare,*** *Romeo and Juliet,* act 5, scene 3

"The terrible 'ifs' accumulate."

—***Winston Churchill,*** on the causes of World War I

"There cannot be a crisis next week. My schedule is already full."

—***Henry Kissinger***

"There is such a thing as a man being too proud to fight. There is such a thing as a nation being so right that it does not need to convince others by force."

—***Woodrow Wilson,*** requesting a formal declaration of war against Germany, April 2, 1917

"The time to repair the roof is when the sun is shining."

—***John F. Kennedy***

"The use of force alone is but *temporary*. It may subdue for a moment; but it does not remove the necessity of subduing again; and a nation is not governed, which is perpetually to be conquered."

—***Edmund Burke,*** *On Conciliation with America,* 1775

"We have petitioned and our petitions have been disregarded, we have entreated and our entreaties have been scorned. We beg no more, we petition no longer, we now defy."

—***William Jennings Bryan,*** "Cross of Gold" speech to the Democratic National Convention, Chicago, 1896

"We learn geology the morning after the earthquake."

—***Ralph Waldo Emerson,*** *The Conduct of Life,* 1860

"Well, everyone can master a grief but he that has it."

—***William Shakespeare,*** *Much Ado about Nothing,* act 3, scene 2

"We shall not escape our dangers by recoiling from them."

—***Winston Churchill***

"We shall not flag or fail. We shall go on to the end. We shall fight in France, we shall fight on the seas and oceans, we shall fight with growing confidence and growing strength in the air, we shall defend our island, whatever the cost may be, we shall fight on the beaches, we shall fight on the landing grounds, we shall fight in the fields and in the streets, we shall fight in the hills; we shall never surrender."

—***Winston Churchill,*** speech regarding the Battle of Dunkirk, House of Commons, June 4, 1940

"When evil men plot, good men must plan."

—***Martin Luther King, Jr.***

"When written in Chinese, the word 'crisis' is composed of two characters. One represents danger and the other represents opportunity."

—***John F. Kennedy***

"You can hear the fabric ripping."

—***Robert F. Kennedy***

9 DEATH AND EULOGIES

"After the first death, there is no other."

—***Dylan Thomas,*** "A Refusal to Mourn the Death, by Fire, of a Child in London," 1945

"Angels are bright still, though the brightest fell."

—***William Shakespeare,*** *Macbeth,* act 4, scene 3

Because I could not stop for Death—
He kindly stopped for me—
The Carriage held but just Ourselves—
And Immortality.

—***Emily Dickinson,*** "Because I Could Not Stop for Death"

But at my back I always hear
Time's winged chariot hurrying near:
And yonder all before us lie
Deserts of vast eternity.

—***Andrew Marvell,*** "To His Coy Mistress," 1681

"But he who is joined with all the living has hope, for a living dog is better than a dead lion."

—***Ecclesiastes 9:4***

"Dear Mrs., Mr., Miss, or Mr. and Mrs. Daneeka: Words cannot express the deep personal grief I experienced when your husband, son, father, or brother was killed, wounded, or reported missing in action."

—***Joseph Heller,*** *Catch-22,* 1961

"Death has made his darkness beautiful with thee."

—***Alfred, Lord Tennyson,*** *In Memoriam A.H.H.*, canto 7, 1850

"Death is a dress that, at some point or another, everyone has to wear."

—***African proverb***

"Death is nothing, but to live defeated is to die every day."

—***Napoleon Bonaparte,*** upon his defeat at Waterloo, 1815

"Death is the only inevitable truth."

—***James Dean***

"Die young, and I shall accept your death—but not if you have lived without glory, without being useful to your country, without leaving a trace of your existence: for that is not to have lived at all."

—***Napoleon Bonaparte,*** to his brother Jérôme, August 6, 1802

> Do not go gentle into that good night,
> Old age should burn and rave at close of day;
> Rage, rage against the dying of the light.

—***Dylan Thomas,*** "Do Not Go Gentle into That Good Night," 1952

"Don't let it end like this. Tell them I said something."

—***Pancho Villa,*** last words

"Each person is born to one possession which out-values all his others—his last breath."

—***Mark Twain***

"Fame is a vapor; popularity an accident; the only earthly certainty is oblivion."

—***Mark Twain***

"For what is to die but to stand naked in the wind and melt into the sun? And what is to cease breathing, but to free the breath from its restlessness, that it may rise and expand and seek God unencumbered?"

—***Kahlil Gibran,*** *The Prophet,* 1923

"Friends and comrades, the light has gone out of our lives and there is darkness everywhere. I do not know what to tell you and how to say it. Our beloved leader, Bapu, as we called him, the Father of the Nation, is no more. Perhaps I am wrong to say that. Nevertheless, we will not see him again as we have seen him for these many years. . . . The light has gone out, I said, and yet I was wrong. For the light that shone in this country was no ordinary light. The light that has illuminated this country for these many years will illumine this country for many more years, a thousand years later that light will still be seen in this country, and the world will see it and it will give solace to innumerable hearts."

—***Jawaharlal Nehru,*** announcing the assassination of Mohandas Gandhi, January 30, 1948

Friends, Romans, countrymen, lend me your ears;
I come to bury Caesar, not to praise him.

—***William Shakespeare,*** Mark Antony's funeral oration, *Julius Caesar,* act 3, scene 2

Give me my Romeo, and when I shall die
Take him and cut him out in little stars
And he will make the face of heaven so fine
That all the world will be in love with night
And pay no worship to the garish sun.

—***William Shakespeare,*** *Romeo and Juliet,* act 3, scene 2

"God's finger touch'd him, and he slept."

—***Alfred, Lord Tennyson,*** *In Memoriam A.H.H,* canto 85, 1850

"Grandfather, you were the pillar of fire in front of the camp and now we are left in the camp alone, in the dark; and we are so cold and so sad."

—***Noa Ben-Artzi,*** granddaughter of Yitzhak Rabin, delivering his eulogy, November 6, 1995

"He added to the sum of human joy; and were everyone to whom he did some loving service to bring a blossom to his grave, he would sleep tonight beneath a wilderness of flowers."

—***Robert G. Ingersoll,*** at his brother's graveside, 1899

"He had every gift but length of years."

—***Edward Kennedy,*** eulogy for his nephew John F. Kennedy, Jr., July 23, 1999

"He notes the fall of a sparrow, and numbers the hairs of our heads; and He will not forget the dying man who puts trust in Him."

—***Abraham Lincoln,*** letter to his dying father, 1850

"How can they tell?"

—***Dorothy Parker,*** on being told that Calvin Coolidge had died, 1933

"I am dying with the help of too many physicians."

—***Alexander the Great***

"I am ready to meet my Maker. Whether my Maker is prepared for the great ordeal of meeting me is another matter."

—***Winston Churchill***

"I did not attend his funeral; but I wrote a nice letter saying I approved of it."

—***Mark Twain,*** on the recent death of a politician

If I should die, think only this of me:
That there's some corner of a foreign field
That is forever England.

—***Rupert Brooke,*** "The Soldier," 1914

"If you have tears, prepare to shed them now."

—***William Shakespeare,*** Mark Antony's funeral oration, *Julius Caesar,* act 3, scene 2

"It is one of the mysteries of our nature that a man, all unprepared, can receive a thunder-stroke like that and live. There is but one reasonable explanation of it. The intellect is stunned by the shock and but gropingly gathers the meaning of the words. The power to realize their full import is mercifully lacking."

—***Mark Twain,*** on the death of his daughter Suzy

"It's only the inspiration of those who die that makes those who live realize what constitutes a useful life."

—***Will Rogers***

"Life is a narrow vale between the cold and barren peaks of two eternities. We strive in vain to look beyond the heights. We cry aloud, and the only answer is the echo of our wailing cry. From the voiceless lips of the unreplying dead there comes no word; but in the night of death hope sees a star, and listening love can hear the rustle of a wing."

—***Robert G. Ingersoll,*** at his brother's graveside, 1899

Life's but a walking shadow, a poor player,
That struts and frets his hour upon the stage,
And then is heard no more.

—***William Shakespeare,*** *Macbeth,* act 5, scene 5

"The living have envy to contend with, while those who are no longer in our path are honored with a goodwill into which rivalry does not enter."

—***Thucydides,*** *History of the Peloponnesian War,* 403 B.C.

"Mr. Nixon stood on pinnacles that dissolved in the precipice. He achieved greatly and he suffered deeply. But he never gave up. In his solitude he envisaged a new international order that would reduce lingering enmities, strengthen historic friendships, and give new hope to mankind."

—***Henry Kissinger,*** eulogy for Richard M. Nixon, Yorba Linda, California, April 27, 1994

"My brother need not be idealized or enlarged in death beyond what he was in life; rather he should be remembered simply as a good and decent man, who saw wrong and tried to right it, saw suffering and tried to heal it, saw war and tried to stop it."

—***Edward Kennedy,*** eulogy for his brother Robert F. Kennedy, June 1968

"Not often in the story of mankind does a man arrive on earth who is both steel and velvet, who is as hard as a rock and soft as drifting fog, who holds in his heart and mind the paradox of terrible storm and peace unspeakable and perfect."

—***Carl Sandburg,*** on Abraham Lincoln

Now cracks a noble heart. Good night, sweet prince,
And flights of angels sing thee to thy rest.

—***William Shakespeare,*** *Hamlet,* act 5, scene 2

"Now he belongs to the ages."

—***Edwin McMasters Stanton,*** immediately following Abraham Lincoln's death, April 15, 1865

Oh I have slipped the surly bonds of earth
And danced the skies on laughter-silvered wings.

—***John Gillespie Magee, Jr.,*** killed in the Battle of Britain at age nineteen. Quoted by President Ronald Reagan after the explosion of the *Challenger* spacecraft, January 28, 1986

"The reports of my death are greatly exaggerated."

—***Mark Twain,*** 1897

Our revels now are ended. . . .
We are such stuff
As dreams are made on, and our little life
Is rounded with a sleep.

—***William Shakespeare,*** *The Tempest,* act 4, scene 1

Soldier, scholar, horseman, he,
As 'twere all life's epitome.
What made us dream that he could comb grey hair?

—***William Butler Yeats,*** "In Memory of Major Robert Gregory"

That we shall die, we know; 'tis but the time
And drawing days out, that men stand upon.

—***William Shakespeare,*** *Julius Caesar,* act 3, scene 1

This was the most unkindest cut of all;
For when the noble Caesar saw him stab,
Ingratitude, more strong than traitors' arms,
Quite vanquish'd him.

—***William Shakespeare,*** Mark Antony's funeral oration, *Julius Caesar,* act 3, scene 2

The time you won your town the race
We chaired you through the market-place;
Man and boy stood cheering by,
And home we brought you shoulder-high.

Today, the road all runners come,
Shoulder-high we bring you home,
And set you at your threshold down,
Townsman of a stiller town.

—***A. E. Housman,*** "To an Athlete Dying Young," 1896

"To die will be an awfully big adventure."

—***J. M. Barrie,*** *Peter Pan,* 1911

"Tragedy is the difference between what is and what could have been."

—***Abba Eban,*** on the death of John F. Kennedy, 1963

"Very few people ever really are alive, and those that are never die, no matter if they are gone. No one you love is ever dead."

—***Ernest Hemingway,*** letter to Gerald and Sara Murphy on the death of their son, March 19, 1935

"We know that men are ready to die in war, but there are a great many things harder than to die. Everybody must die sometime, and it does not make so much difference perhaps as to the number of days we live as it does to the manner in which we live the days we do live."

—***Anna Howard Shaw,*** May 1919

Were a star quenched on high,
For ages would its light,
Still traveling downward from the sky,
Shine on our mortal sight.
So when a great man dies
For years beyond our ken,
The light he leaves behind him lies
Upon the paths of men.

—***Henry Wadsworth Longfellow,*** "Charles Sumner"

"When it came, that last breath, it was as though a lamp in whose circle of light I had lived all my life had been extinguished. Now I was free to live anywhere. In the dark."

—***Richard Selzer,*** on the death of his mother

When there were difficulties, you sustained him.
When there were periods of crisis, you stood beside him.
When there were periods of happiness, you laughed with him.
And when there were periods of sorrow, you comforted him.

—***Robert F. Kennedy,*** thanking young people for their support of his brother John F. Kennedy, Democratic National Convention, Atlantic City, New Jersey, August 27, 1964

"Where dead men meet, on lips of living men."

—***Samuel Butler,*** "Not on Sad Stygian Shore," 1904

"You do not understand life. How can you understand death?"

—***Confucius,*** *The Analects*

The young dead soldiers do not speak.
Nevertheless, they are heard in the still houses: who has not heard them?
They have a silence that speaks for them at night and when the clock counts.

—***Archibald MacLeish,*** "The Young Dead Soldiers," 1944

10 DEMOCRACY

"As I would not be a *slave*, so I would not be a *master*. This expresses my idea of democracy."

—***Abraham Lincoln***, August 1, 1858

"The constant free flow of communication among us—enabling the free interchange of ideas—forms the very bloodstream of our nation. It keeps the mind and body of our democracy eternally vital, eternally young."

—***Franklin Delano Roosevelt***

"The contest, for ages, has been to rescue Liberty from the grasp of executive power."

—***Daniel Webster***, speech to the U.S. Senate, May 27, 1834

"Democracy . . . is a charming form of government, full of variety and disorder, and dispensing a sort of equality to equals and unequals alike."

—***Plato***, *The Republic*

"Democracy is based upon the conviction that there are extraordinary possibilities in ordinary people."

—***Harry Emerson Fosdick***

"Democracy is never a final achievement. It is a call to untiring effort, to continual sacrifice."

—***John F. Kennedy***

"Democracy is no easy form of government. Few nations have been able to sustain it. For it requires that we take the chances of freedom; that the liberating play of reason be brought to bear on events filled with passion; that dissent be allowed to make its appeal for acceptance; that men chance error in their search for truth."

—***Robert F. Kennedy,*** "Admitting the Enemy into the Political Process," press release, February 19, 1966

"Democracy means government by discussion, but it is only effective if you can stop people talking."

—***Clement Attlee,*** speech at Oxford University, June 14, 1957

"Democracy means government by the uneducated, while aristocracy means government by the badly educated."

—***G. K. Chesterton***

"Democratic nations care but little for what has been, but they are haunted by visions of what will be."

—***Alexis de Tocqueville,*** *Democracy in America,* 1835–1840

"Gentlemen, the select classes of mankind are no longer the governors of mankind. The fortunes of mankind are now in the hands of the plain people of the whole world. Satisfy them, and you have not only justified their confidence, but established peace. Fail to satisfy them, and no arrangement that you can make will either set up or steady the peace of the world."

—***Woodrow Wilson,*** speech given to the League of Nations, January 25, 1919

"A government of laws, and not of men."

—***John Adams,*** opening clause of the Massachusetts state constitution, 1779

"The health of a democratic society may be measured by the quality of functions performed by private citizens."

—***Alexis de Tocqueville,*** *Democracy in America,* 1835–1840

"I believe in democracy, because it releases the energy of every human being."

—***Woodrow Wilson***

"If one man can be allowed to determine for himself what is law, every man can. That means first chaos, then tyranny. Legal process is an essential part of the democratic process."

—***Felix Frankfurter,*** concurring in the Supreme Court decision on *United States v. Mine Workers,* 330 U.S. 312, 1946

"I have sworn upon the altar of God, eternal hostility against every form of tyranny over the mind of man."

—*Thomas Jefferson,* letter to Dr. Benjamin Rush affirming his opposition to the establishment of a state-sponsored church, September 23, 1800

"In the great enterprise of making democracy workable we are all partners."

—*Charles Evans Hughes,* speech as a Supreme Court justice to a joint session of Congress

"In the multitude of the people is the king's glory. But in the want of people is the ruin of the prince."

—*Proverbs 14:28*

"I respect the aristocracy of learning; I deplore the plutocracy of wealth; but thank God for the democracy of the heart."

—*Franklin Delano Roosevelt,* speech at Roanoke Island, North Carolina, August 18, 1937

"It had been understood by Cleon, who, in the fifth century B.C., had reminded the citizens of another imperial power, Athens, that 'a democracy is incapable of empire.' "

—*James Lawrence,* during the War of 1812

"Men write many fine and plausible arguments in support of monarchy, but the fact remains that where every man in a State has a vote, brutal laws are impossible."

—*Mark Twain,* *A Connecticut Yankee in King Arthur's Court,* 1889

"Nobody pretends that democracy is perfect or all-wise. Indeed, it has been said that democracy is the worst form of Government except for all other forms that have been tried from time to time."

—*Winston Churchill,* speech to the House of Commons, November 11, 1947

"One person with a belief is equal to a force of ninety-nine who have only interests."

—*John Stuart Mill*

"On one occasion I remarked . . . that democracy had at least one merit, namely, that a Member of Parliament cannot be stupider than his constituents, for the more stupid he is, the more stupid they were to elect him."

—*Bertrand Russell*

"A republican government is slow to move, yet when once in motion its momentum becomes irresistible."

—***Thomas Jefferson***

"Self-criticism is the secret weapon of democracy, and candor and confession are good for the public soul."

—***Adlai Stevenson,*** address to the Democratic National Convention, Chicago, July 16, 1952

"The sun never shined on a cause of greater worth."

—***Thomas Paine,*** *Common Sense,* 1776

II ECONOMY

"Balancing the budget is like going to heaven. Everybody wants to do it, but nobody wants to do what you have to do to get there."

—***Phil Gramm,*** television interview, 1990

"A banker is a person who lends you his umbrella when the sun is shining and wants it back the minute it rains."

—***Mark Twain***

"The borrower is servant to the lender."

—***Proverbs 22:7***

"But while they prate of economic laws, men and women are starving. We must lay hold of the fact that economic laws are not made by nature. They are made by human beings."

—***Franklin Delano Roosevelt,*** accepting the presidential nomination, Democratic National Convention, 1932

"By itself, economics affords no solution to any of the important problems of life."

—***Lionel Robbins,*** *An Essay on the Nature and Significance of Economic Science,* 1935

"Capitalism is about turning luxuries into necessities."

—***Andrew Carnegie***

"Capitalism is the extraordinary belief that the nastiest of men, for the nastiest of reasons, will somehow work for the benefit of us all."

—***John Maynard Keynes***

"The corrosive effects of inflation eat away at ties that bind us together as a people."

—***Jimmy Carter***

"The customer is always right."

—***Marshall Field***

"Economic growth without social progress lets the great majority of the people remain in poverty, while a privileged few reap the benefits of rising abundance."

—***John F. Kennedy,*** address to Congress on the Inter-American Fund for Social Progress, 1961

"Economic perfection lies in the absolute independence of the workers, just as political perfection consists in the absolute independence of the citizens."

—***Pierre Joseph Proudhon,*** *La Révolution sociale,* 1852

"Economic policy can result from governmental inaction as well as governmental action."

—***John F. Kennedy***

"Financial storm definitely passed."

—***Bernard Baruch,*** cablegram to Winston Churchill, November 15, 1929

"The first panacea for a mismanaged nation is inflation of the currency; the second is war. Both bring a temporary prosperity; both bring a permanent ruin. But both are the refuge of political and economic opportunists."

—***Ernest Hemingway,*** "Notes on the Next War: A Serious Topical Letter," *Esquire,* 1935

"For the same reason that pilot keeps the plane's engines running when we are already in the air."

—***William Wrigley, Jr.,*** when asked why, despite its established success, he continued to advertise his chewing gum

"Freedom of trade should be restored only by slow gradations, and with a good deal of reserve and circumspection. Were those high duties and prohibitions taken away all at once, the disorder which this would occasion might no doubt be very considerable."

—***Adam Smith,*** *The Wealth of Nations,* 1776

"Gentlemen, you have come sixty days too late. The depression is over."

—***Herbert Hoover,*** responding to a request for a public works program to aid in economic recovery, June 1930

"If all economists were laid end to end, they would not reach a conclusion."

—***George Bernard Shaw***

"If Karl, instead of writing a lot about Capital, made a lot of Capital, it would have been much better."

—***Henrietta Marx,*** mother of Karl Marx

"If the unemployed could eat plans and promises they would be able to spend the winter on the Riviera."

—***W.E.B. Du Bois,*** "As the Crow Flies," *The Crisis,* 1931

"I have maintained from first to last that the laws of economics are the laws of life."

—***Philip H. Wicksteed,*** *The Common Sense of Political Economy,* 1950

"I have no fears for the future of our country. It is bright with hope."

—***Herbert Hoover,*** commenting on the nation's flourishing economy, New York City, October 22, 1928

"The income tax has made more liars out of the American people than golf has."

—***Will Rogers***

"Income tax returns are the most imaginative fiction being written today."

—***Herman Wouk***

"Inflation is the one form of taxation that can be imposed without legislation."

—***Milton Friedman,*** *Observer,* 1974

"The inherent vice of capitalism is the unequal sharing of blessings; the inherent virtue of socialism is the equal sharing of miseries."

—***Winston Churchill,*** remarks at a White House luncheon, June 26, 1954

"In our time, the curse is monetary illiteracy, just as inability to read plain print was the curse of earlier centuries."

—***Ezra Pound,*** *Guide to Kulchur,* 1938

"In the long run we are all dead."

—***John Maynard Keynes,*** *A Tract on Monetary Reform,* 1923

"It is not possible for this nation to be at once politically internationalist and economically isolationist. This is just as insane as asking one Siamese twin to high dive while the other plays the piano."

—***Adlai Stevenson,*** speech in New Orleans, 1952

"It's a recession when your neighbor loses his job, it's a depression when you lose your own."

—***Harry S. Truman***

"It takes a certain brashness to attack the accepted economic legends but none at all to perpetuate them. So they are perpetuated."

—***John Kenneth Galbraith,*** *The Liberal Hour,* 1960

"The man who dies this rich dies disgraced."

—***Andrew Carnegie***

"Money is coined liberty."

—***Feodor Dostoevsky,*** *House of the Dead,* 1862

"Money, it turned out, was exactly like sex; you thought of nothing else if you didn't have it and thought of other things if you did."

—***James Baldwin,*** "Black Boy Looks at the White Boy," *Esquire,* May 1961

"Money . . . ranks with love as man's greatest joy. And it ranks with death as his greatest source of anxiety."

—***John Kenneth Galbraith,*** *The Age of Uncertainty,* 1977

"The most basic law of economics [is] . . . that one cannot get something for nothing."

—***Roy Harrod,*** *Towards a Dynamic Economics,* 1948

"The name of political economy has been constantly invoked against every effort of the working classes to increase their wages or decrease their hours of labor."

—***Henry George,*** lecture, University of California, 1877

"[1930 will be] a splendid employment year."

—***United States Department of Labor,*** New Year's Labor Forecast, December 1929

"No country can long endure if its foundations are not laid deep in the material prosperity which comes from thrift, from business energy and enterprise, from hard unsparing effort in the fields of industrial activity; but neither was any nation ever yet truly great if it relied upon material prosperity alone."

—***Theodore Roosevelt,*** speech at the Hamilton Club, Chicago, April 10, 1899

"No free people can for long cling to any privilege or enjoy any safety in economic solitude."

—***Dwight D. Eisenhower,*** First Inaugural Address, January 20, 1953

"Reaganomics, that makes sense to me. It means if you don't have enough money, it's because poor people are hoarding it."

—***Kevin Rooney***

"Render therefore unto Caesar the things which are Caesar's."

—***Matthew 22:21***

"Saving is a very fine thing. Especially when your parents have done it for you."

—***Winston Churchill***

"The Sears, Roebuck catalog."

—***Franklin Delano Roosevelt,*** answer to the question of what single book he'd put in the hands of a Russian Communist

"This island is made mainly of coal and surrounded by fish. Only an organizing genius could produce a shortage of coal and fish at the same time."

—***Aneurin Bevan,*** speech in Blackpool, England, May 24, 1945

"This is the end of Western civilization."

—***Lewis Douglas,*** reacting to President Roosevelt's announcement that the United States was going off the gold standard, April 18, 1933

"Those who have never seen the inhabitants of a nineteenth-century London slum can have no idea of the state to which dirt, drink, and economics can reduce human beings."

—***Leonard Woolf,*** *Sowing,* 1960

"To tax and to please, no more than to love and be wise, is not given to men."

—***Edmund Burke,*** *On American Taxation,* 1774

"Trickle-down theory—the less-than-elegant metaphor that if one feeds the horse enough oats, some will pass through to the road for the sparrows."

—***John Kenneth Galbraith,*** *The Culture of Contentment,* 1992

"True individual freedom cannot exist without economic security and independence. People who are hungry and out of a job are the stuff of which dictatorships are made."

—***Franklin Delano Roosevelt,*** message to Congress, 1944

"Very much of the literature of economics strikes me as rationalization after the event."

—***John H. Williams,*** "An Economist's Confessions," *American Economic Review,* 1952

"Wealth is the relentless enemy of understanding."

—***John Kenneth Galbraith,*** *The Affluent Society,* 1958

"We have always known that heedless self-interest was bad morals; we know now that it is bad economics."

—***Franklin Delano Roosevelt,*** Second Inaugural Address, 1937

"We women don't care too much about getting our pictures on money as long as we can get our hands on it."

—***Ivy Baker Priest,*** Treasurer of the United States, *Look,* 1954

12 EDUCATION

"A child miseducated is a child lost."

—*John F. Kennedy,* State of the Union Address, January 11, 1962

"Education is an admirable thing, but it is well to remember from time to time that nothing worth knowing can be taught."

—*Oscar Wilde,* "The Critic as an Artist," 1890

"Education is not a problem. Education is an opportunity."

—*Lyndon B. Johnson*

"Education is that which remains when one has forgotten everything he learned in school."

—*Albert Einstein, Out of My Later Years,* 1936

"Education is the best provision for old age."

—*Aristotle*

"Education is the guardian genius of democracy. It is the only dictator that free men recognize, and the only ruler that free men require."

—*Mirabeau Buonaparte Lamar*

"Education . . . is the mainspring of our economic and social progress. . . . It is the highest expression of achievement in our society, ennobling and enriching human life."

—*John F. Kennedy*

"Education is the transmission of civilization."

—***Will Durant***

"Education is what survives when what has been learned is forgotten."

—***B. F. Skinner,*** "Education in 1964," *New Scientist,* May 21, 1964

"Every educated person is a future enemy."

—***Martin Bormann***

"Every man, every man sent out from a university should be a man of his nation, as well as a man of his time."

—***Woodrow Wilson***

"The free man cannot be long an ignorant man."

—***William McKinley***

"Great as were the material obstacles in the path of the United States, the greatest obstacle of all was the human mind."

—***Henry Adams***

"He who asks is a fool for five minutes, but he who does not ask remains a fool forever."

—***Chinese proverb***

"A human being is not a human being till he is educated."

—***Horace Mann***

"Human history becomes more and more a race between education and catastrophe."

—***H. G. Wells,*** *The Outline of History,* 1920

"I am not a teacher but an awakener."

—***Robert Frost***

"If you feel that you have both feet planted on level ground, then the university has failed you."

—***Robert Goheen,*** baccalaureate address, Princeton University, June 23, 1961

"I have never let my schooling interfere with my education."

—***Mark Twain***

"I learned much from teachers; more from my colleagues; but from my disciples I learned the most."

—*The Talmud*

"In the conditions of modern life the rule is absolute; the race which does not value trained intelligence is doomed."

—*Alfred North Whitehead,* "The Aims of Education: A Plea for Reform," 1929

"In the first place God made idiots. This was for practice. Then he made school boards."

—*Mark Twain, Following the Equator,* 1898

"It is better to keep one's mouth shut and be thought a fool than to open it and remove all doubt."

—*Abraham Lincoln*

"It might be said now that I have the best of both worlds: a Harvard education and a Yale degree."

—*John F. Kennedy,* on receiving an honorary degree from Yale, June 12, 1962

"The man who doesn't read good books has no advantage over the man who can't read them."

—*Mark Twain*

"A man who has never gone to school may steal a freight car; but if he has a university education, he may steal the whole railroad."

—*Theodore Roosevelt*

"The most deadly of all possible sins is the mutilation of a child's spirit."

—*Erik Erikson*

"The object of education is to prepare the young to educate themselves throughout their lives."

—*Robert Hutchins*

"One good head is better than a hundred strong hands."

—*Thomas Fuller*

"The only sure weapon against bad ideas is better ideas. The source of better ideas is wisdom. The surest path to wisdom is liberal education."

—*Alfred Whitney Griswold, Essays on Education,* 1954

"The preservation of the means of knowledge among the lowest ranks is of more importance to the public than all the property of all the rich men in the country."

—***John Adams,*** letter written as vice president, 1789

"A professor is one who talks in someone else's sleep."

—***W. H. Auden***

"Take fast hold of instruction; let her not go: keep her; for she is thy life."

—***Proverbs 4:13***

"A teacher affects eternity; he can never tell where his influence stops."

—***Henry Adams,*** *The Education of Henry Adams,* 1907

"Teaching is not a lost art, but regard for teaching is a lost tradition."

—***Jacques Barzun,*** *Newsweek,* 1955

"Teaching is the art of casting false pearls before real swine."

—***Irwin Edman***

"There is nothing as stupid as an educated man if you get him off the thing he was educated in."

—***Will Rogers***

"The university is the archive of the Western ideal, the keeper of the Western culture, the guardian of our heritage, the dwelling place of the free mind, the teacher of teachers."

—***Adlai Stevenson***

"What nobler employment, or more valuable to the state, than that of the man who instructs the rising generation."

—***Marcus Tullius Cicero***

"When asked how much educated men were superior to those uneducated, Aristotle answered, 'As much as the living are to the dead.'"

—***Diogenes Laertius***

13 THE ENVIRONMENT AND AGRICULTURE

"The American farmer is the only man in our economy who buys everything he buys at retail, sells everything he sells at wholesale, and pays the freight both ways."

—***John F. Kennedy,*** campaign speech, Des Moines, Iowa, September 22, 1960

"The American farmer, living on his own land, remains our ideal of self-reliance and spiritual balance—the source from which the reservoirs of the nation's strength are constantly renewed."

—***Franklin Delano Roosevelt***

"Conservation means development as much as it does protection. I recognize the right and duty of this generation to develop and use the natural resources of our land; but I do not recognize the right to waste them, or to rob, by wasteful use, the generations that come after us."

—***Theodore Roosevelt,*** speech, Osawatomie, Kansas, August 31, 1910

"The conservation of our natural resources and their proper use constitute the fundamental problem which underlies almost every other problem of our national life."

—***Theodore Roosevelt,*** message to Congress, December 3, 1907

"The 'control of nature' is a phrase conceived in arrogance, born of the Neanderthal age of biology and philosophy, when it was supposed that nature exists for the convenience of man."

—***Rachel Carson,*** *Silent Spring,* 1962

"Even in warfare, you shall not destroy the trees."

—***Deuteronomy 20:19***

"Everybody needs beauty as well as bread, places to play in and pray in, where nature may heal and give strength to body and soul alike."

—***John Muir,*** *The Yosemite,* 1912

"Everything is perfect coming from the hands of the Creator; everything degenerates in the hands of man."

—***Jean Jacques Rousseau,*** *Emile,* 1762

"God has lent us the earth for our life; it is a great entail. It belongs as much to those who are to come after us, and whose names are already written in the book of creation, as to us; and we have no right, by anything that we do or neglect, to involve them in unnecessary penalties or deprive them of benefits which it was in our power to bequeath."

—***John Ruskin,*** "The Lamp of Memory," 1907

"The great cities rest upon our broad and fertile prairies. Burn down your cities and leave our farms, and your cities will spring up again as if by magic; but destroy our farms and the grass will grow on the streets of every country."

—***William Jennings Bryan,*** "Cross of Gold" speech to the Democratic National Convention, 1896

"Into every empty corner, into all forgotten things and nooks, Nature struggles to pour life, pouring life into the dead; life into life itself."

—***Henry Beston,*** "Lantern on the Beach," 1928

I think that I shall never see
A poem lovely as a tree.
A tree whose hungry mouth is prest
Against the Earth's sweet flowering breast;
A tree that looks at God all day,
And lifts her leafy arms to pray.
A tree that may in Summer wear
A nest of robins in her hair;
Upon whose bosom snow has lain;
Who intimately lives with rain.
Poems are made by fools like me,
But only God can make a tree.

—***Joyce Kilmer,*** "Trees," 1914

"It is our task in our time and in our generation to hand down undiminished to those who come after us, as was handed down to us by those who went before, the natural wealth and beauty which is ours."

—***John F. Kennedy,*** March 1961

"Land is not something you inherit from your parents. It is something you borrow from your children."

—***Elmer H. MacKay***

"Like music or art, love of nature is a common language that can transcend political or social boundaries."

—***Jimmy Carter,*** *Outdoor Journal: Adventures and Reflections,* 1988

"Man is a complex being: he makes deserts bloom—and lakes die."

—***Gil Stern,*** 1970

"More and more, as it becomes necessary to preserve the game, let us hope that the camera will largely supplant the rifle."

—***Theodore Roosevelt,*** Oyster Bay, New York, May 31, 1901

"The most unhappy thing about conservation is that it is never permanent. Save a priceless woodland or an irreplaceable mountain today, and tomorrow it is threatened from another quarter. Man, our most ingenious predator, sometimes seems determined to destroy the precious treasures of his own environment."

—***Hal Borland,*** *New York Times Book Review,* February 25, 1964

"The nation that destroys its soil destroys itself."

—***Franklin Delano Roosevelt,*** letter to the governors urging uniform soil conservation laws, February 26, 1937

"Nature is the art of God."

—***Dante Alighieri,*** *On World Government,* c. 1313

"Never before has man had such capacity to control his own environment, to end thirst and hunger, to conquer poverty and disease, to banish illiteracy and massive human misery. We have the power to make this the best generation of mankind in the history of the world—or to make it the last."

—***John F. Kennedy,*** address before the General Assembly of the United Nations, New York City, September 20, 1963

"No other human occupation opens so wide a field for the profitable and agreeable combination of labor with cultivated thought, as agriculture."

—***Abraham Lincoln***

"No synonym for God is so perfect as Beauty. Whether as seen carving the lines of mountains with glaciers, or gathering matter into stars, or planning the movements of water, or gardening—still all is Beauty."

—***John Muir***

"Our ideals, laws and customs should be based on the proposition that each generation in turn becomes the custodian rather than the absolute owner of our resources—and each generation has the obligation to pass this inheritance on to the future."

—***Alden Whitman***

"Over increasingly large areas of the United States, spring now comes unheralded by the return of the birds, and the early mornings are strangely silent where once they were filled with the beauty of bird song."

—***Rachel Carson,*** *Silent Spring,* 1962

"Remember the land, and its gifts which endure."

—***William Faulkner***

"A river is more than an amenity, it is a treasure."

—***Oliver Wendell Holmes, Jr.,*** Supreme Court decision in *New Jersey v. New York, et al.,* 283 U.S. 342, 1931

"The roaring of the wind is my wife and the stars through the window pane are my children."

—***John Keats,*** letter, October 14, 1818

"Show me a farmer and I'll show you a man who feels the sweat of God."

—***Robert Frost***

"There is an old saying here that a man must do three things during life: plant trees, write books, and have sons. I wish they would plant more trees and write more books."

—***Luis Muñoz Marin***

"The throwing out of balance of the resources of nature throws out of balance also the lives of men."

—***Franklin Delano Roosevelt***

To see a world in a grain of sand,
And a heaven in a wild flower,
Hold infinity in the palm of your hand,
And eternity in an hour.

—***William Blake,*** "Auguries of Innocence," c. 1803

"Whatever befalls the Earth befalls the sons of the Earth. Man does not weave the web of life, he is merely a strand in it. Whatever he does to the web he does to himself."

—***Chief Seattle***

"Whenever I see so many country people in a big city like this, I think of that old definition of a farmer: 'A person who occasionally visits the city to see where his sons and his profits went.'"

—***Lyndon B. Johnson***

"Why, land's the only thing in the world worth working for, worth fighting for, worth dying for, because it's the only thing that lasts."

—***Thomas Mitchell as Gerald O'Hara*** in the movie adaptation of Margaret Mitchell's *Gone With the Wind,* 1939

Woodman, spare that tree!
Touch not a single bough!
In youth it sheltered me,
And I'll protect it now.

—***George Pope Morris,*** "Woodman, Spare That Tree," 1830

14 EQUALITY

"All animals are equal, but some animals are more equal than others."

—*George Orwell, Animal Farm,* 1945

"America did not invent human rights. In a very real sense . . . human rights invented America."

—*Jimmy Carter,* Farewell Address, January 14, 1981

"And a great silence descended for many decades."

—*Paul Johnson,* on the suppression of African Americans after Reconstruction

"The appointment of a woman to office is an innovation for which the public is not prepared, nor am I."

—*Thomas Jefferson*

"Drive out prejudices through the door, and they will return through the window."

—*Frederick the Great,* letter to Voltaire, March 19, 1771

"Equal rights for all, special privileges for none."

—*Thomas Jefferson*

"Every man a king."

—*Huey P. Long,* title of speech given on February 23, 1934

"'Freedom from fear' could be said to sum up the whole philosophy of human rights."

—*Dag Hammarskjöld,* on the 180th anniversary of the Virginia Declaration of Human Rights, 1956

"The gifts of our colors may be different, but God has so placed us as to journey in the same path."

—***James Fenimore Cooper,*** *The Last of the Mohicans,* 1826

"If I were asked . . . to what the singular prosperity and growing strength of [Americans] ought mainly to be attributed, I should reply: To the superiority of their women."

—***Alexis de Tocqueville,*** *Democracy in America,* 1835–1840

"If the American dream is for Americans only, it will remain our dream and never be our destiny."

—***René de Visme Williamson***

"If there is no struggle, there is no progress."

—***Frederick Douglass,*** letter to Gerrit Smith, March 30, 1849

"I have a dream that one day on the red hills of Georgia the sons of former slaves and the sons of former slave owners will be able to sit down together at the table of brotherhood."

—***Martin Luther King, Jr.,*** address at the March on Washington, Lincoln Memorial, Washington, D.C., August 28, 1963

"Injustice anywhere is a threat to justice everywhere. . . . We are caught in an inescapable network of mutuality tied in a single garment of destiny. Whatever affects one directly affects all indirectly."

—***Martin Luther King, Jr.,*** "Letter from the Birmingham Jail," April 16, 1963

"In the final analysis, I must not ignore the wounded man on life's Jericho Road, because he is a part of me and I am a part of him. His agony diminishes me and his salvation enlarges me."

—***Martin Luther King, Jr.***

"In view of the Constitution, in the eye of the law there is in this country no superior, dominant, ruling class of citizens. There is no caste here. Our Constitution is colorblind, and neither knows nor tolerates classes among citizens. In respect of civil rights, all citizens are equal before the law. The humblest is the peer of the most powerful."

—***John Marshall Harlan,*** dissenting opinion in the Supreme Court decision *Plessy v. Ferguson,* 163 U.S. 537, 559, 1896

"It behooves every man who values liberty of conscience for himself, to resist invasions of it in the cases of others; or their case, by change of circumstances, may become his own."

—***Thomas Jefferson***

"It is a wise man who said that there is no greater inequality than the equal treatment of unequals."

—***Felix Frankfurter,*** dissenting opinion in the Supreme Court decision *Dennis v. United States,* 339 U.S. 184, 1949

"It is never too late to give up your prejudices."

—***Henry David Thoreau,*** *Walden,* 1854

"It is not enough just to open the gates of opportunity. All our citizens must have the ability to walk through those gates. This is the next, and the most profound stage of the battle for civil rights."

—***Lyndon B. Johnson***

"Let us have faith that right makes might, and in that faith let us to the end dare to do our duty as we understand it."

—***Abraham Lincoln,*** speech at Cooper Union, New York, February 27, 1860

"Men, their rights and nothing more; women, their rights and nothing less."

—***Susan B. Anthony,*** *Women's Rights to Suffrage,* 1873

"No civil liberties battle is ever won—permanently."

—***Roger Baldwin,*** founder of the American Civil Liberties Union

"No man can put a chain about the ankle of his fellow man, without at least finding the other end of it around his own neck."

—***Frederick Douglass,*** *Life and Times of Frederick Douglass,* 1895

"No man is good enough to govern another man without that other's consent."

—***Abraham Lincoln,*** speech in Peoria, Illinois, October 16, 1854

"Our flag is red, white, and blue, but our nation is rainbow—red, yellow, brown, black, and white—we're all precious in God's sight."

—***Jesse Jackson,*** address to the Democratic National Convention, July 17, 1984

"Since my little son is only half-Jewish, would it be all right if he went into the pool only up to his waist?"

—***Groucho Marx,*** addressed to a country club that would not admit Jews

"The sufferings that are endured patiently as being inevitable become intolerable the moment it appears there might be an escape. Reform then only serves to reveal more clearly what still remains oppressive and now all the more unbearable. The suffering, it's true, has been reduced if one's sensitivity has become more acute."

—*Alexis de Tocqueville*

"Tell them that the sacrifice was not in vain. Tell them that by the way of the shop, the field, the skilled hand, habits of thrift and economy, by way of industrial school and college, we are coming. We are crawling up, working up, yea, bursting up. Often through oppression, unjust discrimination, and prejudice, but through them we are coming up, and with proper habits, intelligence, and property, there is no power on earth that can permanently stay our progress."

—*Booker T. Washington*

"They have rights who dare maintain them."

—*James Russell Lowell,* "The Present Crisis," 1844

"This Nation was founded by men of many nations and backgrounds. It was founded on the principle that all men are created equal and that the rights of every man are diminished when the rights of one man are threatened."

—*John F. Kennedy,* radio and television report to the American people on civil rights, June 11, 1963

"Too many people think Martin freed black people; in truth he helped free all people."

—*Martin Luther King, Sr.,* speaking of his son, Martin Luther King, Jr.

"Travel is fatal to prejudice."

—*Mark Twain*

"We are not asking for superiority, for we have always had that. All we ask is equality."

—*Lady Nancy Astor,* on equal rights for women

"We are now faced with the fact that tomorrow is today. We are confronted with the fierce urgency of now. In this unfolding conundrum of life and history there is such a thing as being too late. Procrastination is still the thief of time. . . . The 'tide in the affairs of men' does not remain at the flood; it ebbs. . . . Over the bleached bones and jumbled residues of numerous civilizations are written the pathetic words: 'Too late.'"

—*Martin Luther King, Jr., Where Do We Go from Here: Chaos or Community?* 1967

"We must learn to live together as brothers or we will perish as fools. . . . Racial injustice is still the black man's burden and the white man's shame."

—***Martin Luther King, Jr.***

"We shall be judged more by what we do at home than what we preach abroad."

—***John F. Kennedy,*** State of the Union Address, 1963

"When I hear anyone arguing for slavery, I feel a strong impulse to see it tried on him personally."

—***Abraham Lincoln,*** "Address to an Indiana Regiment," March 17, 1865

"While the races may stand side by side, whites stand on history's mountain and blacks stand in history's hollow. Until we overcome unequal history, we cannot overcome unequal opportunity. . . . It's time we get down to the business of trying to stand black and white on level ground."

—***Lyndon B. Johnson***

"The worst provincialism of which America can be guilty is the provincialism of prejudice, racial prejudice against new and challenging ideas."

—***William O. Douglas,*** address to the Amalgamated Clothing Workers, May 14, 1952

"You can't hold a man down without staying down with him."

—***Booker T. Washington***

"You have to be taught second class; you're not born that way."

—***Lena Horne,*** in her autobiography, *Lena,* 1965

15 FAMILY

"Always obey your parents, when they are present."

—***Mark Twain,*** *Advice to Youth,* 1882

"The American dream begins with the American family."

—***Barbara A. Mikulski,*** address to the Democratic National Convention, Atlanta, Georgia, July 20, 1988

"Am I my brother's keeper?"

—***Genesis 4:9,*** Cain's response to God's inquiry about the whereabouts of his brother, Abel

"As the family goes, so goes the nation."

—***Margaret Mead***

"Bigamy is having one husband too many. Monogamy is the same."

—***Anonymous***

"Blood is thicker than water."

—***Proverb***

Children aren't happy with nothing to ignore
And that's what parents were created for.

—***Ogden Nash***

"Even when poverty and disorientation strike, as over the generations they so often do, it is family strength that most defends individuals against alienation, lassitude, or despair."

—***Michael Novak,*** "Family Out of Favor," *Harper's,* 1976

"The family is one of nature's masterpieces."

—***George Santayana***

"The family is the original Department of Health, Education, and Welfare."

—***William J. Bennett,*** interview on *MacNeil-Lehrer News Hour,* August 9, 1989

"The great advantage of living in a large family is that early lesson of life's essential unfairness."

—***Nancy Mitford,*** *The Pursuit of Love,* 1945

"Healthy families are our greatest national resource."

—***Dolores Curran,*** *Traits of a Healthy Family,* 1983

Home is the place where, when you have to go there,
They have to take you in.

—***Robert Frost,*** "The Death of the Hired Man," *North of Boston,* 1915

"I bequeath all my property to my wife on the condition that she remarry immediately. Then, there will be at least one man to regret my death."

—***Heinrich Heine***

"I love all my children, but some of them I don't like."

—***Lillian Carter,*** mother of President Jimmy Carter

"It is no accident that in a million years of evolution we have emerged with a particular form for the raising of children . . . and it is the human family."

—***Urie Bronfenbrenner***

"It is now quite lawful for a Catholic woman to avoid pregnancy by a resort to mathematics, though she is still forbidden to resort to physics or chemistry."

—***H. L. Mencken,*** *Notebooks,* 1956

"It's never easy keeping your own husband happy. It's much easier to make someone else's husband happy."

—***Zsa Zsa Gabor,*** interview with Merv Griffin, January 1980

"My family history begins with me but yours ends in you."

—***Iphicrates,*** response to a taunt by the nobly born Harmodius regarding his plebeian background

"Never in the history of American politics has there been a constituency so popular but with so little political clout as the American family."

—***Christopher J. Dodd,*** *Washington Post,* October 8, 1988

"Nothing to my son, except my name."

—***Napoleon Bonaparte,*** from a note held in his hand at his death, May 5, 1821

"Paradise lies at the feet of thy mother."

—***Muhammad***

"Parents are the last people on earth who ought to have children."

—***Samuel Butler***

"The particular human chain we're part of is central to our individual identity. Even if we loathe our families, in order to know ourselves, we seem to need to know about them, just as prologue."

—***Elizabeth Stone,*** *Black Sheep and Kissing Cousins,* 1988

"The peace and stability of a nation depend upon the proper relationships established in the home."

—***Jade Snow Wong,*** *Fifth Chinese Daughter,* 1950

"The psychological attitudes which are indispensable in the American market place are disastrous to family life. Family life requires yieldingness, generosity, sympathy, altruism, tenderness—all the qualities, in fact, which lead straight to bankruptcy. The American family is tragically out of gear with the profit structure which has mushroomed up around it."

—***Margaret Halsey,*** *The Folks at Home,* 1952

"Somewhere on this globe, every ten seconds, there is a woman giving birth to a child. She must be found and stopped."

—***Sam Levenson***

"There are three ways to get something done: do it yourself, employ someone, or forbid your children to do it."

—***Monta Crane***

"These are times when parenthood seems nothing but feeding the mouth that bites you."

—***Peter De Vries,*** *Tunnel of Love,* 1954

"The thing that impresses me most about America is the way parents obey their children."

—***Edward VIII,*** 1936

"Though it is fairly easy to describe what constitutes a bad home, there is no simple definition of a good one. Conformity with the traditional pattern certainly is no guarantee of the happiest results."

—***Alva Myrdal and Viola Klein,*** *Women's Two Roles,* 1956

"What families have in common the world around is that they are the place where people learn who they are and how to be that way."

—***Jean Illsley Clarke,*** *Self-Esteem,* 1978

"What has made this nation great? Not its heroes but its households."

—***Sarah J. Hale,*** *Traits of American Life,* 1835

"What ought to be done to the man who invented the celebrating of anniversaries? Mere killing would be too light."

—***Mark Twain***

"Wherever there is lasting love, there is a family."

—***Shere Hite,*** *The Hite Report on the Family,* 1994

"The woman who started it all, the head of the greatest employment agency in America."

—***Adlai Stevenson*** on Rose Kennedy

"Workers have both work responsibilities and family responsibilities, and they need some accommodating of these competing needs."

—***Helen Norton***

"The worst misfortune that can happen to an ordinary man is to have an extraordinary father."

—***Austin O'Malley***

16 FATE

"The bad end unhappily, the good unluckily. That is what tragedy means."

—***Tom Stoppard,*** *Rosencrantz and Guildenstern Are Dead,* 1967

"Boast not thyself of tomorrow; for thou knowest not what a day may bring forth."

—***Proverbs 27:1***

"Chance favors only the prepared mind."

—***Louis Pasteur,*** December 17, 1854

"A consistent man believes in destiny, a capricious man in chance."

—***Benjamin Disraeli,*** *Vivian Grey,* 1826

"Destiny. A tyrant's authority for crime and a fool's excuse for failure."

—***Ambrose Bierce,*** *The Devil's Dictionary,* 1881–1911

"Destiny has two ways of crushing us—by refusing our wishes and by fulfilling them."

—***Henri Frédéric Amiel***

"Destiny is not a matter of chance; it is a matter of choice. It is not something to waited for, it is a thing to be achieved."

—***William Jennings Bryan,*** "America's Mission" speech, February 22, 1899

Do not try to find out—
we're forbidden to know—
what end the gods have in store for me,
or for you.

—***Horace,*** *Odes*

"Each man the architect of his own fate."

—***Appius Claudius,*** *De Civitate*

"Failure or success seem to have been allotted to men by their stars. But they retain the power of wriggling, of fighting with their stars or against it, and in the whole universe the only really interesting movement is this wriggle."

—***E. M. Forster,*** "Our Diversions," *Abinger Harvest,* 1936

"Fate is not an eagle, it creeps like a rat."

—***Elizabeth Bowen,*** *The House in Paris,* 1935

"Fate leads the willing, drags the unwilling."

—***Cleanthes,*** *Fragments*

"For want of a nail."

—***George Herbert,*** *Jacula Prudentum,* 1640, tracing the lack of a horseshoe nail to the loss of a rider

"Heaven from all creatures hides the book of fate."

—***Alexander Pope,*** *An Essay on Man,* 1733

"I defeated armies, but I could not conquer the flames, the frost, stupefaction, and death! I was forced to yield to fate!"

—***Napoleon Bonaparte,*** on the failure of his campaign against Russia

"I do not believe in a fate that falls on men however they act; but I do believe in a fate that falls on them unless they act."

—***G. K. Chesterton,*** "On Holland," *Generally Speaking,* 1928

"If fate means you to lose, give him a good fight anyhow."

—***William McFee,*** *Casuals of the Sea,* 1916

"Into each life some rain must fall."

—***Henry Wadsworth Longfellow,*** "The Rainy Day," 1842

"It does not lie in the power of man to stop the rolling stone of fate, which through neglect or lack of wisdom has been set moving."

—***Adolf Hitler,*** address to the Reichstag, February 20, 1938

"Let your life lightly dance on the edges of time like dew on the tip of a leaf."

—***Rabindranath Tagore***

"Life is like a game of cards. The hand that is dealt you represents determinism; the way you play it is free will."

—***Jawaharlal Nehru***

"Little folks become their little fate."

—***Horace,*** *Epistles,* Book 1

"Man was created so that he might lift up the heavens."

—***Menachem Mendel***

"Many men would take the death-sentence without a whimper to escape the life-sentence which fate carries in her other hand."

—***T. E. Lawrence, also known as "Lawrence of Arabia"***

Our wills and fates do so contrary run
That our devices still are overthrown;
Our thoughts are ours, their ends none of our own.

—***William Shakespeare,*** *Hamlet,* act 3, scene 2

"Persistence. Nothing in the world can take the place of persistence. Talent will not; nothing is more common than unsuccessful men with talent. Genius will not; unrewarded genius is almost a proverb. Education will not; the world is full of educated derelicts. Persistence and determination alone are omnipotent. The slogan 'Press on' has solved and will always solve the problems of the human race."

—***Calvin Coolidge***

"Some people find oil. Others don't."

—***J. Paul Getty,*** on being asked the secret of his success

Tempt not the stars, young man,
thou canst not play
With the severity of fate.

—***John Ford,*** *The Broken Heart,* 1640

"There is a mysterious cycle in human events. To some generations much is given. Of other generations much is expected. This generation of Americans has a rendezvous with destiny."

—***Franklin Delano Roosevelt,*** acceptance speech upon renomination for the presidency, Philadelphia, June 27, 1936

"There is a wheel on which the affairs of men revolve, and its movement forbids the same man to always be fortunate."

—***Croesus,*** king of Lydia, to Cyrus the Great prior to the battle of Thymbra

Things without all remedy
Should be without regard. What's done is done.

—***William Shakespeare,*** *Macbeth,* act 3, scene 2

"Those who lived without hope or blame."

—***Dante Alighieri,*** *The Divine Comedy, Inferno,* 1314. Virgil tells Dante that the anguished sounds he hears are the voices of those who cannot die and can only envy those who have been consigned through death to a punishment.

"'Tis weak and vicious people who cast the blame on Fate."

—***Ralph Waldo Emerson,*** "Fate," *The Conduct of Life,* 1860

"We are not permitted to choose the frame of our destiny. But what we put into it is ours."

—***Dag Hammarskjöld,*** *Markings,* 1964

"We are still masters of our fate. We are still captains of our souls."

—***Winston Churchill,*** paraphrasing W. E. Henley's poem "Invictus" in a speech to the House of Commons on the war situation, September 9, 1941

"We direct our affairs at the beginning, . . . but being once undertaken, they guide and transport us, and we must follow them."

—***Michel de Montaigne,*** *Essays,* 1580–1588

"Whatever limits us, we call Fate."

—***Ralph Waldo Emerson,*** "Fate," *The Conduct of Life,* 1860

What fates impose, that men must needs abide;
It boots not to resist both wind and tide.

—***William Shakespeare,*** *Henry VI, Part III,* act 4, scene 4

"The wheel is come full circle."

—***William Shakespeare,*** *King Lear,* 1608, scene 24

"Wherever the Fates, in their ebb and flow, lead, let us follow."

—*Virgil, Æneid*

"You must believe in free will; there is no choice."

—*Isaac Bashevis Singer*

17 FOUNDING FATHERS

"And when the great account of humanity shall be closed, in the bright list of those who have best adorned and served it, shall be found the names of our Adams and our Jefferson!"

—***Edward Everett,*** memorial address honoring John Adams and Thomas Jefferson (who died on the same day, July 4, 1826), Charlestown, Massachusetts, August 1, 1826

"Avoid the necessity of those overgrown military establishments, which under any form of government, are inauspicious to liberty, and which are to be regarded as particularly hostile to republican liberty."

—***George Washington,*** Farewell Address, September 19, 1796

By the rude bridge that arched the flood,
Their flag to freedom's breeze unfurled
Here once the embattled farmers stood
And fired the shot heard 'round the world.

—***Ralph Waldo Emerson,*** "Concord Hymn," 1837, inscribed on the Minuteman Monument

"The decree has gone and cannot now be recalled, that a more equal liberty than has prevailed in other parts of the earth, must be established in America."

—***John Adams***

"Driven from every other corner of the earth, freedom of thought and the right of private judgment in matters of conscience direct their course to this happy country as their last resort."

—***Samuel Adams***

"Here was buried Thomas Jefferson, Author of the Declaration of American Independence, of the Statute of Virginia for religious freedom, and Father of the University of Virginia, because by these, as testimonials that I have lived, I wish most to be remembered."

—***Thomas Jefferson,*** who wrote this epitaph for himself, does not mention his term as President.

"His physical eye saw a tiny, powerless body of some twenty men, hardly worth, Napoleon would have thought, the whiff of grapeshot that would so easily have sent them flying; but in his mind's eye, Washington saw gathered before him the power that was to grow down the centuries, the dignity of a great nation."

—***James Flexner,*** describing George Washington's view of the Continental Congress, 1783

"If he were put beside any king in Europe, that king would appear to be his lackey."

—***Anonymous,*** on Thomas Jefferson

"If you seek Hamilton's monument, look around. You are living in it. We honor Jefferson, but live in Hamilton's country, a mighty industrial nation with a strong central government."

—***George Will,*** on the absence of a monument dedicated to Alexander Hamilton in Washington, D.C., *Restoration,* 1992

"I pray Heaven to bestow the best of blessings on the house and all that shall hereafter inhabit it. May none but honest and wise men ever rule under this roof."

—***John Adams,*** first letter written in the White House, to his wife, Abigail, November 2, 1800. It is inscribed on the State Dining Room mantelpiece.

"I wander alone, and ponder—I muse, I mope, I ruminate—We have not Men, fit for the Times. We are deficient in Genius, in Education, in Travel, in Fortune—in every Thing."

—***John Adams,*** expressing concern over the quality of the members of the Continental Congress in his diary, autumn 1774

"Jefferson wrote almost a chapter in the Bible in the Declaration of Independence."

—***Menachem Begin***

"The makers of our Constitution undertook to secure conditions favorable to the pursuit of happiness. They recognized the significance of man's spiritual nature, of his feelings and of his intellect. They knew that only a part of the pain, pleasure and satisfactions of life are to be found in material things. They sought to protect Americans in their beliefs, their thoughts, their emotions, and their sensations. They conferred, as against the government, the right to be let alone—the most comprehensive of rights and the right most valued by civilized man."

—***Louis D. Brandeis,*** in the Supreme Court decision
Olmstead v. United States, 1928

"Our union is now complete; our constitution composed, established, and approved. You are now the guardians of your own liberties."

—***Samuel Adams,*** speech before the Continental Congress,
August 1, 1776

Then join hand in hand, brave Americans all!
By uniting we stand, by dividing we fall.

—***John Dickinson***

"There! John Bull can read my name without spectacles, and may now double his reward of 500 pounds for my head. *That* is my defiance."

—***John Hancock,*** on signing his name
to the Declaration of Independence

"They wanted enough power to lead, but they wanted to divide power enough to assure liberty."

—***James Reston,*** on the Constitutional doctrine
of separation of powers

"They wanted me to be another Washington."

—***Napoleon Bonaparte,*** at the end of his life

"Those who won our independence . . . valued liberty both as an end and as a means. They believed . . . that the greatest menace to freedom is an inert people; that public discussion is a political duty; and that this should be a fundamental principle of the American Government."

—***Louis D. Brandeis,*** in the Supreme Court decision
Whitney v. California, 1927

"We hold these truths to be self-evident, that all men are created equal; that they are endowed by their Creator with certain unalienable rights; that among these are Life, Liberty, and the pursuit of Happiness."

—***Thomas Jefferson,*** the Declaration of Independence, 1776

"Well, Doctor, what have we got—a Republic or a Monarchy?"
"A Republic, if you can keep it."

—***Benjamin Franklin,*** reply to a bystander at the close of the Constitutional Convention of 1787

"What do we mean by the American Revolution? Do we mean the American war? The Revolution was effected before the war commenced. The Revolution was in the minds and hearts of the people; a change in their religious sentiments of their duties and obligations."

—***John Adams,*** letter to H. Niles, February 13, 1818

"What is a great man who has made his mark upon history? . . . He is a man who has looked through the confusion of the moment and has seen the moral issue involved; he is a man who has refused to have his sense of justice distorted; he has listened to his conscience until conscience becomes a trumpet call to like-minded men, so that they gather about him, and together, with mutual purpose and mutual aid, they make a new period in history."

—***Jane Addams,*** speech on George Washington to Union League Club of Chicago, February 23, 1903

18 GLOBAL AFFAIRS

"Chronic wrongdoing, or an impotence which results in a general loosening of ties of civilized society, may . . . ultimately require intervention by some civilized nation."

—***Theodore Roosevelt,*** Annual Message to Congress, December 6, 1904

"The cost of freedom is always high—but Americans have always paid it."

—***John F. Kennedy,*** address to the American people regarding the Cuban Missile Crisis, October 22, 1962

"A covenant without a sword."

—***Anonymous,*** on the failure of the United States to join the League of Nations

"The freedom of the city is not negotiable. We cannot negotiate with those who say, 'What's mine is mine and what's yours is negotiable.' "

—***John F. Kennedy,*** on West Berlin, 1961

"A great movement has found a small people."

—***Theodor Herzl*** on Zionism, diary entry, 1900

"The Holy Roman Empire—neither holy, nor Roman, nor an Empire."

—***Ludwig Boerne,*** "Fragmente und Aphorismen," 1840

"I asked Tom if countries always apologized when they had done wrong, and he says, 'Yes, the little ones does.' "

—***Mark Twain,*** *Tom Sawyer Abroad,* 1894

"I believe that a generation of wondrous Jews will grow forth from the earth. The Maccabeans will rise again. The Jews who so desire will have our state. The world will be freed by our liberty, enriched by our wealth, magnified by our greatness."

—***Theodor Herzl***

"I cannot forecast to you the action of Russia. It is a riddle wrapped in a mystery inside an enigma."

—***Winston Churchill,*** first wartime broadcast over the BBC, October 1, 1939

"I don't know about the Nobel Prize, but they certainly deserve an Oscar."

—***Golda Meir,*** response to the the suggestion that Anwar Sadat and Menachem Begin be nominated for the Nobel Peace Prize

"If Algeria introduced a resolution declaring that the Earth was flat and that Israel had flattened it, it would pass by a vote of 164 to 13 with 26 abstentions."

—***Abba Eban*** on United Nations partisanship and Israel

"I feel happier now that we have no allies to be polite to and to pamper."

—***George VI*** to Queen Mary, June 27, 1940

"If socialism does not attain victory, then peace is only a truce."

—***Vladimir Ilyich Lenin***

"If the United Nations is a country unto itself, then the commodity it exports most is words."

—***Ester B. Fein,*** *New York Times,* October 14, 1985

"International incidents should not govern foreign policy, but foreign policy govern incidents."

—***Napoleon Bonaparte,*** *Maxims,* 1804–1815

> I will restore the fortunes of my people Israel
> and they shall rebuild the ruined cities and inhabit them;
> they shall plant vineyards and drink their wine,
> and they shall make gardens and eat their fruit.
> I will plant them upon their land,
> and they shall never again be plucked up
> out of the land which I have given them,
> Says the Lord your God.

—***Amos 9:14–15***

"I would not like to be a political leader in Russia. They never know when they're being taped."

—***Richard Nixon***

"Let us speak courteously, deal fairly, and keep ourselves armed and ready."

—*Theodore Roosevelt,* speech, San Francisco, May 13, 1903

"No foreign policy—no matter how ingenious—has any chance of success if it is born in the minds of the few and carried in the hearts of none."

—*Henry Kissinger,* speech to Boston World Affairs Council, March 11, 1976

"No man can tame a tiger into a kitten by stroking it."

—*Franklin Delano Roosevelt,* decryiing the policy of appeasement toward the Axis powers, "Arsenal of Democracy" speech, December 29, 1940

"No nation can be trusted further than it is bound by interest."

—*George Washington*

"Our interests are those of the open door—a door of friendship and mutual advantage. This is the only door we care to enter."

—*Woodrow Wilson,* address proposing a new foreign policy toward Latin America, March 19, 1913

"Our policy is not directed against any country or doctrine but against hunger, poverty, desperation, and chaos."

—*George C. Marshall,* speech at Harvard University announcing the "Marshall Plan" to rebuild post–World War II Europe, June 5, 1947

"Peace, commerce, and honest friendship with all nations—entangling alliances with none."

—*Thomas Jefferson,* First Inaugural Address, March 4, 1801

"Poor Mexico, so far from God and so close to the United States."

—*Porfirio Díaz*

"The Pope! How many divisions has *he* got?"

—*Joseph Stalin,* reply when asked to encourage Catholicism in Russia by way of conciliating the pope, May 13, 1935

"The seeds of totalitarian regimes are nurtured by misery and want. They spread and grow in the evil soil of poverty and strife. They reach their full growth when the hope of a people for a better life has died. We must keep that hope alive."

—*Harry S. Truman,* "Truman Doctrine" speech, March 12, 1947

"Since this century's beginning, a time of tempest has seemed to come upon the continents of the earth."

—*Dwight D. Eisenhower,* First Inaugural Address, January 20, 1953

"Small states are like indecently dressed women. They tempt the evil-minded."

—*Julius L. Nyerere,* April 1964

"Speak softly but carry a big stick."

—*Theodore Roosevelt,* speech at Minnesota State Fair, September 2, 1901

"A state worthy of the name has no friends—only interests."

—*Charles de Gaulle,* speech at West Point, December 5, 1962

"Success in a lottery is no argument for lotteries."

—*John Kenneth Galbraith,* reflecting on the brinkmanship practiced during the Cuban Missile Crisis

"There is no such thing as a small country. The greatness of a people is no more affected by the number of its inhabitants than the greatness of an individual is measured by his height. Whoever presents a great example is great."

—*Victor Hugo*

"There is solidarity, an interdependence about the modern world, both technically and morally, which makes it impossible for any nation completely to isolate itself from economic and political upheavals in the rest of the world, especially when such upheavals appear to be spreading and not declining."

—*Franklin Delano Roosevelt,* "Quarantine the Aggressors" speech, Chicago, October 5, 1937

"There must be, not a balance of power, but a community of power; not organized rivalries, but an organized peace."

—*Woodrow Wilson,* address to U.S. Senate, January 22, 1917

"They [the Arabs and Jews] should settle this problem in a true Christian spirit."

—*Warren Austin,* offering a solution to Arab-Israeli conflicts during United Nations debate over the partition of Palestine, 1948

"The twentieth century looms before us big with the fate of many nations. If we stand idly by, if we seek merely swollen, slothful ease, and ignoble peace, if we shrink from the hard contests where men must win at hazard of their lives and at the risk of all they hold dear, then the bolder and stronger peoples will pass us by and will win for themselves the domination of the world."

—*Theodore Roosevelt,* speech at the Hamilton Club, Chicago, April 10, 1899

"The United States does not have a choice as to whether it will or will not play a great part in the world. Fate has made that choice for us. The only question is whether we will play that part well or badly."

—*Theodore Roosevelt*

"We Americans have no commission from God to police the world."

—*Benjamin Harrison*

"We are at the beginning of an age, in which it will be insisted that the same standards of conduct and of responsibility for wrong done shall be observed among nations and their governments that are observed among the individual citizens of the United States."

—*Woodrow Wilson,* speech to a Joint Session of Congress, April 2, 1917

"We cannot escape danger, or the fear of danger, by crawling into bed and pulling the covers over our heads."

—*Franklin Delano Roosevelt* warning Americans of the dangers of isolationism, "Arsenal of Democracy" speech, December 29, 1940

"We created this Nation, not to serve ourselves, but to serve Mankind."

—*Woodrow Wilson*

"We have no eternal allies, and we have no perpetual enemies. Our interests are eternal, and those interests it is our duty to follow."

—*Lord Palmerston,* speech to House of Commons, March 1, 1848

"We no longer live in a world where only the actual firing of weapons represents a sufficient challenge to a nation's security to constitute maximum peril."

—*John F. Kennedy,* address to the American people regarding the Cuban Missile Crisis, October 22, 1962

"We're eyeball to eyeball, and I think the other fellow just blinked."

—*Dean Rusk,* on the Cuban Missile Crisis, October 24, 1962

"We should consider any attempt on their part to extend their system to any portion of this hemisphere, as dangerous to our peace and safety."

—*James Monroe,* "Monroe Doctrine," December 2, 1823

"What is necessary is a realization that the United States is a part of the movement of history itself; that it cannot stand apart, attempting to control the world by imposing covenants and treaties and by violent military intervention; that our role is not to police the planet but to use military strength with restraint and within limits, while at the same time we make available to the world the great power of our economy, of our knowledge, and of our good will."

—*Eugene McCarthy,* speech to the Conference of Concerned Democrats, a group organized to oppose the Vietnam War, Chicago, December 2, 1967

"When China awakens, the world will tremble."

—*Attributed to Napoleon Bonaparte,* after reading the journals of Sir George Leonard Staunton and John Barrow about their travels to China

"When Kansas and Colorado have a quarrel over the water in the Arkansas River, they don't call out the National Guard in each state and declare war over it. They bring a suit in the Supreme Court of the United States and abide by the decision. There isn't a reason in the world why we can't do that internationally."

—*Harry S. Truman,* speech, Kansas City, Missouri, April 1945

"Without a country you are the bastards of humanity."

—*Giuseppe Mazzini,* on the need for a Jewish homeland

"The world must be made safe for democracy. Its peace must be planted upon the tested foundations of political liberty. We have no selfish ends to serve. We desire no conquest, no dominion. We seek no indemnities for ourselves, no material compensation for the sacrifices we shall freely make. We are but one of the champions of the rights of mankind. We shall be satisfied when those rights have been made as secure as the faith and the freedom of nations can make them."

—*Woodrow Wilson,* address to Congress asking for a declaration of war, April 2, 1917

"You must master at the outset a simple but unalterable fact in modern foreign relations. When peace has been broken anywhere, peace of all countries everywhere is in danger."

—*Franklin Delano Roosevelt,* radio address proclaiming American neutrality in World War II, September 4, 1939

19 GOVERNMENT

"The best minds are not in government. If any were, business would hire them right away."

—*Ronald Reagan*

"The care of human life and happiness . . . is the first and only legitimate object of good government."

—*Thomas Jefferson,* "To the Republican Citizens of Washington County, Maryland," March 31, 1809

"The country is carried comfortably down the river by the current, and the function of government is merely to put out an oar when there is any danger of its drifting into the bank."

—*Lord Salisbury*

"Do you pray for the senators, Dr. Hale?"
"No, I look at the senators and I pray for the country."

—*Edward Everett Hale*

"The functions of government must be readjusted from time to time to restrain the strong and protect the weak. That is the preservation of liberty itself."

—*Herbert Hoover,* September 17, 1935

"Government can err; Presidents do make mistakes, but the immortal Dante tells us that divine justice weighs the sins of the cold-blooded and the sins of the warm-hearted in different scales. Better the occasional faults of a Government that lives in a spirit of charity than the consistent omissions of a Government frozen in the ice of its own indifference."

—*Franklin Delano Roosevelt,* speech at the Democratic National Convention, June 27, 1936

"[The government] goes on in strange paradox, decided only to be undecided, resolved to be irresolute, adamant for drift, solid for fluidity."

—***Winston Churchill,*** speech, November 12, 1936

"Governments, like clocks, go from the motion that men give them."

—***William Penn***

"A government which robs Peter to pay Paul can always depend on the support of Paul."

—***George Bernard Shaw,*** *Everybody's Political What's What,* 1944

"Great constitutional provisions must be administered with caution. Some play must be allowed for the joints of the machine, and it must be remembered that legislatures are ultimate guardians of the liberties and welfare of the people in quite as great a degree as the courts."

—***Oliver Wendell Holmes, Jr.,*** Supreme Court majority opinion in *Missouri, Kansas and Texas Railway Company v. May,* 194 U.S. 270, 1904

"Having looked to government for bread, on the very first scarcity they will turn and bite the hand that fed them."

—***Edmund Burke,*** *Thoughts and Details on Scarcity,* 1795

"I'd rather entrust the government of the United States to the first 400 people listed in the Boston telephone directory than to the faculty of Harvard University."

—***William F. Buckley, Jr.***

"If men were angels, no government would be necessary. If angels were to govern men, neither external nor internal controls on government would be necessary. In framing a government which is to be administered by men over men, the great difficulty lies in this: you must first enable the government to control the governed; and in the next place oblige it to control itself."

—***James Madison,*** *The Federalist Papers,* No. 51, 1787–1788

"If the government becomes a law-breaker, it breeds contempt for the law, it invites every man to become a law unto himself, it invites anarchy. To declare that in the administration of the criminal law the end justifies the means—to declare that the Government may commit crimes in order to secure the conviction of a private criminal—would bring terrible retribution."

—***Louis D. Brandeis,*** dissenting opinion in the Supreme Court decision *Olmstead et al. v. United States,* 277 U.S. 485, 1928

"If the government is big enough to give you everything you want, it is big enough to take away everything you have."

—*Gerald Ford*

"I have considered the pension list of the republic a roll of honor."

—***Grover Cleveland,*** veto of Dependent Pension Bill

"It is dangerous to be right when the government is wrong."

—*Voltaire*

"It is impossible that the whisper of a faction should prevail against the voice of a nation."

—***Lord John Russell,*** reply to the protest of 150,000 persons in Birmingham over the defeat of the second Reform Bill

"I would have been glad to have lived under my woodside, and to have kept a flock of sheep, rather than to have undertaken this government."

—***Oliver Cromwell,*** address to Parliament, 1658

"The legitimate object of government is to do for a community of people whatever they need to have done, but cannot do at all, or cannot so well do, for themselves, in their separate and individual capacities. In all that the people can individually do as well for themselves, government ought not to interfere."

—***Abraham Lincoln,*** "On Government," July 1, 1854

"Let us begin and create in idea a State; and yet the true creator is necessity, which is the mother of our invention."

—***Plato,*** *The Republic*

"Man is immortal; his salvation is hereafter. The state has no immortality; its salvation is now or never."

—*Cardinal Richelieu*

"Many people consider the things which government does for them as social progress, but they consider the things government does for others as socialism."

—*Earl Warren*

"The moral test of government is how that government treats those who are in the dawn of life, the children; those who are in the twilight of life, the elderly; and those in the shadows of life—the sick, the needy, and the handicapped."

—***Hubert H. Humphrey,*** remarks made at the dedication of the Hubert H. Humphrey Building, Washington, D.C., November 1, 1977

"Necessity is the plea for every infringement of human freedom; it is the argument of tyrants; it is the creed of slaves."

—***William Pitt the Younger,*** "Speech on the India Bill," November 18, 1783

"The object of government is the welfare of the people. The liberty of people to carry on their business should not be abridged unless the larger interests of the many are concerned. When the interests of the many are concerned the interests of the few must yield. It is the purpose of the government to see not only that the legitimate interests of the few are protected but that the welfare and the rights of the many are conserved. These are the principles which we must remember in any consideration of the question. This, I take it, is sound government—not politics. Those are the essential basic conditions under which government can be of service."

—***Franklin Delano Roosevelt,*** campaign speech, Portland, Oregon, September 21, 1932

"The only thing that saves us from the bureaucracy is its inefficiency."

—***Eugene McCarthy***

"Our word *idiot* comes from the Greek name for the man who took no share in public matters."

—***Edith Hamilton,*** *The Greek Way,* 1930

"The people's government made for the people, made by the people, and answerable to the people."

—***Daniel Webster,*** speech, January 26, 1830

"The power to tax involves the power to destroy."

—***John Marshall,*** majority opinion in the Supreme Court decision *McCulloch v. Maryland,* 4 Wheaton 316, 421, 1819

"The ruler is the boat and the common people are the water. It is the water that bears the boat up, and the water that capsizes it."

—***Sun Tzu***

"A State without the means of some change is without the means of its conservation."

—***Edmund Burke,*** *Reflections on the Revolution in France,* 1790

"The test of a government is not how popular it is with the powerful and privileged few, but how honestly and fairly it deals with the many who must depend upon it."

—***Jimmy Carter,*** Inaugural Address as governor of Georgia, 1971

"That government is the strongest of which every man feels himself a part."

—***Thomas Jefferson***

"There are those who use their minds and there are those who use their muscles. The former rule, the latter are ruled."

—***Mencius***

"There's no trick to being a humorist when you have the whole government working for you."

—***Will Rogers***

"Those who are too smart to engage in politics are punished by being governed by those who are dumber."

—***Plato***

"We are rapidly entering the age of no privacy, where everyone is open to surveillance at all times; where there are no secrets from government."

—***William O. Douglas,*** dissenting opinion in the Supreme Court decision *Osborn v. United States,* 385 U.S. 341, 1966

"Well, I think that when statesmen forsake their own private conscience for the sake of their public duties, they lead their country by a short route to chaos."

—***Robert Bolt,*** *A Man for All Seasons,* 1962

"When the government fears the people, there is liberty. When the people fear the government, there is tyranny."

—***Thomas Jefferson***

"Why has the government been instituted at all? Because the passions of men will not conform to the dictates of reason and justice without constraint."

—***Alexander Hamilton,*** *The Federalist Papers,* No. 15, 1787–1788

"Without salaries, public office would become the monopoly of the rich."

—***John Adams***

"The worst thing in the world next to anarchy is government."

—***Henry Ward Beecher,*** *Proverbs from Plymouth Pulpit,* 1887

20 HONESTY AND TRUST

"An abomination unto the Lord, but a very present help in time of trouble."

—***Adlai Stevenson,*** definition of a lie

"All is not gold that glitters."

—***Miguel de Cervantes,*** *Don Quixote,* 1615

"All the strength, except truth, was on his side."

—***Barbara Tuchman,*** referring to General Mercier and his handling of the Dreyfus Affair, *The Proud Tower,* 1966

"Believe those who are seeking the truth; doubt those who find it."

—***André Gide***

"The cruelest lies are often told in silence."

—***Robert Louis Stevenson,*** *Virginibus Puerisque,* 1881

"False face must hide what the false heart doth know."

—***William Shakespeare,*** *Macbeth,* act 1, scene 7

"For my mouth shall utter truth, and wickedness is an abomination to my lips."

—***Proverbs 8:7***

"For the great enemy of the truth is very often not the lie—deliberate, contrived and dishonest—but the myth—persistent, persuasive—of our forebears. We enjoy the comfort of opinion without the discomfort of thought."

—***John F. Kennedy,*** commencement address, Yale University, June 11, 1962

"God offers to everyone his choice between truth and repose. Take which you please—you can never have both."

—***Ralph Waldo Emerson***

"The great masses of people . . . will more easily fall victim to a big lie than to a little one."

—***Adolf Hitler,*** *Mein Kampf,* 1925

"He who permits himself to tell a lie once, finds it much easier to do it a second and a third time, till at length it becomes habitual; he tells lies without attending to it, and truths without the world's believing him. This falsehood of the tongue leads to that of the heart, and in time depraves all its good dispositions."

—***Thomas Jefferson,*** letter to Peter Carr, August 10, 1785

"Honesty is the first chapter of the book of wisdom."

—***Thomas Jefferson***

Hypocrisy, the only evil that walks
Invisible, except to God alone.

—***John Milton,*** *Paradise Lost,* 1667

If any question why we died,
Tell them, because our fathers lied.

—***Rudyard Kipling,*** "Common Form," 1919

"If I were two-faced, would I be wearing this one?"

—***Abraham Lincoln***

"If you tell the truth you don't have to remember anything."

—***Mark Twain***

"I have always noticed that people will never laugh at anything that is not based on truth."

—***Will Rogers***

"I hope I shall possess firmness and virtue enough to maintain what I consider the most enviable of all titles, the character of an 'Honest Man.' Your honesty influences others to be honest."

—***George Washington***

"I never gave them hell, I just tell the truth and they think it's hell."

—***Harry S. Truman,*** interview, 1956

"I would rather be accused of breaking precedents than breaking promises."

—***John F. Kennedy***

"The lady doth protest too much, methinks."

—***William Shakespeare,*** *Hamlet,* act 3, scene 2

"Liars, when they speak the truth, are not believed."

—***Aristotle***

"A lie gets halfway around the world before the truth has a chance to get its pants on."

—***Winston Churchill***

"A lie keeps growing and growing, until it's as plain as the nose on your face."

—***Evelyn Venable as The Blue Fairy*** in Walt Disney's *Pinocchio,* 1940

"Love truth, but pardon error."

—***Voltaire,*** *Discours sur l'Homme,* 1843

"Men are disposed to live honestly if the means of doing so are open to them."

—***Thomas Jefferson***

"Men stumble over the truth from time to time, but most pick themselves up and hurry off as if nothing happened."

—***Winston Churchill,*** speech in the House of Commons, November 29, 1944

"Most writers regard truth as their most valuable possession, and therefore are most economical in its use."

—***Mark Twain***

"No error is so monstrous that it fails to find defenders among the ablest men."

—***Lord Acton,*** letter to Mary Gladstone, April 24, 1881

"No pleasure is comparable to the standing upon the vantage-ground of truth."

—***Francis Bacon,*** *Of Truth,* 1625

"Nothing is more damaging to a new truth than an old error."

—***Johann Wolfgang von Goethe,*** *Proverbs in Prose*

"Now, rumor travels faster, but it don't stay put as long as truth."

—***Will Rogers***

Oh, what a tangled web we weave,
When first we practice to deceive!

—***Walter Scott,*** *Marmion,* 1808

"One of the most striking differences between a cat and a lie is that a cat has only nine lives."

—***Mark Twain,*** *The Tragedy of Pudd'nhead Wilson,* 1893

"People ask you for criticism, but they only want praise."

—***W. Somerset Maugham,*** *Of Human Bondage,* 1915

"Plato is a dear friend but a dearer friend is truth."

—***Aristotle***

"There are three kind of lies—lies, damned lies, and statistics."

—***Benjamin Disraeli***

"There is never a duel with the truth. The truth always wins, and we are not afraid of it. The truth is no coward. The truth does not need the law. The truth does not need the forces of government. The truth is imperishable, eternal, and immortal and needs no human agency to support it."

—***Dudley Field Malone,*** arguing that scientific testimony defending evolution should be admitted in the Scopes "monkey" trial, July 16, 1925

"There is nothing so powerful as truth—and often nothing so strange."

—***Daniel Webster,*** arguing a murder trial, April 6, 1830

"There is only one way to find out if a man's honest: ask him. If he says yes, you know he is crooked."

—***Mark Twain***

To be persuasive, we must be believable,
To be believable, we must be credible,
To be credible, we must be truthful.

—***Edward R. Murrow***

"Truth between candid minds can never do harm."

—***Thomas Jefferson,*** letter to John Adams, 1791

"A truth is not hard to kill and . . . a lie told well is immortal."

—***Mark Twain,*** *Advice to Youth,* 1882

"Truth is not only violated by falsehood; it may be outraged by silence."

—***Henri Frédéric Amiel***

"The truth is rarely pure and never simple."

—***Oscar Wilde,*** *The Importance of Being Earnest,* 1895

"The truth is sometimes a poor competitor in the market place of ideas—complicated, unsatisfying, full of dilemmas, always vulnerable to misinterpretation and abuse."

—***George F. Kennan,*** *American Diplomacy,* 1951

"Truth sits upon the lips of dying men."

—***Matthew Arnold,*** "Sohrab and Rustum," 1853

"We must suffer, suffer into truth."

—***Aeschylus***

"We owe respect to the living; to the dead we owe only truth."

—***Voltaire,*** "Première Lettre sur Oedipe," *Oeuvres,* 1785

"When the truth is in your way, you are on the wrong road."

—***Josh Billings***

"Whoever is careless with the truth in small matters cannot be trusted with important affairs."

—***Albert Einstein***

"Why shouldn't the truth be stranger than fiction? Fiction is obliged to stick to possibilities. Truth isn't."

—***Mark Twain***

"With public trust everything is possible, and without it, nothing is possible."

—***Abraham Lincoln***

"Ye shall know the truth, and the truth shall make you free."

—***John 9:32***

21 HUMANITY

"All the world's a stage, and all the men and women merely players."

—***William Shakespeare,*** *As You Like It,* act 2, scene 7

"And God said: 'Let us make man in our image, after our likeness; and let them have dominion over the fish of the sea, over the fowl of the air, and over every living thing that creepeth upon the earth.' "

—***Genesis 1:26***

"As far as we can discern, the sole purpose of human existence is to kindle a light in the darkness of mere being."

—***Carl Gustav Jung,*** *Memories, Dreams, Reflections,* 1962

"The better part of valor is discretion."

—***William Shakespeare,*** *King Henry IV, Part I,* act 5, scene 4, where Falstaff justifies feigning death on the battlefield to escape combat

"Consistency is contrary to nature, contrary to life. The only completely consistent people are the dead."

—***Aldous Huxley,*** "Wordsworth in the Tropics," *Do What You Will,* 1929

"Death and taxes and childbirth! There's never any convenient time for any of them."

—***Margaret Mitchell,*** *Gone With the Wind,* 1936

"Everybody knows in their bones that *something* is eternal, and that something has to do with human beings. All the greatest people ever lived have been telling us that for five thousand years and yet you'd be surprised how people are always losing hold of it."

—***Thornton Wilder,*** *Our Town,* 1938

"Every one of us is given the gift of life, and what a strange gift it is. If it is preserved jealously and selfishly, it impoverishes and saddens. But if it is spent for others, it enriches and beautifies."

—***Ignazio Silone***

"Fear the time when Manself will not suffer and die for a concept, for this one quality is the foundation of Manself, and this one quality is man, distinctive in the universe."

—***John Steinbeck,*** *The Grapes of Wrath,* 1939

"For man, unlike any other thing organic or inorganic in the universe, grows beyond his work, walks up the stairs of his concepts, emerges ahead of his accomplishments. . . . Having stepped forward, he may slip back, but only a half a step, never the full step back."

—***John Steinbeck,*** *The Grapes of Wrath,* 1939

"For the greatest part of the liberated Jews of Bergen-Belsen, there was no ecstasy, no joy at our liberation. We had lost our families, our homes. We had no place to go to, nobody to hug. Nobody was waiting for us anywhere. We had been liberated from death and the fear of death, but not from the fear of life."

—***Hadassah Rosensaft,*** at the International Liberators' Conference, 1981

"Hate the sin and love the sinner."

—***Mohandas K. Gandhi***

He is a portion of the loveliness
Which once he made more lovely.

—***Percy Bysshe Shelley,*** "Adonais," 1821

"He's not the finest character that ever lived. But he's a human being, and a terrible thing is happening to him. So attention must be paid. He's not to be allowed to fall into his grave like an old dog."

—***Arthur Miller,*** *Death of a Salesman,* 1949. Linda Loman is speaking to her son Biff about his father, Willy.

"He that is without sin among you, let him first cast a stone."

—***John 8:7***

"Hope springs eternal in the human breast."

—*Alexander Pope, An Essay on Man,* 1733

"Human beings may be divided into three classes; those who are toiled to death, those who are worried to death, and those who are bored to death."

—*Winston Churchill*

"Humankind cannot bear very much reality."

—*T. S. Eliot, Murder in the Cathedral,* 1935

"I agree with you that there is a natural aristocracy among men. The grounds of this are virtue and talents."

—*Thomas Jefferson,* letter to John Adams, October 28, 1813

"I am the inferior of any man whose rights I trample under foot. Men are not superior by reason of the accidents of race or color. They are superior who have the best heart—the best brain."

—*Robert G. Ingersoll*

"I decline to believe in the end of man. It is easy enough to say that man is immortal simply because he will endure: that when the last ding-dong of doom has clanged and faded from the last worthless rock hanging tideless in the last red and dying evening, that even then there will still be one more sound: that of his puny, inexhaustible voice, still talking. I refuse to accept this. He will not merely endure, he will prevail."

—*William Faulkner,* accepting the Nobel Prize for Literature, Stockholm, Sweden, December 10, 1950

"I know no safe depositary of the ultimate powers of the society but the people themselves; and if we think them not enlightened enough to exercise their control with a wholesome discretion, the remedy is not to take it from them, but to inform their discretion by education."

—*Thomas Jefferson,* letter to William Jarvis, September 28, 1820

"I know of no rights of race superior to the rights of humanity."

—*Frederick Douglass*

"If a man can build a better book, preach a better sermon, or make a better mousetrap than his neighbor, though he builds his house in the woods, the world will make a beaten path to his door."

—*Ralph Waldo Emerson*

"The last clear definite function of man—muscles aching to work, minds aching to create beyond the single need—this is man."

—***John Steinbeck,*** *The Grapes of Wrath,* 1939

Laugh, and the world laughs with you;
Weep, and you weep alone;
For the sad old earth must borrow its mirth,
But has troubles enough of its own.

—***Ella Wheeler Wilcox,*** *Solitude,* 1883

"Man—a creature made at the end of the week's work when God was tired."

—***Mark Twain***

"Man is the only animal that blushes. Or needs to."

—***Mark Twain,*** "Pudd'nhead Wilson's New Calendar," *Following the Equator,* 1897

"Man is the only creature who refuses to be what he is."

—***Albert Camus***

"Man is what he believes."

—***Anton Chekhov,*** *Notebooks,* 1896

The man who lives for self alone
Lives for the meanest mortal known.

—***Joaquin Miller,*** "Walker in Nicaragua"

"Men should be either treated generously or destroyed, because they take revenge for slight injuries—for heavy ones they cannot."

—***Niccolò Machiavelli,*** *The Prince,* 1513

"My candle burns at both ends."

—***Edna St. Vincent Millay,*** *Figs from Thistles,* 1922

"No man is an island, entire of itself: every man is a piece of the continent, a part of the main; . . . any man's death diminishes me, because I am involved in mankind; and therefore never send to know for whom the bell tolls; it tolls for thee."

—***John Donne,*** *Devotions,* 1624

"Nobody wants to be called Common People, especially common people."

—***Will Rogers***

"Nobody will save us—from us, or for us—but us. In our schools and in our society, it is time for self-reliance to replace the dependency that has victimized too many of us."

—***Jesse Jackson***

"Our problems are man-made, therefore they may be solved by man. . . . No problem of human destiny is beyond human beings."

—***John F. Kennedy,*** speech at American University, Washington, D.C., June 10, 1963

"The people is a great beast."

—***Alexander Hamilton***

"Popularity is the easiest thing in the world to gain and it is the hardest thing to hold."

—***Will Rogers***

"A single candle can light a thousand more without diminishing itself."

—***Hillel the Elder***

"Such is the human race . . . often it seems a pity that Noah and his party didn't miss the boat."

—***Mark Twain***

"Then the Lord God formed man of the dust of the ground, and breathed into his nostrils the breath of life, and man became a living soul."

—***Genesis 2:7***

"The true worth of a race must be measured by the character of its womanhood."

—***Mary McLeod Bethune,*** "A Century of Progress of Negro Women," Chicago Women's Federation, June 30, 1935

"While there's life, there's hope."

—***Theocritus,*** *Idylls,* 4.42

"The worst sin towards our fellow creatures is not to hate them but to be indifferent to them: that's the essence of inhumanity."

—***George Bernard Shaw,*** *The Devil's Disciple,* 1901

"The young man who has not wept is a savage, and the old man who will not laugh is a fool."

—***George Santayana,*** *Dialogues in Limbo,* 1926

22 IDEALISM

"All hope abandon, ye who enter here."

—*Dante Alighieri, The Divine Comedy, Inferno,* 1314

"Behind the cloud the sun is still shining."

—***Abraham Lincoln***

"Behold, the dreamer cometh."

—***Genesis 37:19.*** Spoken derisively by Joseph's brothers upon his approach, before they sell him into slavery

"Be practical as well as generous in your ideals. Keep your eyes on the stars, but remember to keep your feet on the ground."

—***Theodore Roosevelt,*** speech at the Groton School, Groton, Massachusetts, May 24, 1904

"But I guess . . . I'm like the everlasting optimist who fell off the skyscraper. As he passed the twentieth floor, the horrified spectators in the windows heard him shout, 'So far, so good!' "

—***Adlai Stevenson,*** speech delivered at an Illinois Democratic rally after the defeat of his budget plan by the state legislature, spring 1949

"Cynicism is disappointed idealism."

—***Harry Kemelman***

Don't let it be forgot
that once there was a spot

for one brief shining moment
that was known as Camelot.

—***Alan Jay Lerner,*** title song of *Camelot,* 1960

"Don't part with your illusions. When they are gone, you may still exist, but you have ceased to live."

—***Mark Twain,*** *Following the Equator,* 1898

"Dream and deed are not as different as many think. All the deeds of men are dreams at first, and become dreams in the end."

—***Theodor Herzl***

"An era can be said to end when its basic illusions are exhausted."

—***Arthur Miller***

"Hope is a good breakfast, but it is a bad supper."

—***Francis Bacon,*** *Apophthegms,* 1624

"I believe a leaf of grass is no less than the journey-work of the stars."

—***Walt Whitman,*** "Song of Myself," 1855

"An idealist without illusions."

—***John F. Kennedy,*** describing himself, 1953

"I do not believe that any of us would exchange places with any other people of any other generation."

—***John F. Kennedy,*** Inaugural Address, January 20, 1961

"If a man hasn't discovered something that he will die for, he isn't fit to live."

—***Martin Luther King, Jr.,*** speech in Detroit, Michigan, June 23, 1963

"If you would hit the mark, you must aim a little above it; every arrow that flies feels the attraction of the earth."

—***Henry Wadsworth Longfellow***

"I hope always, I desire much, I expect little."

—***Vladimir Jabotinsky***

"I look forward to a great future for America—a future in which our country will match its military strength with our moral restraint, its wealth with our wisdom, its power with our purpose."

—***John F. Kennedy,*** address at Amherst College, Amherst, Massachusetts, October 26, 1963

"Important principles may and must be inflexible."

—***Abraham Lincoln,*** "Reconstruction of the Union," final public address, April 11, 1865

"In each of us, there is a private hope and dream which, fulfilled, can be translated into benefit for everyone."

—***John F. Kennedy***

"In spite of everything I still believe that people are really good at heart."

—***Anne Frank,*** *The Diary of a Young Girl,* entry for July 15, 1944

"In the past we have had a light which flickered, in the present we have a light which flames, and in the future there will be a light which shines over all the land and sea."

—***Winston Churchill,*** speech to the House of Commons, December 8, 1941

"It is the right of the people that they shall not be deprived of hope."

—***Broderick Crawford as Willie Stark,*** in the film version of Robert Penn Warren's *All the King's Men,* 1949

"Let our age be the age of improvement. In a day of peace let us advance the arts of peace and the works of peace. Let us develop the resources of our land, call forth its powers, build up its institutions, promote all its great interests, and see whether we also, in our day and generation, may not perform something worthy to be remembered."

—***Daniel Webster,*** speaking at the dedication of the Bunker Hill Monument, Charlestown, Massachusetts, June 17, 1825

"Lives of great men all remind us we can make our lives sublime."

—***Henry Wadsworth Longfellow,*** *A Psalm of Life,* 1838

"The mark of the immature man is that he wants to die nobly for a cause, while the mark of the mature man is that he wants to live humbly for one."

—***J. D. Salinger,*** *The Catcher in the Rye,* 1951

"The most useful thing about a principle is that it can always be sacrificed to expediency."

—***W. Somerset Maugham,*** *The Circle,* 1921

"Nor be cast down; for it is always dawn. Day breaks forever, and above the eastern horizon the sun is now about to peep. Full light of day? No, perhaps not ever. But yet it grows lighter, and the paths that were so blind, will, if one watches sharply enough, become hourly plainer. We shall learn to walk straighter. Yes, it is always dawn."

—***Learned Hand,*** "Democracy and Its Presumptions," 1932

"One miracle is just as easy to believe as another."

—***William Jennings Bryan,*** at the Scopes "monkey" trial in Dayton, Tennessee, 1925

"The only limit to our realization of tomorrow will be our doubts of today, so let us move forward with strong and active faith."

—***Franklin Delano Roosevelt,*** speech prepared for a Jefferson Day Dinner, but undelivered. He died the day before the event.

"Our brave young men are dying in the swamps of Southeast Asia. Which of them might have written a poem? Which of them might have cured cancer? Which of them might have played in a World Series or given us the gift of laughter from the stage or helped build a bridge or a university? Which of them would have taught a child to read? It is our responsibility to let these men live. . . . It is indecent if they die because of the empty vanity of their country."

—***Robert F. Kennedy,*** campaign speech on the Vietnam War, California, March 24, 1968

"A pessimist sees the difficulty in every opportunity; an optimist sees the opportunity in every difficulty."

—***Winston Churchill,*** *My Early Life,* 1930

"Risk more than others think is safe. Care more than others think is wise. Dream more than others think is practical. Expect more than others think is possible."

—***U.S. Military Academy cadet maxim***

"Sometimes people call me an idealist. Well, that is the way I know I am an American. America, my fellow citizens—I do not say it in disparagement of any other great people—America is the only idealistic nation in the world."

—***Woodrow Wilson,*** speech supporting the League of Nations, Sioux Falls, South Dakota, September 8, 1919

"There will always be dissident voices heard in the land, expressing opposition without alternatives, finding fault but never favor, perceiving gloom on every side and seeking influence without responsibility."

—***John F. Kennedy,*** speech planned for delivery in Dallas, Texas, November 22, 1963

"These are my principles. If you don't like them, I have others."

—***Groucho Marx***

"We are all in the gutter, but some of us are looking at the stars."

—***Oscar Wilde,*** *Lady Windermere's Fan,* 1893

"We have always held to the hope, the belief, the conviction, that there is a better life, a better world, beyond the horizon."

—***Franklin Delano Roosevelt***

"We promise according to our hopes, and perform according to our fears."

—***Dag Hammarskjöld***

"We steer our ship with hope, leaving fear astern."

—***Thomas Jefferson***

"What is objectionable, what is dangerous about extremists is not that they are extreme, but that they are intolerant. The evil is not what they say about their causes, but what they say about their opponents."

—***Robert F. Kennedy,*** *The Pursuit of Justice: Extremism, Left and Right,* 1964

"When one door of happiness closes, another opens; but often we look so long at the closed door that we do not see the one which has been opened for us."

—***Helen Keller***

"A wise man will make more opportunities than he finds."

—***Francis Bacon,*** "Of Ceremonies and Respects," 1625

"You see things as they are; and you say 'Why?' But I dream things that never were; and I say 'why not?'"

—***George Bernard Shaw,*** *Back to Methuselah,* 1921. The serpent says these words to Eve.

23 IDEAS AND WORDS

"After all, we were not beaten on the battlefield by dint of superior arms. We were defeated in the spiritual contest by virtue of a nobler idea."

—***Kase Toshikazu,*** while negotiating the Japanese surrender aboard the U.S.S. *Missouri,* September 2, 1945

"All great truths begin as blasphemies."

—***George Bernard Shaw,*** *Annajanska,* 1919

"All things are at odds when God sets a thinker loose on the planet."

—***Edith Hamilton***

"Any man who afflicts the human race with ideas must be prepared to see them misunderstood."

—***H. L. Mencken***

"As societies grow decadent, the language grows decadent, too. Words are used to disguise, not to illuminate, action: you liberate a city by destroying it. Words are used to confuse, so that at election time people will solemnly vote against their interests."

—***Gore Vidal***

"The best test of truth is the power of the thought to get itself accepted in the competition of the marketplace."

—***Oliver Wendell Holmes, Jr.,*** majority opinion in the Supreme Court decision *Abrams v. United States,* 1919

"Brevity is the sister of talent."

—***Anton Chekhov,*** letter to Alexander Chekhov, April 11, 1889

"Brevity is the soul of wit."

—***William Shakespeare,*** *Hamlet,* act 2, scene 2

"Calvin Coolidge didn't say much, and when he did he didn't say much."

—***Will Rogers***

"Consistency is the last refuge of the unimaginative."

—***Oscar Wilde***

"Do a common thing in an uncommon way."

—***Booker T. Washington,*** *Daily Resolves,* 1896

"Embarrassed, obscure, and feeble sentences are generally, if not always, the result of embarrassed, obscure, or feeble thought."

—***Hugh Blair,*** *Lectures on Rhetoric,* 1783

"Every now and then a man's mind is stretched by a new idea and never shrinks back to its original proportion."

—***Oliver Wendell Holmes, Jr.***

"A fanatic is one who can't change his mind and won't change the subject."

—***Winston Churchill***

"For almost a week pompous phrases marched over this landscape in search of an idea."

—***Adlai Stevenson,*** commenting on the Republican National Convention at the Democratic National Convention, Chicago, Illinois, July 16, 1952

"The Framers [of the Constitution] knew that free speech is the friend of change and revolution. But they also knew that it is always the deadliest enemy of tyranny."

—***Hugo L. Black,*** address to New York University School of Law, 1960

"Genius is one percent inspiration and ninety-nine percent perspiration."

—***Thomas Alva Edison***

"Grasp the subject, the words will follow."

—***Cato the Elder,*** *Ars Rhetorica*

"[Herbert Henry Asquith, Chancellor of the Exchequer] . . . distrusts great thoughts even if . . . [he] thinks them."

—***Alfred Gardiner***

"He was a self-made man who worshiped his creator."

—***Benjamin Disraeli,*** on Napoleon

"I am not one of those who in expressing opinions confine themselves to facts."

—***Mark Twain***

"I am sure that the power of vested interests is vastly exaggerated compared with the gradual encroachment of ideas."

—***John Maynard Keynes***

"An idea that is not dangerous is unworthy of being called an idea at all."

—***Don Marquis***

"Ideas are more dangerous than guns. We wouldn't let our enemies have guns, why should we let them have ideas?"

—***Joseph Stalin***

"If there is any principle of the Constitution that more imperatively calls for attachment than any other, it is the principle of free thought—not free thought for those who agree with us but freedom for the thought that we hate."

—***Oliver Wendell Holmes, Jr.,*** majority opinion in the Supreme Court decision on *United States v. Schwimmer,* 1928

"If you haven't got anything nice to say about anybody, come sit next to me."

—***Alice Roosevelt Longworth***

"If you steal from one author, it's plagiarism; if you steal from many, it's research."

—***Wilson Mizner,*** quoted in *The Legendary Mizners,* 1953

"The intuitive mind is a sacred gift and the rational mind is a faithful servant. We have created a society that honors the servant and has forgotten the gift."

—***Albert Einstein***

"An invasion of armies can be resisted; an invasion of ideas cannot be resisted."

—***Victor Hugo,*** *Histoire d'un crime,* 1877

"I should be glad, if I could flatter myself that I came as near to the central idea of the occasion, in two hours, as you did in two minutes."

—***Edward Everett,*** letter to Abraham Lincoln, November 20, 1863, comparing their respective addresses at Gettysburg

"It is as absurd to argue men, as to torture them, into believing."

—***John Henry Newman,*** "The Usurpations of Reason," 1831

"It is with words as with sunbeams—the more they are condensed, the deeper they burn."

—***Robert Southey***

"It usually takes me more than three weeks to prepare a good impromptu speech."

—***Mark Twain***

"A life's work in the agony and sweat of the human spirit, not for glory and least of all for profit, but to create out of the materials of the human spirit something which did not exist before."

—***William Faulkner,*** accepting the Nobel Prize for Literature, Stockholm, Sweden, December 10, 1950

"The logic of words should yield to the logic of realities."

—***Louis D. Brandeis,*** Supreme Court decision in *Di Santo v. Pennsylvania,* 1927

"A man may die, nations may rise and fall, but an idea lives on. Ideas have endurance without death."

—***John F. Kennedy***

"The man who never alters his opinion is like standing water, and breeds reptiles of the mind."

—***William Blake,*** "The Marriage of Heaven and Hell," 1790

"The mind is its own place, and in itself can make a heaven of hell, a hell of heaven."

—***John Milton,*** *Paradise Lost,* 1667

"Never explain—your friends do not need it and your enemies will not believe you anyway."

—***Elbert Hubbard,*** *The Motto Book,* 1907

"New opinions are always suspected, and usually opposed, without any other reason but because they are not already common."

—***John Locke,*** "Dedicatory Epistle," *Essay concerning Human Understanding,* 1690

"No author is a man of genius to his publisher."

—***Heinrich Heine***

"No generation can write the history of its own time."

—***Anonymous***

"No matter what anybody tells you, words and ideas can change the world."

—***Robin Williams as John Keating*** in *Dead Poets Society,* screenplay by Tom Schulman, 1989

"Once sent out, a word takes wing beyond recall."

—***Horace,*** *Epistles,* book 1

"Only kings, editors, and people with tapeworm have the right to use the editorial 'we.'"

—***Mark Twain***

"Only two things are infinite, the universe and human stupidity, and I'm not sure about the former."

—***Albert Einstein***

"The opposite of a correct statement is a false statement. But the opposite of a profound truth may well be another profound truth."

—***Niels Bohr***

"Our love of what is beautiful does not lead to extravagance; our love of the things of the mind does not make us soft."

—***Pericles,*** Funeral Oration, 430 B.C.

"Our major obligation is not to mistake slogans for solutions."

—***Edward R. Murrow***

"The pen is mightier than the sword."

—***Edward Bulwer-Lytton,*** *Richelieu,* 1839

"A . . . sharp tongue is the only edged tool that grows keener with constant use."

—***Washington Irving,*** "Rip Van Winkle," *The Sketch Book,* 1820

"The thinker dies, but his thoughts are beyond the reach of destruction. Men are mortal; but ideas are immortal."

—***Walter Lippmann,*** *A Preface to Morals,* 1929

"This is one of the cases in which the imagination is baffled by the facts."

—***Winston Churchill,*** in the House of Commons, May 13, 1941, commenting on the parachute descent into Scotland by Rudolf Hess

"We know that he has, more than any other man, the gift of compressing the largest number of words into the smallest amount of thought."

—***Winston Churchill,*** on Ramsay MacDonald, speech, March 23, 1933

"We think in generalities, we live in detail."

—***Alfred North Whitehead***

"Winston [Churchill] has a hundred ideas a day, of which four are good."

—***Franklin Delano Roosevelt***

"[Winston Churchill] mobilized the English language and sent it into battle."

—***Edward R. Murrow***

"A word is not a crystal, transparent and unchanged; it is the skin of a living thought and may vary greatly in color and content according to the circumstances and the time in which it is used."

—***Oliver Wendell Holmes, Jr.,*** Supreme Court decision in *Towne v. Eisner,* 245 U.S. 425, 1918

"Words are chameleons which reflect the color of their environment."

—***Learned Hand***

"Words calculated to catch everyone may catch no one."

—***Adlai Stevenson,*** Democratic National Convention, Chicago, Illinois, July 16, 1952

Yond Cassius has a lean and hungry look;
He thinks too much: such men are dangerous.

—***William Shakespeare,*** *Julius Caesar,* act 1, scene 2

"The young are slaves to dreams; the old, servants of regrets."

—***Hervey Allen,*** *Anthony Adverse,* 1933

24 INDIVIDUALISM

"All good things which exist are the fruits of originality."

—*John Stuart Mill, On Liberty,* 1859

"At the heart of that Western freedom and democracy is the belief that the individual man, the child of God, is the touchstone of value, and all society, groups, the state, exist for his benefit. Therefore the enlargement of liberty for individual human beings must be the supreme goal and the abiding practice of any Western society."

—***Robert F. Kennedy,*** "Day of Affirmation" address, University of Cape Town, South Africa, June 6, 1966

"Conformity is the jailer of freedom and the enemy of growth."

—***John F. Kennedy,*** address to the United Nations General Assembly, 1961

"Could Hamlet have been written by a committee, or the Mona Lisa painted by a club? Could the New Testament have been composed as a conference report? Creative ideas do not spring from groups. They spring from individuals. The divine spark leaps from the finger of God to the finger of Adam, whether it takes ultimate shape in a law of physics or a law of the land, a poem or a policy, a sonata or a mechanical computer."

—***Alfred Whitney Griswold,*** baccalaureate address, Yale University, 1957

"First, is the danger of futility; the belief there is nothing one man or one woman can do against the enormous array of the world's ills—against misery and ignorance, injustice and violence. Yet many of the world's great movements, of thought and action, have flowed from the work of a single man. A young monk began the

Protestant Reformation, a young general extended an empire from Macedonia to the borders of the earth, and a young woman reclaimed the territory of France. It was a young Italian explorer who discovered the New World, and the thirty-two-year-old Thomas Jefferson who proclaimed that all men are created equal."

—***Robert F. Kennedy,*** "Day of Affirmation" address, University of Cape Town, South Africa, 1966

"He who is able to conquer others is powerful; he who is able to conquer himself is more powerful."

—***Lao-tzu,*** *Tao-te-ching*

"If a man does not keep pace with his companions, perhaps it is because he hears a different drummer. Let him step to the music he hears, however measured or far away."

—***Henry David Thoreau,*** *Walden,* 1854

"I hold it the inalienable right of anybody to go to hell in his own way."

—***Robert Frost,*** speech at the University of California at Berkeley, 1935

"An individual is as superb as a nation when he has the qualities which make a superb nation."

—***Walt Whitman,*** Preface to *Leaves of Grass,* 1855

"Individuality of expression is the beginning and end of all art."

—***Johann Wolfgang von Goethe,*** *Proverbs in Prose*

"In every age there have been a few heroic souls who have been in advance of their time, who have been misunderstood, maligned, persecuted—sometimes put to death. Long after their martyrdom, monuments were erected to them and garlands woven for their graves."

—***Eugene V. Debs,*** defending himself in court, September 1, 1918

"It is not the name they call you, but it is the name to which you answer."

—***Mike Espy,*** advice to Bill Clinton during the 1992 presidential campaign

"A man cannot be comfortable without his own approval."

—***Mark Twain***

"Nature never rhymes her children, nor makes two men alike."

—***Ralph Waldo Emerson,*** *Character,* 1844

"People often say that this person or that person has not yet found himself. But the self is not something that one finds. It is something that one creates."

—***Thomas Szasz,*** *The Second Sin,* 1973

"The poorest man may in his cottage bid defiance to all the forces of the Crown. It may be frail—its roof may shake—the wind may blow through it—the storm may enter—the rain may enter—but the King of England cannot enter—all his forces dare not cross the threshold of the ruined tenement."

—***William Pitt the Younger***

"Style is knowing who you are, what you want to say, and not giving a damn."

—***Gore Vidal***

"The surest way to corrupt a youth is to instruct him to hold in higher esteem those who think alike than those who think differently."

—***Friedrich Nietzsche***

"That cause is strong which has not a multitude, but one strong man behind it."

—***James Russell Lowell,*** speech in Chelsea, Massachusetts, 1885

"Towering genius disdains a beaten path."

—***Abraham Lincoln,*** "Lyceum Address," January 27, 1837

"Whatever crushes individuality is despotism, by whatever name it may be called."

—***John Stuart Mill,*** *On Liberty,* 1859

"The will to do, the soul to dare."

—***Walter Scott,*** *The Lady of the Lake,* 1810

"The worth of a state, in the long run, is the worth of the individuals composing it."

—***John Stuart Mill,*** *On Liberty,* 1859

25 JUSTICE

"The administration of justice is the firmest pillar of government."

—***George Washington,*** letter, 1789

"The appearance of justice is just as important as justice itself in terms of maintaining public confidence in our judicial system."

—***William Cohen***

"An eye for an eye only ends up making the whole world blind."

—***Ben Kingsley as Mohandas K. Gandhi,*** in *Gandhi,* 1982

"Father, forgive them; for they know not what they do."

—***Luke 23:34***

"For more than two thousand years the Jewish people, my people, have been dispersed. But wherever they are, wherever Jews are found, every year they have repeated, 'Next year in Jerusalem.' Now when I am farther then ever from my people, from my Avital, facing many arduous years of my imprisonment, I say turning to my people, to my Avital, 'Next year in Jerusalem.'

"Now I turn to you, the court, who are required to confirm a predetermined sentence. To you I have nothing to say."

—***Anatoly Shcharansky,*** statement to a Soviet court during sentencing, July 14, 1978

"Had I so interfered on behalf of the rich, the powerful, the intelligent, the so-called great, or on behalf of their children, or any of that class, and suffered and sacrificed what I have in this interference, it would have been all right, and every man in this Court would have deemed it an act worthy of reward rather than punishment."

—***John Brown,*** addressing the court after being sentenced to be executed, November 2, 1859

"Having done what men could, they suffered what men must."

—***Thucydides***

"He that covereth his transgressions shall not prosper. But whoso confesseth and forsaketh them shall obtain mercy."

—***Proverbs 28:13***

"He who allows oppression shares the crime."

—***Erasmus Darwin,*** *The Botanic Garden,* 1789

"He who is merciful to the cruel will in the end be cruel to the merciful."

—***The Talmud***

"If we are to keep our democracy there must be one commandment: Thou shalt not ration justice."

—***Learned Hand***

"I know there is a God and that He hates injustice. I see the storm coming and I see His hand in it. If He has a place and part for me, I am ready."

—***Abraham Lincoln***

"In the state of nature, indeed, all men are born equal, but they cannot continue in this equality. Society makes them lose it, and they recover it only by the protection of the laws."

—***Baron de Montesquieu,*** *The Spirit of Laws,* 1748

"I should like to be able to love my country and still love justice."

—***Albert Camus,*** "The Value of Dissent," address at Vanderbilt University, Nashville, Tennessee, March 21, 1968

"It is better that ten guilty persons escape than one innocent suffer."

—***William Blackstone,*** *Commentaries on the Laws of England,* 1765–1769

"I tremble for my country when I reflect that God is just, that His justice cannot sleep forever."

—***Thomas Jefferson,*** on the institution of slavery in the United States, *Notes on the State of Virginia,* 1781–1785

"A jury consists of twelve persons chosen to decide who has the better lawyer."

—***Robert Frost***

"Justice, being destroyed, will destroy; being preserved, will preserve; it must never therefore be violated."

—***Manu,*** *The Laws of Manu*

"Justice does not come down from heaven; it must be conquered."

—***Joseph Reinach***

"Justice has nothing to do with expediency."

—***Woodrow Wilson***

"Justice is truth in action."

—***Benjamin Disraeli,*** speech, February 11, 1851

"Justice, sir, is the greatest interest of man on earth."

—***Daniel Webster,*** *Remarks . . . Occasioned by the Death of Hon. Mr. Justice Story,* September 12, 1845

"Justice . . . 'this great cement of society.' "

—***Alexander Hamilton***

"Life for life, eye for eye, tooth for tooth, hand for hand, foot for foot, burning for burning, wound for wound, stripe for stripe."

—***Exodus 21:23***

Mine eyes have seen the glory of the coming of the Lord:
He is trampling out the vintage where the grapes of wrath are stored;
He hath loosed the fateful lightning of his terrible swift sword;
His truth is marching on.

—***Julia Ward Howe,*** "Battle Hymn of the Republic," 1862

Mourn not the dead that in the cool earth lie—
But rather mourn the apathetic throng—
The cowed and the meek—
Who see the world's great anguish and its wrong
And dare not speak.

—***Ralph Chaplin,*** "Solidarity Forever," January 9, 1915

"They have sown the wind, and they shall reap the whirlwind."

—***Hosea 8:7***

"Those who have not known the joy of standing up for a great cause of justice have not known what makes living worthwhile."

—***Paul Painlevé,*** regarding the Dreyfus Affair, 1894

"Under a government which imprisons unjustly, the true place for a just man is also a prison."

—***Henry David Thoreau,*** *Civil Disobedience,* 1849

"When I came back to Dublin, I was court-martialed in my absence and sentenced to death in my absence, so I said they could shoot me in my absence."

—***Brendan Behan,*** *The Hostage,* 1959

"When the judgment day comes, civilization will have an alibi: 'I never took a human life, I only sold the fellow the gun to take it with.'"

—***Will Rogers***

"You should never have your best trousers on when you go out to fight for freedom and truth."

—***Henrik Ibsen,*** *An Enemy of the People,* 1882

26 KNOWLEDGE AND EXPERIENCE

"Ain't we got all the fools in town on our side? And ain't that a big enough majority in any town?"

—*Mark Twain, The Adventures of Huckleberry Finn,* 1884

"Anyone who has never made a mistake has never tried anything new."

—*Albert Einstein*

"Anyone who isn't confused doesn't really understand the situation."

—*Edward R. Murrow,* on the Vietnam War

"The brain is a wonderful organ; it starts working the moment you get up in the morning and does not stop until you get into the office."

—*Robert Frost*

"The confidence of fools shall destroy them. But whoso hearken unto me shall dwell securely, and shall be quiet without fear of evil."

—*Proverbs 1:32–33*

"Consistency requires you to be as ignorant today as you were a year ago."

—*Bernard Berenson*

"A critic is someone who knows the way but can't drive the car."

—*Kenneth Tynan,* 1966

"Discontent comes in proportion to knowledge."

—*Will Rogers*

"Even a fool, when he holdeth his peace, is counted wise; And he that shutteth his lips is esteemed as a man of understanding."

—***Proverbs 17:28***

"Everybody is ignorant, only on different subjects."

—***Will Rogers***

"Everything's got a moral, if only you can find it."

—***Lewis Carroll,*** *Alice's Adventures in Wonderland,* 1865

"Experience is not what happens to a man. It is what a man does with what happens to him."

—***Aldous Huxley,*** *Reader's Digest,* March 1956

"Experience is the name everyone gives to their mistakes."

—***Oscar Wilde,*** *Lady Windermere's Fan,* 1893

"The fellow who thinks he knows it all is especially annoying to those of us who do."

—***Harold Coffin***

"The fool doth think he is wise, but the wise man knows himself to be a fool."

—***William Shakespeare,*** *As You Like It,* act 5, scene 1

"Fools rush in where angels fear to tread."

—***Alexander Pope,*** *An Essay on Criticism,* 1711

For I have neither wit, nor words, nor worth,
Action, nor utterance, nor the power of speech,
To stir men's blood: I only speak right on;
I tell you that which you yourselves do know.

—***William Shakespeare,*** *Julius Caesar,* act 3, scene 2

"For wisdom is better than rubies, and all things desirable are not to be compared to her."

—***Proverbs 8:11***

"Good judgment is usually the result of experience. And experience is frequently the result of bad judgment."

—***Anonymous,*** saying passed from Robert Lovett
to Robert F. Kennedy during the Cuban Missile Crisis

"The great tragedy of Science—the slaying of a beautiful hypothesis by an ugly fact."

—***Thomas Henry Huxley,*** "Biogenesis and Abiogenesis," *Collected Essays,* 1893

"He who learns must suffer. And even in our sleep pain that cannot forget, falls drop by drop upon the heart, and in our own despair, against our will, comes wisdom to us by the awful grace of God."

—***Aeschylus,*** *Agamemnon*

I am a part of all that I have met;
Yet all experience is an arch wherethrough
Gleams the untraveled world, whose margin fades
For ever and for ever when I move.
How dull it is to pause, to make an end,
To rust unburnished, not to shine in use!
As though to breathe were life.

—***Alfred, Lord Tennyson,*** "Ulysses," 1842

"I do not feel obliged to believe that the same God who has endowed us with sense, reason, and intellect has intended us to forgo their use."

—***Galileo Galilei***

"I do not know what I may appear to the world; but to myself I seem to have been only like a boy playing on the seashore, and diverting myself in now and then finding a smoother pebble or a prettier shell than ordinary, whilst the great ocean of truth lay all undiscovered before me."

—***Isaac Newton***

"If Crusoe on his island had the library of Alexandria, and a certainty that he should never again see the face of man, would he ever open a volume?"

—***John Adams***

"If we value the pursuit of knowledge, we must be free to follow wherever that search may lead us. The free mind is no barking dog to be tethered on a ten-foot chain."

—***Adlai Stevenson***

"I have but one lamp by which my feet are guided; and that is the lamp of experience. I know of no way of judging the future but by the past."

—***Patrick Henry,*** speech to the Virginia Convention, March 23, 1775

"Imagination is more important than knowledge. Knowledge is limited. Imagination encircles the world."

—***Albert Einstein,*** 1929

"In a time of turbulence and change, it is more true than ever that knowledge is power."

—***John F. Kennedy,*** speech at the University of California at Berkeley, 1962

"It is not enough to have a good mind. The main thing is to use it well."

—***René Descartes,*** *Discourse on Method,* 1639

"It is the province of knowledge to speak and it is the privilege of wisdom to listen."

— ***Oliver Wendell Holmes,*** *The Poet at the Breakfast-Table,* 1872

"Knowledge comes, but wisdom lingers."

—***Alfred, Lord Tennyson,*** "Locksley Hall," 1842

"Little things affect little minds."

—***Benjamin Disraeli,*** *Sybil,* 1845

"Loyalty to petrified opinion never yet broke a chain or freed a human soul in this world—and never will."

—***Mark Twain***

"A man never reaches that dizzy height of wisdom that he can no longer be led by the nose."

—***Mark Twain***

"A man should never be ashamed to own he has been in the wrong, which is but saying, in other words, that he is wiser to-day than he was yesterday."

—***Alexander Pope,*** *Miscellanies,* vol. 2, 1727

"The Master said, 'It is only the very wisest and the very stupidest who cannot change.'"

—***Confucius,*** *The Analects*

"Maturity of mind is the capacity to endure uncertainty."

—***John Finley***

"The most useful piece of learning for the uses of life is to unlearn what is untrue."

—***Antisthenes,*** *Views of Religion*

"A second-class intellect but a first-class temperament."

—***Oliver Wendell Holmes, Jr.,*** on Franklin Delano Roosevelt

There are three things which are real:
God, human folly, and laughter.
The first two are beyond our comprehension
So we must do what we can with the third.

—***Aubrey Menen,*** *The Ramayana,* 1954

"There is no point in our ancestors speaking to us unless we know how to listen."

—***Mortimer J. Adler***

"They have learned nothing and forgotten nothing."

—***Charles Maurice de Talleyrand-Périgord,*** on the Bourbons

"To be absolutely certain about something, one must know everything or nothing about it."

—***Olin Miller***

"To every complicated question there is a simple answer—which is usually wrong."

—***H. L. Mencken***

To follow knowledge like a sinking star
Beyond the utmost bound of human thought.

—***Alfred, Lord Tennyson,*** "Ulysses," 1842

"Tragedy is a tool for the living to gain wisdom, not a guide by which we live."

—***William Appleman Williams***

"Verily I say unto you, no prophet is accepted in his own country."

—***Luke 4:24***

"We are born to inquire into truth; it belongs to a greater power to possess it."

—***Michel de Montaigne,*** "Of the Art of Conversation," *Essays,* 1580–1588

"We have come out of the time when obedience, the acceptance of discipline, intelligent courage, and resolution were most important, into that more difficult time when it is a man's duty to understand his world rather than to simply fight for it."

—***Ernest Hemingway,*** 1946

"We know nothing of what will happen in [the] future, but by the analogy of experience."

—***Abraham Lincoln,*** speech in the Hall of the House of Representatives, Springfield, Illinois, December 26, 1839

"We should be careful to get out of an experience only the wisdom that is in it—and stop there; lest we be like the cat that sits down on the hot stove-lid. She will never sit down on a hot stove-lid again—and that is well; but also she will never sit down on a cold one anymore."

—***Mark Twain,*** "Pudd'nhead Wilson's New Calendar," *Following the Equator,* 1897

"A whale ship was my Yale College and my Harvard."

—***Herman Melville,*** *Moby-Dick,* 1851

"When a stupid man is doing something he is ashamed of, he always declares that it is his duty."

—***George Bernard Shaw,*** *Caesar and Cleopatra,* 1901

"When a true genius appears in this world you may know him by this sign, that the dunces are all in confederacy against him."

—***Jonathan Swift***

"When I was a boy of fourteen, my father was so ignorant I could hardly stand to be around him. But when I got to be twenty-one, I was amazed by how much he had learned in seven years."

—***Mark Twain***

"When you find that you are on the side of the majority, it is time to reform."

—***Mark Twain***

"Wisdom too often never comes, and so one ought not to reject it merely because it comes late."

—***Felix Frankfurter,*** dissenting opinion in the Supreme Court decision *Henslee v. Union Planters Bank,* 335 U.S. 600, 1948

"Wise men talk because they have something to say; fools, because they have to say something."

—***Plato***

"Wonder is the foundation of all philosophy, inquiry its progress, ignorance its end."

—***Michel de Montaigne,*** "Of Cripples," *Essays,* 1580–1588

"The words of a man's mouth are as deep waters; a flowing brook, a fountain of wisdom."

—***Proverbs 18:4***

27 LABOR

"Anybody who has doubt about the ingenuity or the resourcefulness of a plumber never got a bill from one."

—*George Meany*

Bowed by the weight of centuries he leans
Upon his hoe and gazes on the ground,
The emptiness of the ages in his face,
And on his back the burden of the world.

—*Edwin Markham,* "The Man with the Hoe," 1899

"Capital should be at the service of labor and not labor at the service of capital."

—*John Paul II*

"Clad in the armor of a righteous cause . . . a cause as holy as the cause of liberty—the cause of humanity. . . . You shall not press down upon the brow of labor this crown of thorns; you shall not crucify mankind upon a cross of gold!"

—*William Jennings Bryan,* "Cross of Gold" speech to the Democratic National Convention, Chicago, 1896

"The dictionary is the only place that 'success' comes before 'work.' "

—*Vince Lombardi*

"Don't go around saying the world owes you a living; the world owes you nothing, it was here first."

—*Mark Twain*

"Employers and employees alike have learned that in union there is strength, that a coordination of individual effort means an elimination of waste, a bettering of living conditions, and is, in fact, the father of prosperity."

—***Franklin Delano Roosevelt,*** address to the New York Women's Trade Union League, June 8, 1929

"Except the Lord build the house, they labor in vain that build it; except the Lord keep the city, the watchman waketh but in vain."

—***Psalm 127:1***

"Folks who never do any more than they get paid for, never get paid for any more than they do."

—***Elbert Hubbard***

"Genius begins great works; labor alone finishes them."

—***Joseph Joubert***

"The great struggling unknown masses of the men who are at the base of everything are the dynamic force that is lifting the levels of society. A nation is as great, and only as great, as her rank and file."

—***Woodrow Wilson***

"Hard work spotlights the character of people: some turn up their sleeves, some turn up their noses, and some don't turn up at all."

—***Sam Ewing***

"How could God create the world in six days? No unions."

—***Franklin Delano Roosevelt***

"I believe in building a better world—not just a better house or more material things for myself—but to better people's lives. And I believe trade unions are necessary to preserve the American way of life. I don't think we can have a free democratic society without a free democratic labor movement."

—***Murray Finley***

"I believe in the dignity of labor, whether with head or hand; that the world owes every man an opportunity to make a living."

—***John D. Rockefeller, Jr.***

"If a man tells you he loves America, yet hates labor, he is a liar!"

—***Abraham Lincoln***

"If you are called to be a street sweeper, sweep streets even as Michelangelo painted, or Beethoven composed music, or Shakespeare wrote poetry. Sweep streets so well that all the hosts of heaven and earth will pause to say, here lived a great street sweeper who did his job well."

—***Martin Luther King, Jr.***

"I'm a great believer in luck, and I find the harder I work, the more I have of it."

—***Thomas Jefferson***

"I never did anything worth doing by accident, nor did any of my inventions come by accident."

—***Thomas Alva Edison***

"The interest of every businessman is bound to the interest of every wage earner. Whether he is running a store on the corner or is a stockholder in a corporation, big or little, he is financially better off than when wages and working conditions are poor."

—***Franklin Delano Roosevelt,*** speech in Cleveland, Ohio, October 16, 1936

"In the sweat of thy face shalt thou eat bread, till thou return unto the ground; for out of it wast thou taken."

—***Genesis 3:16***

"It ill behooves one who has supped at labor's table and who has been sheltered in labor's house to curse with equal fervor and fine impartiality both labor and its adversaries when they become locked in deadly embrace."

—***John L. Lewis,*** rallying union members throughout the nation, September 3, 1937

"It is time that all Americans realized that the place of labor is side by side with the businessman and with the farmer, and not one degree lower."

—***Harry S. Truman***

"It is to the real advantage of every producer, every manufacturer and every merchant to cooperate in the improvement of working conditions, because the best customer of American industry is the well-paid worker."

—***Franklin Delano Roosevelt,*** speech, Cleveland, Ohio, October 16, 1936

"I watched a small man with thick calluses on both hands work fifteen and sixteen hours a day. I saw him once literally bleed from the bottoms of his feet, a man who came here uneducated, alone, unable to speak the language, who taught me all I needed to know about faith and hard work by the simple eloquence of his example."

—***Mario Cuomo,*** speaking of his father in an address to Democratic National Convention, July 16, 1984

"A just wage for the worker is the ultimate test of whether any economic system is functioning justly."

—***John Paul II***

"Labor is man's active property."

—***Karl Marx***

"Labor is prior to, and independent of, capital. Capital is the fruit of labor, and could never have existed if labor had not first existed."

—***Abraham Lincoln***

"Labor, therefore, it appears evidently, is the only universal, as well as the only accurate measure of value, or the only standard by which we can compare the values of different commodities, at all times, and at all places."

—***Adam Smith,*** *The Wealth of Nations,* 1776

"Let the ruling classes tremble at a Communist revolution. The proletarians have nothing to lose but their chains. They have a world to win."

—***Karl Marx and Friedrich Engels,*** *The Communist Manifesto,* 1848

"Melancholy is the condition of that people whose government can be sustained only by a system which periodically transfers large amounts from the labor of the many to the coffers of the few."

—***James K. Polk***

"Men everywhere are going to see that the problem of labor is nothing more nor less than the problem of the elevation of humanity."

—***Woodrow Wilson,*** address regarding the League of Nations, September 25, 1919

"The nation's labor force is its most productive asset."

—***Harry S. Truman***

"No business which depends for existence on paying less than living wages to its workers has any right to continue in this country. By living wages I mean more than a bare subsistence level—I mean the wages of decent living."

—***Franklin Delano Roosevelt***

"One man wins success by his words; another gets his due reward by the work of his hands."

—*Proverbs 12:14*

"Organizations of workers, wisely led, temperate in their demands and conciliatory in their attitude, make not for industrial strife, but for industrial peace."

—***Franklin Delano Roosevelt,*** address to the New York Women's Trade Union League, June 8, 1929

"The organized workers of America, free in their industrial life, conscious partners of production, secure in their homes, and enjoying a decent standard of living, will prove the finest bulwark against the intrusion of alien doctrines of government."

—***John L. Lewis,*** rallying union members throughout the nation, September 3, 1937

"A professional is one who does his best work when he feels the least like working."

—***Frank Lloyd Wright***

"The reason why worry kills more people than work is that more people worry than work."

—***Robert Frost***

"The right of workingmen to combine and to form trade unions is no less sacred than the right of the manufacturer to enter into associations and conferences with his fellows. . . . My experience has been that trade unions upon the whole are beneficial both to labor and to capital."

—***Andrew Carnegie***

"The right to work, I had assumed, was the most precious liberty that man possessed. Man has indeed as much right to work as he has to live, to be free, to own property."

—***William O. Douglas,*** dissenting opinion in the Supreme Court decision *Barsky v. Regents,* April 26, 1954

"The rights of one are as sacred as the rights of a million. Suppose you happen to be the one who has no work. This Republic is a failure so far as you are concerned. Every man has the inalienable right to work."

—***Eugene V. Debs***

"The sleep of a laboring man is sweet."

—*Ecclesiastes 5:12*

"Sometimes a bad settlement hurts the public worse than a strike."

—*Willard Wirtz*

"The strongest bond of human sympathy, outside the family relation, should be one uniting all working people, of all nations, and tongues and kindreds."

—*Abraham Lincoln*

"There has never been but one question in all civilization—how to keep a few men from saying to many men: You work and earn bread and we will eat it."

—*Abraham Lincoln*

"The union itself is an elemental response to the human instinct for group action in dealing with group problems."

—*William Green,* speech before the Harvard Union, 1925

"Unions can no more live without democracy than a fish without water."

—*Lane Kirkland*

"We believe that if men have the talent to invent new machines that put men out of work, they have the talent to put those men back to work."

—*John F. Kennedy,* speech, Wheeling, West Virgina, September 27, 1962

"We have the most wealth of any nation because our workers have the skill to create it. We have the best products because they know how to make them. We have the most democratic system because of the values our trade unions have to sustain it."

—*Walter F. Mondale*

"We have too many people who live without working, and we have altogether too many people who work without living."

—*Charles Reynolds Brown*

"What profit hath a man of all his labor which he taketh under the sun? One generation passeth away, and another generation cometh: but the earth abideth for ever."

—*Ecclesiastes 1:3–4*

"When a man tells you that he got rich through hard work, ask him whose."

—*Don Marquis*

"When the rich concern themself with the poor, that's called charity. When the poor concern themself with the rich, that's called revolution."

—***William W. Winpisinger***

"When work is a pleasure, life is a joy! When work is a duty, life is slavery!"

—***Maxim Gorky,*** *The Lower Depths,* 1903

"With all their faults, trade unions have done more for humanity than any other organization that ever existed. They have done more for decency, for honesty, for education, for the developing of character, than any other association."

—***Clarence Darrow***

"The world is full of willing people, some willing to work, the rest willing to let them."

—***Robert Frost***

"You knew that what is given or granted can be taken away, that what is begged can be refused; but that what is earned is kept."

—***Robert F. Kennedy,*** launching the Bedford-Stuyvesant Restoration Effort, Brooklyn, New York, December 10, 1966

"You should not confuse your career with your life."

—***Dave Barry***

28 LATIN QUOTATIONS

"Amicitiae immortales, mortales inimicitias debere esse."
"Our friendships should be immortal, our enmities mortal."

—***Livy,*** *Ab Urbe Condita*

"Amor patriae, ratione valentior."
"Love of country is more powerful than reason itself."

—***Ovid,*** *Epistolae ex Ponto* 1.3

"Annuit Coeptis."
"God has favored our undertakings."

—One of three Latin phrases that appear on the walls of the Senate Chamber

"Audentes fortuna iuvat."
"Fortune favors the brave."

—***Terence,*** *Phormio*

"Ave Caesar, morituri te salutamus."
"Hail Caesar, we who are about to die salute you."

—***Roman gladiator salutation*** upon entering the arena

"Beneficium accipere libertatem est vendere."
"To accept a favor is to sell one's freedom."

—***Publilius Syrus***

"Brevis a natura nobis vita data est; at memoria bene redditae vitae sempiterna."
"It is a brief period of life that is granted us by nature, but the memory of a well-spent life never dies."

—***Marcus Tullius Cicero,*** *Philippic* 14.12

"Carpe diem, quam minimum credula postero."
"Seize the day, trusting as little as you may to tomorrow."

—***Horace,*** *Odes* 1.11.8

"Cogito ergo sum."
"I think, therefore I am."

—***René Descartes,*** *Discourse on Method,* 1637

"Corruptissima re publica plurimae leges."
"Laws were most numerous when the commonwealth was most corrupt."

—***Marcus Claudius Tacitus,*** *Annales,* 3.27

"Cuiusvis hominis est errare, nullius nisi insipientis in errore perseverae."
"Any man is liable to err, only a fool persists in error."

—***Marcus Tullius Cicero,*** *Philippic* 12.2

"Cum tacent, clamant."
"Their very silence is a loud cry."

—***Marcus Tullius Cicero,*** *Catilinam* 1.21

"De inimico non loquaris male sed cogites."
"Don't speak ill of our enemy; plot it."

—***Publilius Syrus***

"Dimidium facti qui coepit habet."
"A task begun is half done."

—***Horace,*** *Epistulae* 2.40

"Dulce et decorum est pro patria mori."
"Sweet and fitting it is to die for one's country."

—***Horace,*** *Odes* 3.2.13

"E Pluribus Unum."
"One out of many."

—One of three Latin phrases that appear on the walls of the Senate Chamber. Official motto on the Great Seal of the United States.

"Eripuit coelo fulmen sceptrumque tyrannis."
"He snatched the lightning from heaven and the scepter from the tyrants."

—***Anonymous.*** These words appeared on the medal struck in honor of Benjamin Franklin when he was U.S. ambassador to France.

"Errare mehercule malo cum Platone . . . quam cum istis vera sentire."
"I would rather err with Plato, by God . . . than to be correct with those men."

—***Marcus Tullius Cicero,*** *Tusculanae Disputationes* 1.17.39

"Et tu, Brute?"
"You too, Brutus?"

—***William Shakespeare,*** *Julius Caesar,* act 3, scene 1. Julius Caesar to Brutus, one of his assassins, as he dies

"Fere libenter homines id quod volunt credunt."
"Men willingly believe what they wish."

—***Julius Caesar***

"Festina lente."
"Make haste slowly."

—***Augustus Caesar.*** A favorite maxim of the emperor.

"Fortunam citius reperias quam retineas."
"One can more quickly meet with good fortune than hold on to it."

—***Publilius Syrus***

"Haec Manus Inimica Tyrannis."
"This Company is an enemy to tyranny."

—***Marquis de Lafayette,*** slogan on a Revolutionary War infantry banner, October 7, 1781

"Homines enim ad deos nulla re propius accedunt quam slautem hominibus dando."
"In nothing are men more like gods than in coming to the rescue of their fellow men."

—***Marcus Tullius Cicero,*** *Pro Ligario*

"Iacta alea est."
"The die is cast."

—***Julius Caesar,*** at the crossing of the Rubicon

"Ignis aurum probat, miseria fortes viros."
"Fire tests gold, misfortune brave men."

—***Seneca,*** *De Providentia* 5.10

"In causa facili cuivis licet esse diserto."
"In an easy cause anyone may be eloquent."

—***Ovid,*** *Tristia* 11.21

"Male facere qui vult numquam non causam invenit."
"Those who mean to do ill never fail to find a reason."

—***Publilius Syrus***

"Mea mihi conscientia pluris est quam omnium sermo."
"My own conscience is more to me than what the world says."

—***Marcus Tullius Cicero,*** *Epistulae ad Familiares* 12.28.2

"Mendacem memorem esse oportere."
"A liar should have a good memory."

—***Quintilian,*** *Institutio Oratoria* 4.2

"Nescire autem quid ante quam natus sis acciderit, id est semper esse puerum."
"To be ignorant of what occurred before you were born is to remain always a child."

—***Marcus Tullius Cicero,*** *De Oratore*

"Nihil tam incertum nec tam inaestimabile est quam animi multitudinis."
"Nothing is so uncertain or so incalcuable as the disposition of a crowd."

—***Livy***

"Non qui parum habet, sed qui plus cupit, pauper est."
"It is not the man who has little, but the man who craves more, that is poor."

—***Seneca,*** *Epistulae Morales* 2.6

"Novus Ordo Seclorum."
"A new order of the ages."

—One of three Latin phrases that appear on the walls of the Senate Chamber. It also appears on the Great Seal of the United States.

"Nullumst iam dictum quod not sit dictum prius."
"Nothing is ever said that has not been said before."

—***Terence,*** *Eunuchus*

"Oderint, dum metuant."
"Let them hate me, so long as they fear me."

—***Lucius Accius,*** *Atreus*

"Omnia amor vincit: et nos cedamus amori."
"Love conquers all things; let us too surrender to love."

—***Virgil,*** *Ecologues* 10.69

"Proprium humani ingenii est odisse quem laeseris."
"It is human nature to hate the man you have injured."

—***Marcus Claudius Tacitus,*** *Agricola*

"Quis custodiet ipsos custodes?"
"Who will watch the watchmen?"

—***Juvenal,*** *Satire 6*

"Satis est superare inimicum, ninium est perdere."
"It is enough to defeat an enemy, too much to ruin him."

—***Publilius Syrus***

"Segnius homines bona quam mala sentire."
"Men are slower to become aware of blessings than evils."

—***Livy***

"Silent enem leges inter arma."
"During war, the laws are silent."

—***Marcus Tullius Cicero,*** *Pro Milone* 4.11

"Ubi vinci necesse est, expedit cedere."
"Where defeat is inevitable, it is wisest to yield."

—***Quintilian,*** *Institutio Oratoria* 6.4.16

"Ut sementem feceris, ita metes."
"As you sow, so shall you reap."

—***Marcus Tullius Cicero***

"Veni, vidi, vici."
"I came, I saw, I conquered."

—***Julius Caesar***

"Vincere scis, Hannibal, victoria uti nescis."
"You know how to vanquish, Hannibal, but you do not know how to profit from victory."

—***Livy***

"Vivere tota vita discendum est et, quod mafis fortasse moraberis, tota vita discendum est mori."
"It takes the whole of life to learn how to live, and—what will perhaps make you wonder more—it takes the whole of life to learn how to die."

—***Seneca,*** *De Brevitate Vitae* 7.3

"Vox populi vox Dei."
"The voice of the people is the voice of God."

—***Alcuin,*** letter to Charlemagne

29 LAW

Any fool can make a rule,
And every fool will mind it.

—*Henry David Thoreau,* journal entry, February 3, 1860

"Bad laws are the worst sort of tyranny."

—*Edmund Burke,* speech in Bristol, England, 1780

"Constitutions should consist only of general provisions; the reason is that they must necessarily be permanent, and that they cannot calculate for the possible change of things."

—*Alexander Hamilton*

"Crime is contagious. If the government becomes a lawbreaker, it breeds contempt for the law."

—*Louis D. Brandeis,* Supreme Court decision in *Olmstead v. U.S.,* 1928

"Every law is an infraction of liberty."

—*Jeremy Bentham, Principles of Morals and Legislation,* 1789

"The execution of the laws is more important than the making of them."

—*Thomas Jefferson,* letter to Abbé Arnoux, 1789

"Facts are stubborn things; and whatever may be our wishes, our inclinations, or the dictates of our passions, they cannot alter the state of facts and evidence."

—*John Adams,* "Argument in Defense of the Soldiers in the Boston Massacre Trials," December 1770

"For him [Lincoln], law was more than a profession; it was a faith."

—***Arthur Goodhart***

"Good laws lead to the making of better ones; bad ones bring about worse."

—***Jean Jacques Rousseau,*** *The Social Contract,* 1762

"I don't see what's wrong with giving Bobby a little experience before he starts to practice law."

—***John F. Kennedy,*** on appointing his brother Robert attorney general

"The illegal we do immediately, the unconstitutional takes a little more time."

—***Henry Kissinger,*** commenting to reporters about the Nixon Administration

"It is futile to seek safety beyond geographical barriers. Real security will be found only in law and in justice."

—***Harry S. Truman,*** addressing the nation upon the death of President Franklin Delano Roosevelt

"A judge is just a law student who gets to mark his own papers."

—***H. L. Mencken***

"Law is the great civilizing machinery. It liberates the desire to build and subdues the desire to destroy. And if war can tear us apart, law can unite us—out of fear, or love, or reason, or all three. Law is the greatest human invention. All the rest give man mastery over his world. Law gives him mastery over himself."

—***Lyndon B. Johnson***

"The law is the only sure protection of the weak and the only efficient restraint upon the strong."

—***Millard Fillmore***

"The law: It has honored us; may we honor it."

—***Daniel Webster,*** speech at the Charleston Bar Dinner, May 10, 1847

"Laws are like sausages. It's better not to see them being made."

—***Otto von Bismarck***

"Laws can restrain the heartless; they cannot restrain the heart."

—***Martin Luther King, Jr.***

"Laws do not persuade just because they threaten."

—***Seneca***

"The laws of this country are the great barriers that protect the citizen from the winds of evil and tyranny."

—***Robert Bolt,*** *A Man for All Seasons,* 1962

"A lawyer with his briefcase can steal more than a hundred men with guns."

—***Mario Puzo,*** *The Godfather,* 1969

"Liberty to make our laws does not give us license to break them."

—***William McKinley***

"The life of the law has not been logic; it has been experience."

—***Oliver Wendell Holmes, Jr.,*** *The Common Law,* 1881

"A man who is his own lawyer has a fool for a client."

—***Anonymous***

"Manners are of more importance than laws. Upon them, in a great measure, the laws depend. The law touches us but here and there, and now and then. Manners are what vex or smooth, corrupt or purify, exalt or debase, barbarize or refine us, by a constant, steady, uniform, insensible operation, like that of the air we breathe in. They give their whole form and color to our lives. According to their quality, they aid morals, they support them, or they totally destroy them."

—***Edmund Burke,*** *Letters on a Regicide Peace,* 1797

"The Master said, 'Guide them by edicts, keep them in line with punishments, and the common people will stay out of trouble, but will have no sense of shame. Guide them by virtue . . . and they will, besides having a sense of shame, reform themselves.' "

—***Confucius,*** *The Analects*

"The more laws and orders are multiplied, the more theft and violence increase."

—***Lao-tzu,*** *Tao-te-ching*

"No laws are binding on the human subject which assault the body or violate the conscience."

—***William Blackstone,*** *Commentaries on the Laws of England,* 1765–1769

"One who breaks an unjust law that conscience tells him is unjust, and who willingly accepts the penalty of imprisonment in order to arouse the conscience of the community over its injustice, is in reality expressing the highest respect for law."

—***Martin Luther King, Jr.,*** "Letter from the Birmingham City Jail," 1963

"Only a respect for the law makes it possible for free men to dwell together in peace and progress. . . . Law is the adhesive force in the cement of society, creating order out of chaos and coherence in place of anarchy."

—***John F. Kennedy,*** convocation speech, Vanderbilt University, Nashville, Tennessee, May 18, 1963

"A verbal agreement isn't worth the paper it's printed on."

—***Samuel Goldwyn***

"We have a criminal jury system which is superior to any in the world; and its efficiency is only marred by the difficulty of finding twelve men every day who don't know anything and can't read."

—***Mark Twain,*** speech, London, July 4, 1873

"What we are this day justifying by precedents will be itself a precedent."

—***Marcus Claudius Tacitus,*** *Annals*

"Where law ends, tyranny begins."

—***William Pitt the Younger***

30 LEADERSHIP

"The absence of alternatives clears the mind marvelously."

—***Henry Kissinger***

"Although prepared for martyrdom, I preferred that it be postponed."

—***Winston Churchill,*** *My Early Life,* 1930

"American public opinion is like the ocean—it cannot be stirred by teaspoon."

—***Hubert H. Humphrey,*** speech at Gannon College,
Erie, Pennsylvania, October 11, 1966

"An army of lions commanded by a deer will never be an army of lions."

—***Napoleon Bonaparte***

"As President, I have constitutional eyes; I cannot see you."

—***Abraham Lincoln,*** reply to the South Carolina commissioners
following the state's secession from the Union

"The ayes have it."

—***Abraham Lincoln,*** upon hearing that his Cabinet
had voted "no" on emancipation

"Better to reign in hell, than to serve in heaven."

—***John Milton,*** *Paradise Lost,* 1667. Lucifer declares his
rebellion against God with this line.

"Brandeis is a name that cannot be merely adopted. It must be achieved."

—***Albert Einstein,*** commenting on the founding of Brandeis
University, named for Justice Louis D. Brandeis, in 1948

"But the Emperor has nothing on at all!"

—***Hans Christian Andersen,*** *The Emperor's New Clothes,* 1837

"[Caesar] had rather be first in a village than second at Rome."

—***Francis Bacon,*** *Advancement of Learning,* 1605

"Do not follow where the path may lead. Go instead where there is no path and leave a trail."

—***Harold R. McAlindon***

"Early this morning I signed my death warrant."

—***Michael Collins,*** after signing the treaty establishing the Irish Free State, December 6, 1921

"Every great man has his disciples, and it is always Judas who writes the biography."

—***Oscar Wilde,*** *The Critic as Artist,* 1891

"Every man can make a contribution, for even a fool can set an example for others."

—***Scottish proverb***

"Father always wanted to be the bride at every wedding and the corpse at every funeral."

—***Alice Roosevelt Longworth,*** quoted in Nicholas Roosevelt, *A Front Row Seat,* 1953

"First in war, first in peace, and first in the hearts of his countrymen."

—***Richard Henry Lee,*** funeral oration and tribute to George Washington

"For if the trumpet give an uncertain sound, who shall prepare himself to the battle?"

—***1 Corinthians 14:8***

"Franklin, even the Lord took six days."

—***Winston Churchill,*** to Franklin Delano Roosevelt, who wanted to finish the plans for the new world order at Yalta within five days

"The gentleman need not be disturbed; he will never be either."

—***Thomas B. Reed,*** comments directed to Congressman Springer of Illinois upon the latter's announcement to the House that he would rather be right than be President

"Good man; wrong job."

—***Sam Rayburn,*** on the election of Dwight D. Eisenhower to the presidency

"The graveyards are full of indispensable men."

—***Napoleon Bonaparte***

"The greatest man who ever came out of Plymouth Corner, Vermont."

—***Clarence Darrow,*** on Calvin Coolidge

"Great men are like meteors; they consume themselves and light the world."

—***Napoleon Bonaparte***

"The hand that rocks the cradle rules the world."

—***William Ross Wallace,*** "The Hand That Rocks the Cradle Is the Hand That Rules the World," 1865

"He could receive counsel from a child and give counsel to a sage. The simple approached him with ease, and the learned approached him with deference."

—***Frederick Douglass,*** tribute to Abraham Lincoln

"He did not know all the answers. But, more than other politicians of the day, he knew the questions."

—***Arthur M. Schlesinger, Jr.,*** on Robert F. Kennedy

"He is one of those men of whom Nature is sparing, and whom she does not throw upon the earth but with centuries between them."

—***Andoche Junot,*** on Napoleon, in a letter to his father, 1794

"Herzl managed to build a façade without a house and believed that it would not occur to anyone to look behind it. He could do so because he had such immense faith in himself. I am a different man."

—***Max Nordau,*** refusing to assume Theodor Herzl's mantle as president of the Zionist Organization

"He was a Caesar without his ambition, a Frederick without his tyranny, a Napoleon without his selfishness, and a Washington without his reward."

—***Benjamin H. Hill,*** commenting on Robert E. Lee, 1894

"The history of the world is but the biography of great men."

—***Thomas Carlyle,*** *Heroes and Hero-Worship,* 1846

"I am not the kind of man to stand on ceremony. 'His Excellency' will suffice."

—***Henry Kissinger,*** when asked by reporters how to address him after being appointed secretary of state

"I am the law."

—***"Boss" Frank Hague,*** November 1937

"I claim not to have controlled events, but confess plainly that events have controlled me."

—***Abraham Lincoln,*** letter to A. G. Hodges, April 4, 1864

"I desire so to conduct the affairs of this administration that if at the end, when I come to lay down the reins of power, I have lost every other friend on earth, I shall at least have one friend left, and that friend shall be down inside of me."

—***Abraham Lincoln,*** reply to a peace-now committee, 1864

"If Churchill had a speech writer in 1940, Britain would be speaking German today."

—***James C. Humes,*** *New York Times,* June 15, 1986

"If I were to read, much less answer, all the attacks made on me, this shop might as well be closed for any other business. I do the very best I know how—the very best I can; and I mean to keep doing so until the end. If the end brings me out all right, what is said against me won't amount to anything. If the end brings me out wrong, ten angels swearing I was right would make no difference."

—***Abraham Lincoln***

"I have climbed to the top of the greasy pole."

—***Benjamin Disraeli,*** on becoming prime minister of Britain

"I know I have the body of a weak and feeble woman; but I have the heart and stomach of a king, and of a King of England, too."

—***Elizabeth I,*** speech to Royal Navy at Tilbury while awaiting the Spanish Armada, 1588

"In every dark hour of our national life a leadership of frankness and vigor has met with that understanding and support of the people themselves, which is essential to victory."

—***Franklin Delano Roosevelt,*** First Inaugural Address, March 4, 1933

"An institution is the lengthened shadow of one man."

—***Ralph Waldo Emerson,*** "Self-Reliance," 1841

"In the country of the blind the one-eyed man is king."

—***Desiderius Erasmus,*** *Adages*

"I shall be an autocrat: that's my trade. And the good Lord will forgive me: that's his."

—***Catherine the Great***

"Is there anything we can do for you? For you are the one in trouble now."

—***Eleanor Roosevelt,*** response to Harry S. Truman upon his offer of assistance following the death of Franklin Delano Roosevelt, April 22, 1945

"I *succeed* him; no one can *replace* him."

—***Thomas Jefferson,*** on succeeding Benjamin Franklin as ambassador to France, 1785

"It is much safer for a prince to be feared than loved, if he is to fall in one of the two."

—***Niccolò Machiavelli,*** *The Prince,* 1513

"It was worse than a crime—it was a blunder."

—***Antoine Boulay de la Meurthe,*** in reference to Napoleon's failed seizure of the Spanish throne

"I walk on untrodden ground. There is scarcely any part of my conduct which may not hereafter be drawn into precedent."

—***George Washington***

"I will not change my beliefs to win votes; I will offer a choice, not an echo."

—***Barry Goldwater,*** presidential campaign speech, January 3, 1964

"A leader is a dealer in hope."

—***Napoleon Bonaparte***

"A leader takes people where they want to go. A great leader takes people where they don't necessarily want to go but ought to be."

—***Rosalynn Carter***

"Leadership is convincing people they can do something they shouldn't be able to do."

—***Al Roberts***

"Leaders make things possible. Exceptional leaders make them inevitable."

—***Lance Morrow***

"Let him who elevates himself above humanity, above its weakness, its infirmities, its wants, its necessities, say, if he pleases, he will never compromise; but let no one who is not above the frailties of our common nature disdain compromises."

—***Henry Clay,*** speech on radical abolitionism, 1839

"Lincoln had faith in time and time has justified his faith."

—***Benjamin Harrison,*** Lincoln Day address, Chicago, Illinois, 1898

"Lincoln has become for us the test of human worth."

—***Stephen Wise,*** on the anniversary of Lincoln's birth, February 12, 1914

Lives of great men all remind us
We can make our lives sublime,
And, departing, leave behind us
Footprints on the sands of time.

—***Henry Wadsworth Longfellow,*** "A Psalm of Life," 1839

"Magnanimity in politics is not seldom the truest wisdom; and a great empire and little minds go ill together."

—***Edmund Burke,*** *On Conciliation with America,* 1775

"The measure of a man is what he does with power."

—***Greek proverb***

"The minds of some of our statesmen, like the pupil of the human eye, contract themselves the more, the stronger light there is shed upon them."

—***Thomas Moore,*** Preface to *Corruption and Intolerance,* 1813

"My only ambition is to do my duty in this world as well as I am capable of performing it, and to merit the good opinion of all good men."

—***George Washington,*** on the eve of his election as President, 1789

"Never did a prisoner released from his chains feel such relief as I shall on shaking off the shackles of power."

—***Thomas Jefferson,*** letter dated March 2, 1809

"No man is a hero to his valet. This is not because the hero is no hero, but because the valet is a valet."

—***Georg Wilhelm Friedrich Hegel***

O Captain! my Captain! our fearful trip is done,
The ship has weathered every rack, the prize we sought is won,
The port is near, the bells I hear, the people all exulting,
While follow eyes the steady keel, the vessel grim and daring;
But O heart! heart! heart!
O the bleeding drops of red,
Where on the deck my captain lies,
Fallen cold and dead.

—***Walt Whitman,*** "O Captain! My Captain!," 1865

"Power tends to corrupt and absolute power corrupts absolutely."

—***Lord Acton,*** letter to Bishop Mandell Creighton discussing the unquestioned authority of the popes, April 3, 1887

"Some are born great, some achieve greatness, and some have greatness thrust upon them."

—***William Shakespeare,*** *Twelfth Night,* act 2, scene 5

"A statesman is a politician who is dead."

—***Thomas B. Reed***

"Statistics are no substitute for judgment."

—***Henry Clay,*** speech on radical abolitionism, 1839

"Tactically aggressive, strength of character, steadiness of purpose, acceptance of responsibility, energy, and good health and strength."

—***George S. Patton,*** notion of the six qualities of a good general, found scribbled in the margin of his copy of Fieberger's *Elements of Strategy*

"There go the people. I must follow them for I am their leader."

—***Alexandre Ledru-Rollin***

"They are ill discoverers that think there is not land, when they can see nothing but sea."

—***Francis Bacon,*** *The Advancement of Learning,* 1605

"They never open their mouths without subtracting from the sum of human knowledge."

—***Thomas B. Reed,*** commenting on colleagues in Congress

"The tyrant dies and his rule ends, the martyr dies and his rule begins."

—***Søren Kierkegaard***

"Uneasy lies the head that wears the crown."

—***William Shakespeare,*** *King Henry IV, Part II,* act 3, scene 1

"Viewed from the genuine abolition ground, Mr. Lincoln seemed tardy, cold, dull and indifferent; but measuring him by the sentiment of his country, a sentiment he was bound as a statesman to consult, he was swift, zealous, radical and determined."

—***Frederick Douglass,*** 1876

"We do not lack leaders. Various trumpets are always being sounded. We lack sufficient followers. That is always the problem with leadership."

—***Garry Wills,*** *Certain Trumpets,* 1994

"We don't propose, like some people, to meet today's problems by saying that they don't exist, and tomorrow's problems by wishing that tomorrow wouldn't come."

—***Harry S. Truman***

"We love him for the enemies he has made."

—***Edward Stuyvesant Bragg,*** "Seconding Speech for Grover Cleveland," July 9, 1884. This became a Cleveland campaign slogan.

"What is a rebel? A man who says 'no.'"

—***Albert Camus***

"When a man assumes a public trust, he should consider himself as public property."

—***Thomas Jefferson***

"When the eagles are silent, the parrots begin to jabber."

—***Winston Churchill,*** speech in the House of Commons, directly following the collapse of France, June 18, 1940

"Where there is no vision, the people perish."

—***Proverbs 29:18***

"[Wendell] Wilkie sprang from the grass roots of American country clubs."

—***Alice Roosevelt Longworth***

"The worst ruler is one who cannot rule himself."

—*Cato the Elder*

"You cannot be a leader, and ask other people to follow you, unless you know how to follow, too."

—*Sam Rayburn*

"You must love soldiers in order to understand them, and understand them in order to lead them."

—*Henri de La Tour d'Auvergne Turenne*

31 LIBERTY

"Among free men, there can be no successful appeal from the ballot to the bullet; and those who take such appeal are sure to lose their case and pay the cost."

—***Abraham Lincoln,*** "On the Mindless Menace of Violence," Cleveland, Ohio, April 5, 1858

"Beware how you trifle with your marvelous inheritance, this great land of ordered liberty, for if we stumble and fall, freedom and civilization everywhere will go down in ruin."

—***Henry Cabot Lodge,*** opposing America's joining the League of Nations, August 12, 1919

"The boisterous sea of liberty is never without a wave."

—***Thomas Jefferson***

"Despotism may govern without faith but liberty cannot."

—***Alexis de Tocqueville,*** *Democracy in America,* 1835–1840

"The difference between Liberty and liberties is as great as between God and gods."

—***Ludwig Boerne,*** "Fragmente und Aphorismen," 1840

"Easier were it to hurl the rooted mountain from its base, than force the yoke of slavery upon men determined to be free."

—***Robert Southey***

"The essential characteristic of true liberty is that under its shelter, many different types of life and character and opinion and belief can develop unmolested and unobstructed."

—***Charles Evans Hughes***

"Eternal vigilance by the people is the price of liberty, and . . . you must pay the price if you wish to secure the blessing."

—***Andrew Jackson***

"Every dictatorship has ultimately strangled in the web of repression it wove for its people, making mistakes that could not be corrected because criticism was prohibited."

—***Robert F. Kennedy,*** "The Value of Dissent," speech at Vanderbilt University, Nashville, Tennessee, March 21, 1968

"Freedom by itself is not enough. 'Freedom is a good horse,' said Matthew Arnold, 'but a horse to ride somewhere.' What counts is the use to which men put freedom; what counts is how liberty becomes the means of opportunity and growth and justice."

—***Robert F. Kennedy***

"Freedom's fame finds wings on every wind."

—***George Gordon, Lord Byron,*** "Sonnet on Chillon," 1816

"The God who gave us life, gave us liberty at the same time: the hand of force may destroy, but cannot disjoin them."

—***Thomas Jefferson,*** "Summary View of the Rights of British America," 1774

"The ground of liberty is to be gained by inches. It will not be won overnight."

—***Thomas Jefferson***

"He only earns his freedom and existence who daily conquers them anew."

—***Johann Wolfgang von Goethe,*** *Faust,* 1832

"History teaches that no oppressed class has ever come into power, and cannot come into power, without passing through a period of dictatorship."

—***Vladimir Ilyich Lenin,*** speech to the Communist International Congress, 1919

"How shall freedom be defended? By arms when it is attacked by arms; by truth when it is attacked by lies; by democratic faith when it is attacked by authoritarian dogma. Always, and in the final act, by dedication and faith."

—***Archibald MacLeish***

"I believe there are more instances of the abridgment of the freedom of the people by gradual and silent encroachments of those in power than by violent and sudden usurpations."

—***James Madison,*** speech to the Virginia Convention, 1788

"If you try to deprive even a savage or a barbarian of his just rights you can never do it without becoming a savage or a barbarian yourself."

—***George F. Hoar,*** speech to the Senate opposing the annexation of the Philippines, May 1902

"Is life so dear, or peace so sweet, as to be purchased at the price of chains and slavery? Forbid it, Almighty God! I know not what course others may take, but as for me . . . give me liberty or give me death!"

—***Patrick Henry,*** speech to the Virginia Convention of Delegates, March 23, 1775

"I would rather belong to a poor nation that was free than a rich nation that had ceased to be in love with liberty."

—***Woodrow Wilson***

"The last hopes of mankind, therefore, rest with us; and if it should be proclaimed that our example had become an argument against the experiment, the knell of popular liberty would be sounded throughout the earth."

—***Daniel Webster,*** speaking at the dedication of the Bunker Hill Monument, June 17, 1825

"Let me remind you that extremism in the defense of liberty is no vice. And let me also remind you that moderation in the pursuit of justice is no virtue."

—***Barry Goldwater,*** accepting the presidential nomination at the Republican National Convention, July 16, 1964

"Let my people go."

—***Exodus 9:1***

"The liberties of mankind and the glory of human nature are in our keeping."

—***John Adams,*** revolutionary pamphlet, 1765

"Liberty can no more exist without virtue and independence than the body can live and move without a soul."

—***John Adams,*** commenting on corruption in British politics

"Liberty cannot be preserved without a general knowledge among the people."

—***John Adams,*** *Dissertation on Canon and Feudal Law,* 1765

"Liberty has never come from the government. Liberty has always come from the subjects of it. The history of liberty is the history of resistance. The history of liberty is a history of limitations of governmental power, not the increase of it."

—***Woodrow Wilson,*** speech, New York, September 9, 1912

"Liberty lies in the hearts of men and women; when it dies there, no Constitution, no law, no Court can save it; no Constitution, no law, no Court can even do much to help it. While it lies there it needs no Constitution, no law, no Court to save it."

—***Learned Hand,*** "Spirit of Liberty," May 1944

"Liberty means responsibility. That is why most men dread it."

—***George Bernard Shaw,*** "Maxims for Revolutionists," *Man and Superman,* 1903

"Liberty, when it begins to take root, is a plant of rapid growth."

—***George Washington***

"Liberty without learning is always in peril and learning without liberty is always in vain."

—***John F. Kennedy,*** speech at Vanderbilt University, Nashville, Tennessee, May 18, 1963

"Man is free, but not if he doesn't believe it."

—***Casanova,*** *Memoires,* 1826–1838

"Most of all of us favor free enterprise for business. Let us also favor free enterprise for the mind."

—***Adlai Stevenson,*** address to the American Legion Convention, New York, August 27, 1952

"My definition of a free society is a society where it is safe to be unpopular."

—***Adlai Stevenson,*** speech in Detroit, Michigan, 1952

"Nations around the world look to us for leadership not merely by strength of arms but by the strength of our convictions."

—***Robert F. Kennedy***

"No man or country can be really free unless all men and all countries are free."

—***Thomas Paine***

"Our strength lies, not alone in our proving grounds and our stockpiles, but in our ideals, our goals, and their universal appeal to all men who are struggling to breathe free."

—***Adlai Stevenson***

"The real threat of crime is what it does to ourselves and our communities. No nation hiding behind locked doors is free, for it is imprisoned by its own fear."

—***Robert F. Kennedy,*** "Crime in America" speech, Indianapolis, Indiana, April 26, 1968

"The saddest epitaph which can be carved in memory of a vanished liberty is that it was lost because its possessors failed to stretch forth a saving hand while yet there was time."

—***George Sutherland,*** dissenting opinion, Supreme Court decision in *Associated Press v. National Labor Relations Board,* 301 U.S. 141, 1938

"A society in which men recognize no check upon their freedom soon becomes a society where freedom is the possession of only a savage few."

—***Learned Hand,*** "Spirit of Liberty," May 1944

"Someone who expresses a view that is contrary to the view of the overwhelming majority should be allowed to stand undisturbed as a monument to our commitment to free speech."

—***Albert Gore, Jr.***

"The sound of tireless voices is the price we pay for the right to hear the music of our own opinions."

—***Adlai Stevenson,*** speech, New York, August 28, 1952

"The spirit of liberty is the spirit of him who, near two thousand years ago, taught mankind that lesson it has never learned, but has never quite forgotten—that there may be a kingdom where the least shall be heard and considered side by side with the greatest."

—***Learned Hand,*** "Spirit of Liberty," May 1944

"Systems political or religious or racial or national—will not just respect us because we practice freedom, they will fear us because we do."

—***William Faulkner***

"There are those who will say that the liberation of humanity, the freedom of man and mind, is nothing but a dream. They are right. It is the American dream."

—***Archibald MacLeish***

There is no despot in our land, no man
Who rules and makes laws at his own desire.
Free is our city, here the people rule,
rich man and poor held equal by the law.

—***Euripides***

"They count on our freedom—our individual freedom, our individual interests, our individual pursuit of pleasure and happiness—as the means of our destruction of ourselves."

—***Dorothy Thompson***

"They that can give up essential liberty to obtain a little temporary safety deserve neither liberty nor safety."

—***Benjamin Franklin,*** *Historical Review of Pennsylvania,* 1759

"Those who deny freedom to others deserve it not for themselves, and under a just God cannot long retain it."

—***Abraham Lincoln,*** letter, April 6, 1859

"Those who profess to favor freedom, and yet depreciate agitation, are men who want rain without the thunder and lightning."

—***Frederick Douglass***

"Those who won our independence by revolution were not cowards. They did not fear political change. They did not exalt order at the cost of liberty."

—***Louis D. Brandeis***

"The tree of liberty must be refreshed from time to time with the blood of patriots and tyrants."

—***Thomas Jefferson,*** letter to William Stevens Smith, November 13, 1787

"The voices from Eastern Europe, speaking so plainly and simply of freedom and truth, sounded like an ultimate affirmation that human nature is unchangeable, that nihilism will be futile, that even in the absence of all teaching and in the presence of overwhelming indoctrination, a yearning for freedom and truth will rise out of man's heart and mind forever."

—***Hannah Arendt***

"We are not to be expected to be translated from despotism to liberty in a featherbed."

—***Thomas Jefferson,*** letter to Lafayette, April 2, 1790

"We believe that the only whole man is a free man."

—***Franklin Delano Roosevelt***

"We have buried the putrid corpse of liberty."

—***Benito Mussolini***

"We know that if one man's rights are denied, the rights of all are endangered."

—***Robert F. Kennedy,*** address at the University of Georgia Law School, Athens, May 6, 1961

"You can only protect your liberties in this world by protecting the other man's freedom. You can only be free if I am free."

—***Clarence Darrow,*** address to the jury, trial of Communists, Chicago, Illinois, 1920

"You have power over people as long as you don't take *everything* away from them. But when you've robbed a man of *everything* he's no longer in your power—he's free again."

—***Alexander Solzhenitsyn,*** *The First Circle,* 1968

32 LOVE AND FRIENDSHIP

"All comedies are ended by a marriage."

—***George Gordon, Lord Byron,*** *Don Juan,* 1818–1824

All love that has not friendship for its base,
Is like a mansion built upon the sand.

—***Ella Wheeler Wilcox,*** "Upon the Sand," 1883

"All mankind loves a lover."

—***Ralph Waldo Emerson,*** "Love," *Essays,* 1841

"Beauty is unbearable, drives us to despair, offering us for a minute the glimpse of an eternity that we should like to stretch out over the whole of time."

—***Albert Camus,*** *Notebooks 1935–1942*

Before I built a wall I'd ask to know
What I was walling in or walling out,
And to whom I was like to give offence.

—***Robert Frost,*** "Mending Wall," 1914

"By the accident of fortune a man may rule the world for a time, but by virtue of love he may rule the world forever."

—***Lao-tzu,*** *Tao-te-ching*

Count where man's glory begins and ends
And say my glory was I had such friends.

—***William Butler Yeats,*** "The Municipal Gallery Revisited," *New Poems,* 1938

"Distance lends enchantment."

—***Thomas Campbell,*** *The Pleasures of Hope,* 1799

"Don't marry for money; you can borrow it cheaper."

—***Scottish proverb***

"A friend may well be reckoned the masterpiece of Nature."

—***Ralph Waldo Emerson,*** "Friendship," *Essays,* 1841

"Friend. The finest word in any language."

—***Franchot Tone as Midshipman Byam*** in the film version of Charles Nordhoff and James Hall's *Mutiny on the Bounty,* 1935

Friendship is constant in all other things
Save in the office and affairs of love.

—***William Shakespeare,*** *Much Ado about Nothing,* act 2, scene 1

"Greater love hath no man than this, that he lay down his life for his friends."

—***John 15:13***

"Grief can take care of itself; but to get the full value of a joy you must have somebody to divide it with."

—***Mark Twain***

"The heart of marriage is memories."

—***Bill Cosby,*** *Love and Marriage,* 1989

He who has a thousand friends has not a friend to spare,
And he who has one enemy will meet him everywhere.

—***Ali Ibn Abu Talib***

"He who plays alone never loses. And, of course, never wins."

—***Anonymous***

"How do I love thee? Let me count the ways."

—***Elizabeth Barrett Browning,*** *Sonnets from the Portuguese,* 1850

"Immature love says: 'I love you because I need you.' Mature love says: 'I need you because I love you.'"

—***Erich Fromm,*** *The Art of Loving,* 1955

"It is a truth universally acknowledged that a single man in possession of a good fortune must be in want of a wife."

—***Jane Austen,*** opening sentence, *Pride and Prejudice,* 1813

"It's very hard to get your heart and head together in life. In my case, they're not even friendly."

—***Woody Allen,*** *Husbands and Wives,* 1992

"It takes your enemy and your friend, working together, to hurt you to the heart; the one to slander you and the other to get the news to you."

—***Mark Twain***

"Kindness is the language which the deaf can hear and the blind can see."

—***Mark Twain***

"Life has no blessing like a prudent friend."

—***Euripides***

"Love conquers all things—except poverty and toothache."

—***Mae West***

"Love does not consist in gazing at each other but in looking outward together in the same direction."

—***Antoine de Saint-Exupéry,*** *Wind, Sand, and Stars,* 1939

"Love is blind, but marriage restores its sight."

—***Georg Christoph Lichtenberg***

"Love itself is love's chief nourishment."

—***Propertius,*** *Elegies*

"Love makes all men orators."

—***Robert Greene***

"Love makes time pass. Time makes love pass."

—***French proverb***

"Love means never having to say you're sorry."

—***Erich Segal,*** *Love Story,* 1970

"Love turns one person into two; and two into one."

—***Judah ben Isaac Abravenel***

"The magic of first love is our ignorance that it can ever end."

—***Benjamin Disraeli,*** *Henrietta Temple,* 1837

"Marriage is a lot like the army: everyone complains, but you'd be surprised at the large number that re-enlist."

—***James Garner***

"Marriage is the only adventure open to the cowardly."

—***Voltaire***

"Men should take care not to make women weep, for God counts their tears."

—***The Talmud***

"Needing someone is like needing a parachute. If they are not there the first time you need them, chances are you won't be needing them again."

—***Scott Adams***

"No one loves the man whom he fears."

—***Aristotle***

"Occasionally in life there are moments . . . which cannot be completely explained by words. Their meaning can only be articulated by the inaudible language of the heart."

—***Martin Luther King, Jr.***

"Of all forms of caution, caution in love is perhaps the most fatal to true happiness."

—***Bertrand Russell,*** *The Conquest of Happiness,* 1930

"One friend in a lifetime is much; two are many; three are hardly possible."

—***Henry Adams,*** *The Education of Henry Adams,* 1907

"Only a life lived for others is a life worthwhile."

—***Albert Einstein,*** *Youth,* 1932

"The only reward of virtue is virtue; the only way to have a friend is to be one."

—***Ralph Waldo Emerson,*** "Friendship," *Essays,* 1841

"The only whole heart is a broken one."

—***Menachem Mendel***

"Parting is such sweet sorrow."

—***William Shakespeare,*** *Romeo and Juliet,* act 2, scene 2

"Persons are to be loved, things are to be used."

—***Reuel Howe***

"The proper office of a friend is to side with you when you are in the wrong. Nearly everybody will side with you when you are in the right."

—***Mark Twain***

"Sir, if you were my husband, I would poison your coffee."
"Madam, if you were my wife, I'd drink it."

—***Nancy Astor and Winston Churchill,*** exchange in the House of Commons

"Someday, after mastering the winds, the waves, the tides and gravity, we shall harness for God the energies of love. And then, for the second time in the history of the world . . . man will have discovered fire."

—***Pierre Teilhard de Chardin***

"The supreme happiness of life is the conviction that we are loved."

—***Victor Hugo,*** *Les Misérables,* 1862

"There is only one happiness in life, to love and be loved."

—***George Sand,*** letter to Lina Calamatta, March 31, 1862

"A thing of beauty is a joy forever."

—***John Keats,*** "Endymion," 1817

Though lovers be lost love shall not;
And death shall have no dominion.

—***Dylan Thomas,*** "And Death Shall Have No Dominion," 1933

"To be wise, and love, exceeds man's might."

—***William Shakespeare,*** *Troilus and Cressida,* act 3, scene 2

"The tragedy of love is indifference."

—***W. Somerset Maugham,*** *The Trembling of Leaf,* 1921

"We are shaped and fashioned by what we love."

—***Johann Wolfgang von Goethe***

"What a woman says to her ardent lover should be written in wind and running water."

—***Catullus,*** *Carmina*

> What's in a name? that which we call a rose
> By any other name would smell as sweet.

—***William Shakespeare,*** *Romeo and Juliet,* act 2, scene 2

"You can give without loving, but you cannot love without giving."

—***Amy Carmichael***

33 THE MEDIA

"According to American principle and practice the public is the ruler of the State, and in order to rule rightly it should be informed correctly."

—***William Randolph Hearst***

"Censorship reflects a society's lack of confidence in itself."

—***Potter Stewart***

"An editor is one who separates the wheat from the chaff, and then prints the chaff."

—***Adlai Stevenson***

"Evil news rides post, while good news baits."

—***John Milton,*** *Samson Agonistes,* 1671

"For the newspaper is in all literalness the bible of democracy, the book out of which a people determines its conduct. It is the only serious book most people read. It is the only book they read every day."

—***Walter Lippmann,*** *Liberty and the News,* 1920

"A free press is not a privilege but an organic necessity in a great society."

—***Walter Lippmann,*** address at the International Press Institute Assembly, London, 1965

"The freedom of the press is one of the great bulwarks of liberty, and can never be restrained but by despotic governments."

—***George Mason,*** Virginia Bill of Rights, Article I, 1776

"Freedom of the press is to the machinery of the state what the safety valve is to the steam engine."

—***Arthur Schopenhauer***

"A good newspaper is a nation talking to itself."

—***Arthur Miller,*** *London Observer,* November 26, 1961

"The hand that rules the press, the radio, the screen, and the far-spread magazine rules the country."

—***Learned Hand,*** memorial address for Justice Louis D. Brandeis, 1942

"I'll know my career's going bad when they start quoting me correctly."

—***Lee Marvin***

"In America the President reigns for four years, and journalism governs for ever and ever."

—***Oscar Wilde,*** "The Soul of Man under Socialism," 1881

"In old days men had the rack. Now they have the Press."

—***Oscar Wilde,*** "The Soul of Man under Socialism," 1881

"In order to enjoy the inestimable benefits that the liberty of the press ensures, it is necessary to submit to the inevitable evils that it creates."

—***Alexis de Tocqueville,*** *Democracy in America,* 1835–1840

"I wish I could sue the *New York Post,* but it's awfully hard to sue a garbage can."

—***Paul Newman***

"The mass production of distraction is now as much a part of the American way of life as the mass production of automobiles."

—***C. Wright Mills***

"Men with the muck-rake are often indispensable to the well-being of society; but only if they know when to stop raking the muck."

—***Theodore Roosevelt,*** speech, Washington, D.C., April 14, 1906

"Mr. Brady, it is the duty of a newspaper to comfort the afflicted and afflict the comfortable."

—***Gene Kelly*** as newspaper reporter ***E. K. Hornbeck,*** to Matthew Brady (Fredric March), the leading prosecutor in the trial in Jerome Lawrence and Robert Lee's *Inherit the Wind,* 1960

"News is the first rough draft of history."

—***Ben Bradlee***

"Newspapers are the schoolmasters of the common people. That endless book, the newspaper, is our national glory."

—***Henry Ward Beecher,*** *Proverbs from Plymouth Pulpit,* 1887

"No government ought to be without censors; and where the press is free none ever will."

—***Thomas Jefferson***

"Our liberty depends on the freedom of the press, and that cannot be limited without being lost."

—***Thomas Jefferson,*** letter to Dr. J. Curie, 1786

"Popular government, without popular information, or the means of acquiring it, is but a prologue to a farce or a tragedy; or perhaps both. Knowledge will forever govern ignorance; and a people who mean to be their own governors must arm themselves with the power which knowledge gives."

—***James Madison***

"The sources of information are the springs from which democracy drinks."

—***Adlai Stevenson,*** speech in Cincinnati, Ohio, 1956

"Sunlight is the best of [all] disinfectants."

—***Louis D. Brandeis***

"Television—a medium. So called because it is neither rare nor well done."

—***Ernie Kovacs***

"There are only two forces that can carry light to all corners of the globe—the sun in the heavens and the Associated Press."

—***Mark Twain,*** speech in New York City, 1906

"There is only one thing in the world worse than being talked about, and that is not being talked about."

—***Oscar Wilde,*** *The Picture of Dorian Gray,* 1891

"This instrument [television] can teach, it can illuminate—yes, it can even inspire. But it can do so only to the extent that humans are determined to use it to those ends. Otherwise it is merely wires and lights in a box."

—***Edward R. Murrow,*** speaking to the Radio and Television News Directors in Chicago, Illinois, October 15, 1958

"To the press alone, chequered as it is with abuses, the world is indebted for all the triumphs which have been gained by reason and humanity over error and oppression."

—***James Madison***

"Were it left to me to decide whether we should have a government without newspapers, or newspapers without a government, I should not hesitate a moment to prefer the latter."

—***Thomas Jefferson,*** letter to Edward Carrington, January 16, 1787

"When the press is free and every man able to read, all is safe."

—***Thomas Jefferson***

"Wherever books are burned, sooner or later men are also burned."

—***Heinrich Heine,*** "Almansor," 1821

"Where there is a great deal of free speech there is always a certain amount of foolish speech."

—***Winston Churchill***

34 PAST, PRESENT, AND FUTURE

"The admiration of the present and succeeding ages will be ours, since we have not left our power without witness, but have shown it by mighty proofs."

—*Thucydides, History of the Peloponnesian War,* 403 B.C.

"After all, tomorrow is another day."

—*Vivien Leigh as Scarlett O'Hara,* last line of the film version of Margaret Mitchell's *Gone With the Wind,* 1939

"All history becomes subjective; in other words, there is properly no history; only biography."

—*Ralph Waldo Emerson,* "History," *Essays,* 1841

Bliss in possession will not last;
Remember'd joys are never past;
At once the fountain, stream, and sea,
They were,—they are,—they yet shall be.

—*James Montgomery, The Little Cloud,* 1835

"God cannot alter the past, but historians can."

—*Samuel Butler*

"The great use of a life is to spend it for something that outlasts it."

—*William James*

"History [is] a distillation of rumor."

—*Thomas Carlyle, History of the French Revolution,* 1837

"History is a gallery of pictures in which there are few originals and many copies."

—***Alexis de Tocqueville,*** *L'Ancien Régime,* 1856

"History is a set of lies agreed upon."

—***Napoleon Bonaparte***

"History is not a web woven with innocent hands. Among all the causes which degrade and demoralize men, power is the most constant and the most active."

—***Lord Acton,*** *Essays on Freedom and Power,* 1862

"History is the essence of innumerable biographies."

—***Thomas Carlyle,*** "On History," *Critical and Miscellaneous Essays,* 1838

"History is the record of an encounter between character and circumstance."

—***Donald Grant Creighton***

"History will be kind to me for I intend to write it."

—***Winston Churchill***

"I don't know who my grandfather was; I am more concerned to know what his grandson will be."

—***Abraham Lincoln***

"If we open a quarrel between the past and the present, we shall find that we have lost the future."

—***Winston Churchill,*** speech in the House of Commons, June 18, 1940

"If you don't know where you're going, you'll end up someplace else."

—***Yogi Berra***

"I like the dreams of the future better than the history of the past."

—***Thomas Jefferson***

"I never think of the future. It comes soon enough."

—***Albert Einstein,*** interview on the *Belgenland,* December 1930

"It is fun to be in the same decade with you."

—***Franklin Delano Roosevelt,*** cablegram to Winston Churchill, January 30, 1942

"It is not for us to forecast the future, but to shape it."

—***Antoine de Saint-Exupéry***

"The kind of events that once took place will by reason of human nature take place again."

—***Thucydides***

"Not much longer shall we have time for reading the lessons of the past. An inexorable present calls us to the defense of a great future."

—***Henry Luce,*** Foreword to *Why England Slept* by John F. Kennedy, 1940

"Now, gentlemen, let us do something today which the world may talk of hereafter."

—***Cuthbert Collingwood,*** before the Battle of Trafalgar, October 21, 1805

"Now is the winter of our discontent."

—***William Shakespeare,*** *King Richard III,* act 1, scene 1

"A page of history is worth a volume of logic."

—***Oliver Wendell Holmes, Jr.,*** in the Supreme Court decision *New York Trust Co. v. Eisner,* 256 U.S. 345, 349, 1921

"People will not look forward to posterity, who never look backward to their ancestors."

—***Edmund Burke,*** *Reflections on the Revolution in France,* 1790

"Perfection of means and confusion of ends seems to characterize our age."

—***Albert Einstein***

"The present is never tidy, or certain, or reasonable, and those who try to make it so, once it has become the past, succeed only in making it seem implausible."

—***William Manchester***

"Present things are less than horrible imaginings."

—***William Shakespeare,*** *Macbeth,* act 1, scene 3

"Read no history: nothing but biography, for that is life without theory."

—***Benjamin Disraeli,*** *Contarini Fleming,* 1832

"That is the supreme value of history. The study of it is the best guarantee against repeating it."

—*John Buchan, Baron Tweedsmuir*

"That which seems the height of absurdity in one generation becomes the height of wisdom in another."

—*Adlai Stevenson*

"There are people in every time and every land who want to stop history in its tracks. They fear the future, mistrust the present, and invoke the security of a comfortable past which, in fact, never existed."

—*Robert F. Kennedy,* speech at the California Institute of Technology, Pasadena, California, June 8, 1964

"There are times in history where the business of one is the business of all, when life or death is a matter of choice, and when no one alive can avoid making that choice. These times occur seldom in history, these times of inevitable decisions. But this is one of those times."

—*Dorothy Thompson,* addressing a convention in Toronto, May 2, 1941

"[This is] the century of the common man."

—*Henry A. Wallace, The Price of Free World Victory,* 1943

"The time for extracting a lesson from history is ever at hand for those who are wise."

—*Demosthenes*

"Time is the great physician."

—*Benjamin Disraeli*

"Tomorrow night is nothing but one long sleepless wrestle with yesterday's omissions and regrets."

—*William Faulkner, Intruder in the Dust,* 1949

"The twentieth century has proven to be a terrible disappointment."

—*Winston Churchill,* words spoken in 1922, prior to the Great Depression, World War II, and the Cold War

"Unless there is the most intimate association between those who look to the far horizons and those who deal with our daily problems, then . . . we shall not pass through these stormy times with success."

—*John F. Kennedy*

"We have come too far, we have sacrificed too much, to disdain the future now."

—***John F. Kennedy***

"We have forced every sea and land to be the highway of our daring, and everywhere, whether for evil or for good, have left imperishable monuments behind us."

—***Thucydides,*** *History of the Peloponnesian War,* 403 B.C.

"We've reached the end of history."

—***Francis Fukuyama,*** on the end of the Cold War and the broad acceptance of liberal democratic principles, *The End of History,* 1989

"You must live in the world as it is."

—***Dean Acheson,*** to a stunned Evelyn Shuckburgh on the loss of British influence in Iran a few weeks after the evacuation of Abadan Island

35 PATRIOTISM

"An American is one who loves justice and believes in the dignity of man. An American is one who will fight for his freedom and that of his neighbor. An American is one who will sacrifice prosperity, ease, and security in order that he and his children may retain the rights of free men."

—***Harold L. Ickes***

"Americans, indeed all free men, remember that in the final choice, a soldier's pack is not so heavy a burden as a prisoner's chains."

—***Dwight D. Eisenhower***

"The fabulous country—the place where miracles not only happen, but where they happen all the time."

—***Thomas Wolfe,*** *Of Time and the River,* 1935

"Feed your eyes upon her from day to day, till love of her fills your hearts; and when all her greatness shall break upon you, you must reflect that it was by courage, sense of duty, and a keen feeling of honor in action that men were enabled to win all this, and that no personal failure in an enterprise could make them consent to deprive their country of their valor."

—***Thucydides,*** *History of the Peloponnesian War,* 403 B.C.

"From these honored dead we take increased devotion to that cause for which they gave the last full measure of devotion; that we here highly resolve that these dead shall not have died in vain; that this nation, under God, shall have a new birth of freedom; and that government of the people, by the people, for the people, shall not perish from the earth."

—***Abraham Lincoln,*** Gettysburg Address, November 19, 1863

"Gentlemen, you will permit me to put on my spectacles, for I have not only grown gray, but almost blind in the service of my country."

—***George Washington***

"He loved his country as no other man has loved her."

—***Edward Everett Hale,*** *The Man without a Country,* 1863

"How hard it is to die and leave one's country no better than if one had never lived for it."

—***Abraham Lincoln***

"I am a citizen, not of Athens, nor of Greece, but of the whole world. The world is my parish."

—***Socrates***

"If a man is going to be an American at all let him be so without any qualifying adjectives."

—***Henry Cabot Lodge,*** at a dinner for the New England Society, New York, December 21, 1888

"I only regret that I have but one life to lose for my country."

—***Nathan Hale,*** spoken before his execution for espionage during the American Revolution, September 22, 1776

"I pray that our Heavenly Father may assuage the anguish of your bereavement, and leave you only to the cherished memory of the loved and lost, and the solemn pride that must be yours, to have laid so costly a sacrifice upon the altar of freedom."

—***Abraham Lincoln,*** letter to Mrs. Lydia Bixby upon the death of her five sons in defense of the Union, November 21, 1864

"It was the nation and the races dwelling all around the globe that had the lion's heart. I had the luck to be called upon to give the roar."

—***Winston Churchill,*** eightieth-birthday speech, November 1954

"It would seem that men always need some idiotic fiction in the name of which they can hate one another. Once it was religion. Now it is the State."

—***Albert Einstein***

"Let every man honor and love the land of his birth and the race from which he springs and keep their memory green. It is a pious and honorable duty."

—***Henry Cabot Lodge,*** at a dinner for the New England Society, New York, December 21, 1888

"Let our patriotism be reflected in the creation of confidence in one another, rather than in crusades of suspicion. Let us prove we think our country great, by striving to make it greater."

—***John F. Kennedy,*** speech at the Democratic Party of California dinner, November 18, 1961

"Let us therefore brace ourselves to our duties and so bear ourselves that if the British Empire and its Commonwealth last for a thousand years men will still say, 'This was their finest hour.'"

—***Winston Churchill,*** speech in the House of Commons preparing the nation for the impending German assault upon Britain following the defeat of France, June 18, 1940

"Lives of nations are determined, not by the count of years, but by the lifetime of the human spirit. The life of a man is three score years and ten, a little more, a little less. But the life of a nation is the fullness of its will to live."

—***Franklin Delano Roosevelt,*** Third Inaugural Address, January 20, 1941

"The long gray line has never failed us. Were we to do so, a million ghosts in olive drab, in brown khakis, in blue and gray, would rise from their white crosses, thundering those magic words: duty, honor, country."

—***Douglas MacArthur,*** address at the U.S. Military Academy at West Point, May 12, 1962

"Men may speculate as they will, they make talk of patriotism . . . but whoever builds upon it as a sufficient basis for conducting a long and bloody war will find themselves deceived in the end. . . . For a time it may of itself push men to action, to bear much, to encounter difficulties, but it will not endure unassisted by interest."

—***George Washington***

"Men who have offered their lives for their country know that patriotism is not the *fear* of something; it is the *love* of something."

—***Adlai Stevenson,*** address to the American Legion Convention, Madison Square Garden, New York, August 27, 1952

"The mystic chords of memory, stretching from every battlefield and patriot grave to every living heart and hearthstone all over this broad land, will yet swell the chorus of the Union, when again touched, as surely they will be, by the better angels of our nature."

—***Abraham Lincoln,*** First Inaugural Address, March 4, 1861

"A nation reveals itself not only by the men it produces but also by the men it honors, the men it remembers."

—***John F. Kennedy,*** speech in praise of Robert Frost, Amherst College, Amherst, Massachusetts, October 27, 1963

"Not that I loved Caesar less, but that I loved Rome more."

—***William Shakespeare,*** *Julius Caesar,* act 3, scene 2. Brutus, after his assassination of Caesar, justifies the act to the people of Rome.

"Now the trumpet summons us again—not as a call to bear arms, though arms we need—not as a call to battle, though embattled we are—but a call to bear the burden of a long twilight struggle year in and year out 'rejoicing in hope, patient in tribulation'—a struggle against the common enemies of man: tyranny, poverty, disease and war itself."

—***John F. Kennedy,*** Inaugural Address, January 20, 1961

"Now we are engaged in a great civil war, testing whether this nation, or any nation so conceived and so dedicated, can long endure. We are met on a great battlefield of that war. We have come to dedicate a portion of that field as a final resting place for those who here gave their lives that this nation might live. It is altogether fitting and proper that we should do this.

"But, in a larger sense, we cannot dedicate—we cannot consecrate—we cannot hallow—this ground. The brave men, living and dead, who struggled here have consecrated it far above our poor power to add or to detract. The world will little note nor long remember what we say here, but it can never forget what they did here."

—***Abraham Lincoln,*** Gettysburg Address, November 19, 1863

"Patriotism is the last refuge of a scoundrel."

—***Samuel Johnson,*** Boswell's *Life of Johnson,* April 7, 1775

"Sarah, my love for you is deathless. It seems to bind me with mighty cables that nothing but Omnipotence could break; and yet my love of Country comes over me like a strong wind and bears me irresistibly on with all these chains to the battlefield."

—***Sullivan Ballou,*** a major in the Second Rhode Island Volunteers, last letter to his wife, Sarah, prior to the Battle of Bull Run, July 14, 1861

"A strict observance of the written laws is doubtless one of the high virtues of a good citizen, but it is not the highest. The laws of necessity, of self-preservation, of saving our country when in danger, are of higher obligation."

—***Thomas Jefferson,*** letter, 1810

"There is a debt of service due from every man to his country, proportioned to the bounties which nature and fortune have measured on him."

—***Thomas Jefferson***

Those heroes that shed their blood and lost their lives.
You are now lying in the soil of a friendly country,
Therefore rest in peace.
There is no difference between the Johnnies
And the Mehmets to us where they lie side by side
Here in this country of ours.
You the mothers
Who sent their sons from faraway countries
Wipe away your tears.
Your sons are now lying in our bosom
And are at peace.
After having lost their lives on this land they have
Become our sons as well.

—***Kemal Pasha Ataturk,*** memorial tablet honoring the British, Australian, and New Zealander soldiers killed in the 1915 Dardanelles Campaign, Gallipoli, Turkey

"Ultimately no nation can be great unless its greatness is lain on foundations of righteousness and decency."

—***Theodore Roosevelt***

"We are at the beginning of an age in which it will be insisted that the same standards of conduct and of responsibility for wrong done shall be observed among nations and their governments that are observed among the individual citizens of civilized states."

—***Woodrow Wilson,*** address to Congress, April 2, 1917

"We mutually pledge to each other our Lives, our Fortunes, and our sacred Honor."

—***Declaration of Independence,*** last line, July 4, 1776

"With a good conscience our only sure reward, with history the final judge of our deeds, let us go forth to lead the land we love."

—***John F. Kennedy,*** Inaugural Address, January 20, 1961

36 PEACE

"Blessed are the peacemakers: for they shall be called the children of God."

—*Matthew 5:9*

"But peace does not rest in the charters and covenants alone. It lies in the hearts and minds of all people. And if it is cast out there, then no act, no pact, no treaty, no organization can hope to preserve it without the support and wholehearted commitment of all people. So let us not rest all our hopes on parchments and on paper—let us strive to build peace, a desire for peace, a willingness to work for peace in the hearts and minds of all of our people."

—***John F. Kennedy,*** address to the United Nations, September 20, 1963

"Come now, and let us reason together."

—***Isaiah 1:18***

"Even peace may be purchased at too high a price."

—***Benjamin Franklin***

"The god of Victory is said to be one-handed, but peace gives victory to both sides."

—***Ralph Waldo Emerson,*** *Journals,* 1867

"If peace cannot be maintained with honor, it is no longer peace."

—***Lord John Russell,*** speech, Greenock, England, September 19, 1853

"If you want to stop war, you gather such an aggregation of force on the side of peace that the aggressor, whoever he may be, will not dare challenge."

—***Winston Churchill***

"In His will is our peace."

—***Dante Alighieri,*** *The Divine Comedy, Paradiso,* canto 3, 1321

"Let us dedicate ourselves to what the Greeks wrote so many years ago: to tame the savageness of man and to make gentle the life of this world. Let us dedicate ourselves to that, and say a prayer for our country and for our people."

—***Robert F. Kennedy,*** speech to an audience of African Americans in Indianapolis, Indiana, upon the assassination of Martin Luther King, Jr., April 4, 1968

"Peace can be a cover whereby evil men can perpetrate diabolical wrongs."

—***John Foster Dulles,*** April 11, 1955

"Peace cannot be kept by force, it can only be achieved by understanding."

—***Albert Einstein***

"Peace hath her victories no less renowned than war."

—***John Milton,*** *To the Lord General Cromwell,* 1694

"Peace is like a delicate plant. It has to be constantly tended to and nurtured if it is to survive. If we neglect it, it will wither and die."

—***Richard Nixon,*** *Beyond Peace,* 1994

"Peace is never long preserved by weight of metal or by an armament race. Peace can be made tranquil and secure only by understanding and agreement fortified by sanctions. We must embrace international cooperation or international disintegration."

—***Bernard Baruch,*** speech to the United Nations Atomic Energy Commission on Atomic Control, 1946

"Peace is not a relationship of nations. It is a condition of mind brought about by a serenity of soul. Peace is not merely the absence of war. It is also a state of mind. Lasting peace can come only to peaceful people."

—***Jawaharlal Nehru***

A peace is of the nature of a conquest;
For then both parties nobly are subdued,
And neither party loser.

—***William Shakespeare,*** *Henry IV, Part II,* act 4, scene 2

"A soft answer turneth away wrath; but harsh words stir up anger."

—***Proverbs 15:1***

"So let us persevere. Peace need not be impracticable—and war need not be inevitable. By defining our goal more clearly, by making it seem more manageable and less remote, we can help all peoples to see it, to draw hope from it, and to move irresistibly towards it."

—***John F. Kennedy,*** speech, American University, Washington, D.C., 1963

"A steadfast concert for peace can never be maintained except by a partnership of democratic nations. No autocratic government could be trusted to keep faith within it or observe its covenants. It must be a league of honor, a partnership of opinion. . . . Only free peoples can hold their purpose and their honor steady to a common end and prefer the interests of mankind to any narrow interest of their own."

—***Woodrow Wilson,*** speech, April 2, 1917

"Teach them politics and war so that their sons may study medicine and mathematics in order to give their children a right to study painting, poetry, music, and architecture."

—***John Adams***

"There never was a good war or a bad peace."

—***Benjamin Franklin,*** letter to Josiah Quincy, September 11, 1783

"They made a desert and called it peace."

—***Marcus Claudius Tacitus,*** *Agricola*

"They shall beat their swords into plowshares, and their spears into pruning hooks; nation shall not lift up sword against nation, neither shall they learn war any more."

—***Isaiah 2:4***

"Those who make peaceful revolution impossible will make violent revolution inevitable."

—***John F. Kennedy,*** the White House, Washington, D.C., March 3, 1962

'Tis not hard, I think,
For men so old as we to keep the peace.

—***William Shakespeare,*** *Romeo and Juliet,* act 1, scene 2

"To be prepared for war is one of the most effectual means of preserving peace."

—***George Washington,*** First State of the Union Address, January 8, 1790

"Victory would mean peace forced upon the loser, a victor's terms imposed upon the vanquished. It would be accepted in humiliation, under duress, at an intolerable sacrifice, and would leave a sting, a resentment, a bitter memory, upon which terms of peace would rest, not permanently, but only as upon quicksand. Only a peace between equals can last; only a peace the very principle of which is equality and a common participation in a common benefit."

—***Woodrow Wilson,*** speech to Senate, January 21, 1917

"War makes rattling good history; but Peace is poor reading."

—***Thomas Hardy,*** *The Dynasts,* 1904

"We are going to win the war, and we are going to win the peace that follows."

—***Franklin Delano Roosevelt,*** radio address to the American people following the Japanese attack on Pearl Harbor, December 9, 1941

"What a beautiful fix we are in now; peace has been declared."

—***Napoleon Bonaparte,*** after the Treaty of Amiens

"When peace comes, we will perhaps in time be able to forgive the Arabs for killing our sons, but it will be harder for us to forgive them for having forced us to kill their sons."

—***Golda Meir,*** interview following the Six Day War of 1967

"You cannot shake hands with a clenched fist."

—***Golda Meir***

37 POLITICAL PARTIES

"All free governments are party governments."

—*James A. Garfield,* speech in the House of Representatives, 1878

"All political parties die at last of swallowing their own lies."

—*John Arburthnot,* 1887

"The conduct of a losing party never appears right: at least it never can possess the only infallible criterion of wisdom to vulgar judgements—success."

—*Edmund Burke, Letter to a Member of the National Assembly,* 1791

"Conservatism is the policy of make no change and consult your grandmother when in doubt."

—*Woodrow Wilson*

"The country is Republican until five o'clock."

—*Theodore H. White*

"Damn your principles! Stick to your party."

—*Benjamin Disraeli*

"The Democratic Party . . . presents its case on a strong platform and strong candidates, on a proven record of past accomplishment, on the evidence that it alone has the vision and boldness to meet the challenge of leadership of the free world."

—*Robert F. Kennedy,* New England Democratic Party meeting, Boston, Massachusetts, August 2, 1960

"Democrats give away their old clothes; Republicans wear theirs. Republicans employ exterminators; Democrats step on the bugs. Democrats eat the fish they catch; Republicans stuff 'em and hang 'em on the wall."

—***Sean Donlon,*** *Washington Post,* October 23, 1981

"The Democrats of this day and age are providing this Nation with the kind of leadership that the world requires. Ours is a party that is responsible and is responsive, that is progressive and prudent. It is a party of vision and a party of common sense. It is a party where all expect full hearing and all receive fair play."

—***Lyndon B. Johnson,*** remarks before the Democratic National Convention, Atlantic City, New Jersey, August 28, 1964

"The disagreement among American political parties, with only a few exceptions, has been over the practical question of how to secure the agreed objective, while conciliating different interests, rather than over ultimate values or over what interest is paramount."

—***Daniel Boorstin,*** *The Genius of American Politics,* 1953

"Every Harvard class should have one Democrat to rescue it from oblivion."

—***Will Rogers,*** *The Autobiography of Will Rogers,* 1949

"He serves his party best who serves the country best."

—***Rutherford B. Hayes,*** Inaugural Address, March 5, 1877

"Honor is not the exclusive property of any political party."

—***Herbert Hoover***

"I don't belong to any organized political party. I'm a Democrat."

—***Will Rogers***

"If I could not go to heaven but with a party, I would not go there at all."

—***Thomas Jefferson,*** letter to Francis Hopkinson, 1789

"If parties in a republic are necessary to secure a degree of vigilance sufficient to keep the public functionaries within the bounds of law and duty, at that point their usefulness ends."

—***William Henry Harrison,*** Inaugural Address, 1841

"If the Republicans will stop telling lies about the Democrats, we will stop telling the truth about them."

—***Adlai Stevenson***

"If you want to live like a Republican, vote Democratic."

—*Alben Barkley*

"I long for the time when the public service will get onto a higher plane than that of serving political parties, and come to serve the public interest instead."

—*Robert M. La Follette*

I never dared be radical when young
For fear it would make me conservative when old.

—*Robert Frost,* "Precaution," 1936

"In every critical hour when they wanted to march into the future, the people have turned to the Democratic Party for leadership. The finger of destiny beckons us once again to resume the vigorous leadership of the free world. The Democratic Party is ready for its rendezvous with destiny."

—*Sam Rayburn*

"In the fullness of time and service to the nation, the Democratic Party has become more than a political party. It has become an idea, an essential part of the American idea. Political parties have their ups and downs. But great ideas go on forever."

—*Sam Rayburn*

"In this entire century the Democratic Party has never been invested with power on the basis of a program which promised to keep things as they were. We have won when we pledged to meet the new challenges of each succeeding year. We have triumphed not in spite of controversy, but because of it; not because we avoided problems, but because we faced them. We have won, not because we bent and diluted our principles, but because we stood fast to the ideals which represent the most noble and generous portion of the American spirit."

—*Robert F. Kennedy*

"I shall give the Republican orators some more opportunities to say 'Me, too.'"

—*Franklin Delano Roosevelt,* in one of his last campaign speeches, 1944

"It doesn't matter whether you're riding an elephant or a donkey if you're going in the wrong direction."

—*Jesse Jackson*

"Lincoln was right about not fooling all the people all of the time. But the Republicans haven't given up trying."

—*Lyndon B. Johnson,* October 7, 1966

"A Majority is always the best repartee."

—***Benjamin Disraeli,*** *Tancred,* 1847

"More important than winning the election is governing the nation. That is the test of a political party—the acid, final test."

—***Adlai Stevenson,*** acceptance speech, Democratic National Convention, Chicago, Illinois, July 26, 1952

"The most radical revolutionary will become a conservative the day after the revolution."

—***Hannah Arendt,*** *The New Yorker,* September 12, 1970

"Mr. Nixon, in the last seven days, has called me an economic ignoramus, a Pied Piper, and all the rest. I've just confined myself to calling him a Republican, but he says that is getting low."

—***John F. Kennedy,*** New York City, November 5, 1960

"No party has a monopoly over what is right."

—***Mikhail Gorbachev,*** speech to the Congress of the Soviet Communist Party, Moscow, 1986

"Now there is an old and somewhat lugubrious adage that says: 'Never speak of rope in the house of a man who has been hanged.' In the same way, if I were a Republican leader speaking to a mixed audience, the last word in the whole dictionary that I think I would use is that word 'Depression.'"

—***Franklin Delano Roosevelt,*** campaign speech at a dinner for the International Teamsters, Washington, D.C., September 23, 1944

"Our duty as a party is not to our party alone, but to the nation and, indeed, to all mankind. Our duty is not merely the preservation of political power but the preservation of peace and freedom."

—***John F. Kennedy,*** speech planned for delivery in Dallas, Texas, November 22, 1963

"Parties are instruments of government. . . . The business of parties is not just to win elections. It is to govern. And a party cannot govern if it is disunited."

—***Robert F. Kennedy,*** speech at the Kings County Democratic Party dinner, Brooklyn, New York, 1965

"Party divisions, whether on the whole operating for good or evil, are things inseparable from free government."

—***Edmund Burke,*** *Observations on a Publication, "The Present State of a Nation,"* 1769

"Party is organized opinion."

—***Benjamin Disraeli,*** speech at Oxford, reported in *The Times,* November 26, 1864

"Permanent political parties have been born in this country after, and not before, national campaigns, and they have come from the people, not from the proclamations of individual leaders."

—***Robert M. La Follette,*** platform statement presented to the Progressive Conference, 1924

"The radical invents the views. When he has worn them out, the conservative adopts them."

—***Mark Twain***

"[Republicans] approve of the American farmer, but they are willing to help him go broke. They stand four-square for the American home—but not for housing. They are strong for labor—but they are stronger for restricting labor's rights. They favor minimum wage—the smaller the minimum wage the better. They endorse educational opportunity for all—but they won't spend money for teachers or for schools. They think modern medical care and hospitals are fine—for the people who can afford them. They consider electric power a great blessing—but only when the private power companies get their rake-off. They think the American standard of living is a fine thing—so long as it doesn't spread to all the people. And they admire the Government of the United States so much that they would like to buy it."

—***Harry S. Truman***

"Republicans are the party that says government doesn't work, and then they get elected and prove it."

—***P. J. O'Rourke,*** *Parliament of Whores,* 1991

"Republicans have been accused of abandoning the poor. It's the other way around. They never vote for us."

—***Dan Quayle***

"Republicans lobby; Democrats march."

—***Donna Brazile,*** quoted in *Campaigns & Elections,* 1989

"Saying we should keep the two-party system simply because it is working is like saying the *Titanic* voyage was a success because a few people survived on life rafts."

—***Eugene McCarthy***

"A sect or party is an elegant incognito devised to save a man from the vexation of thinking."

—***Ralph Waldo Emerson,*** *Journals,* 1831

"There are but two parties. There never have been but two parties, founded in the radical question, whether people or property shall govern?"

—***Thomas Hart Benton,*** speech to the Senate, 1835

"There are two ideas of government. There are those who believe that, if you will only legislate to make the well-to-do prosperous, their prosperity will leak through on those below. The Democratic idea, however, has been that if you make the masses prosperous, their prosperity will find its way up through every class which rests upon them."

—***William Jennings Bryan,*** seeking the presidential nomination at the Democratic National Convention, 1896

"To me, party platforms are contracts with the people."

—***Harry S. Truman,*** *Memoirs,* 1955

"The two political parties in our history have always been divided . . . into the party of hope and into the party of memory."

—***Ralph Waldo Emerson***

"We Democrats can run on our record, but we cannot rest on it. We will win if we continue to take the initiative and if we carry the message of hope and action throughout the country."

—***Robert F. Kennedy***

"What counts now is not just what we are against, but what we are for. Who leads us is less important than what leads us—what convictions, what courage, what faith—win or lose. A man doesn't save a century or a civilization, but a militant party wedded to a principle can."

—***Adlai Stevenson,*** speech to the Democratic National Convention, Chicago, Illinois, July 16, 1952

"What is a Democrat? One who believes that the Republicans have ruined the country. What is a Republican? One who believes that the Democrats would ruin the country."

—***Ambrose Bierce,*** *Wasp,* 1884

"You may elect whatever candidates you please to office, if you will allow me to select the candidates."

—***"Boss" William Marcy Tweed***

"You've got to be an optimist to be a Democrat, and you've got to be a humorist to stay one."

—***Will Rogers,*** *Good Gulf* radio show, June 24, 1934

38 POLITICS AND DIPLOMACY

"All the wisdom in the world consists of shouting with the majority."

—*Thomas B. Reed*

"Are you aware that Claude Pepper is known all over Washington as a shameless extrovert? Not only that, but this man is reliably reported to practice nepotism with his sister-in-law, and he has a sister who was once a Thespian in Greenwich Village. He has a brother who was a practicing homo sapien. And he went to college where he matriculated. Worst of all, it is an established fact that Mr. Pepper, before his marriage, practiced celibacy."

—*Campaign leaflet in the Smathers-Pepper senatorial contest,* 1950. Mr. Pepper lost the election.

"Being in politics is like being a football coach. You have to be smart enough to understand the game . . . and dumb enough to think it's important."

—*Eugene McCarthy*

"Candidates without ideas, hiring consultants without convictions to run campaigns without content. . . ."

—*Gerald Ford*

"A conservative government is an organized hypocrisy."

—*Benjamin Disraeli,* speech, March 17, 1845

"The cure for admiring the House of Lords is to go and look at it."

—*Walter Bagehot*

"Defeat, like victory, is only a passing phenomenon in a political career. The battle for one's ideals and beliefs must go on, and I mean to pursue mine."

—*Hubert H. Humphrey,* letter to a friend following his defeat in the presidential election of 1968

Diplomacy is to do and say
The nastiest thing in the nicest way.

—***Isaac Goldberg,*** *The Reflex,* 1927

"Diplomacy—lying in state."

—***Oliver Herford***

"A diplomat is a man who always remembers a woman's birthday but never remembers her age."

—***Robert Frost***

"[A diplomat is] a man who thinks twice before saying nothing."

—***Frederick Sawyer***

"[A diplomat is] a person who can tell you to go to hell in such a way that you actually look forward to the trip."

—***Caskie Stinett,*** *Out of the Red,* 1960

"A diplomat's life is made up of three ingredients: protocol, Geritol, and alcohol."

—***Adlai Stevenson***

"Do you realize the responsibility I carry? I'm the only person standing between Nixon and the White House."

—***John F. Kennedy***

"Do you want to trace your family tree? Run for public office."

—***Patricia H. Vance***

"Forgive your enemies, but never forget their names."

—***John F. Kennedy***

"Glory is fleeting, but obscurity is forever."

—***Napoleon Bonaparte***

"The hardest thing about any political campaign is how to win without proving that you are unworthy of winning."

—***Adlai Stevenson***

"He knows all the facts, and he's against all the solutions."

—***Robert F. Kennedy,*** referring to Daniel Patrick Moynihan

"He knows nothing; and he thinks he knows everything. That points clearly to a political career."

—***George Bernard Shaw,*** *Major Barbara,* 1907

"He's the kind of politician who would cut down a redwood tree, then mount the stump and make a speech on conservation."

—***Adlai Stevenson,*** on Richard Nixon

"His opinions are like water in the bottom of a canoe, going from side to side."

—***African proverb***

"An honest man in politics shines more than he would elsewhere."

—***Mark Twain***

"I always cheer up immensely if an attack is particularly wounding because I think, well, if they attack one personally, it means they have not a single political argument left."

—***Margaret Thatcher,*** *Daily Telegraph,* March 21, 1986

"I could not be leading a religious life unless I identified myself with the whole of mankind, and that I could not do unless I took part in politics."

—***Mohandas K. Gandhi,*** *Non-Violence in Peace and War,* 1948

"Ideas are great arrows, but there has to be a bow. And politics is the bow of idealism."

—***Bill Moyers,*** *Time,* October 29, 1965

"If elected, I shall be thankful; if not, it will be all the same."

—***Abraham Lincoln,*** first political speech, 1832

"I have always noticed in politics how often men are ruined by having too good a memory."

—***Alexis de Tocqueville***

"I have come to the conclusion that politics are too serious a matter to be left to the politicians."

—***Charles de Gaulle***

"I have just received the following telegram from my generous daddy. It says, 'Dear Jack: Don't buy a single vote more than necessary. I'll be damned if I'm going to pay for a landslide.'"

—***John F. Kennedy,*** Gridiron Dinner, Washington, D.C., 1958

"In politics, there are no friends, only allies."

—***John F. Kennedy***

"In this country people don't vote for; they vote against."

—***Will Rogers***

"In Washington, if you want a friend, get a dog."

—***Anonymous***

"I only wish that I could be as sure of anything as my opponent is of everything."

—***Benjamin Disraeli,*** on William E. Gladstone

"I thought for a time about becoming a minister. But then I read that little-known passage from the Bible: 'Thou shalt walk among the false prophets, and bargain with the money-changers, and dwell in the house of strife and discord.' So I decided to go into politics."

—***Walter F. Mondale***

"It is grievously hurtful to our society when vilification becomes an accepted form of political debate, when negative campaigning becomes a full-time occupation, when members of each party become self-appointed vigilantes carrying out personal vendettas against members of the other party."

—***Jim Wright,*** resignation speech from the House of Representatives, May 31, 1989

"It is not the hand that signs the laws that holds the destiny of America. It is the hand that casts the ballot."

—***Harry S. Truman***

"It's not what you do, Ben. . . . It's who you know and the smile on your face—it's contacts, Ben, contacts."

—***Arthur Miller,*** *Death of a Salesman,* 1949

"It was said [of William McKinley] that his strongest conviction was to be liked."

—***Barbara Tuchman,*** *The Proud Tower,* 1966

"It would be premature to ask your support in the next election and it would be inaccurate to thank you for it in the past."

—***John F. Kennedy,*** speech to the National Industrial Conference Board, Washington, D.C., February 13, 1961

"I've come to wonder how anyone can presume to talk about 'America' until he has done some campaigning."

—***Adlai Stevenson,*** letter to longtime friend Mrs. Edison (Jane) Dick, written while campaigning in Illinois, March 1948

"Listening to a speech by Chamberlain is like paying a visit to Woolworth's. Everything is in its place and nothing above sixpence."

—***Aneurin Bevan,*** speech in the House of Commons, 1937

"The most important quality of political success is sincerity. When you can fake that, you've got it made."

—***Groucho Marx***

"Mothers may still want their sons to grow up to be President, but according to a famous Gallup poll of some years ago, some 73 percent do not want them to become politicians in the process."

—***John F. Kennedy,*** *Profiles in Courage,* 1956

"My brother Bob doesn't want to be in government—he promised Dad he'd go straight."

—***John F. Kennedy***

"Ninety percent of politicians give the other ten percent a bad reputation."

—***Henry Kissinger***

"Now of course that's not perjury . . . I'll tell you what that is: it's wanting to win too badly."

—***Dale Bumpers,*** referring to the House managers while defending President Bill Clinton at his impeachment hearings, January 21, 1999

"Open each session with a prayer and close it with a probe."

—***Clarence Brown,*** statement after a Republican victory, November 1946

"'Poli' is a Greek prefix meaning many, and 'tics' are blood-sucking animals."

—***James Carville***

"Political ability is the ability to foretell what is going to happen tomorrow, next week, next month, and next year. And to have the ability afterward to explain why it didn't happen."

—***Winston Churchill***

"Politics, as a practice, whatever its professions, has always been the systematic organization of hatreds."

—***Henry Adams,*** *The Education of Henry Adams,* 1907

"Politics has got so expensive that it takes lots of money to even get beat with."

—***Will Rogers***

"Politics is almost as exciting as war, and quite as dangerous. In war you can only be killed once, but in politics many times."

—***Winston Churchill***

"Politics is supposed to be the second oldest profession. I have come to realize that it bears a very close resemblance to the first."

—***Ronald Reagan***

"Politics is the art of the possible."

—***Otto von Bismarck,*** in conversation with Meyer von Waldeck, August 11, 1867

"Politics is the pursuit of the possible, not of the ideal."

—***Herbert Agar***

"Politics is war without bloodshed while war is politics with bloodshed."

—***Mao Tse-tung,*** *Selected Works,* vol. 2, 1965

"Successful . . . politicians are insecure and intimidated men. They advance politically only as they placate, bribe, seduce, bamboozle or otherwise manage to manipulate the demanding and threatening elements of their constituencies."

—***Walter Lippmann,*** 1955

"That's the trouble with a politician's life—somebody is always interrupting it with an election."

—***Will Rogers***

"They asked [Lincoln] how he felt once after an unsuccessful election. He said he felt like a little boy who had stubbed his toe in the dark. He said that he was too old to cry, but it hurt too much to laugh."

—***Adlai Stevenson,*** concession speech after his first presidential defeat, Springfield, Illinois, November 4, 1952

"Too bad all the people who know how to run the country are busy driving taxi cabs and cutting hair."

—*George Burns*

"University politics are vicious precisely because the stakes are so small."

—*Henry Kissinger*

"Vote for the man who promises least; he'll be the least disappointing."

—*Bernard Baruch,* quoted in Meyer Berger's *New York,* 1960

"When people are least sure they are often most dogmatic."

—*John Kenneth Galbraith*

"When you're abroad, you're a statesman; when you're at home, you're just a politician."

—*Harold Macmillan*

"Whenever you find that you are on the side of the majority, it is time to pause and reflect."

—*Mark Twain*

"You campaign in poetry. You govern in prose."

—*Mario Cuomo*

"Your representative owes you, not his industry only, but his judgement; and he betrays, instead of serving you, if he sacrifices it to your opinion."

—*Edmund Burke,* on the responsibilities of a member of Parliament, speech to the Electors of Bristol, November 3, 1774

39 POVERTY

"And there was not only the violence of the shot in the night. Slower but just as deadly, [Martin Luther King, Jr.] said, was 'the violence of institutions. . . . This is the violence that afflicts the poor, that poisons relations between men because their skin has different colors. This is a slow destruction of a child by hunger . . . the breaking of a man's spirit by denying him the chance to stand as a father and as a man among men.' So much at least was clear: 'Violence breeds violence, repression brings retaliation, and only a cleaning of our whole society can remove this sickness from our soul.'"

—***Robert F. Kennedy,*** address to African Americans at the Cleveland City Club, April 5, 1968

"Anyone who had ever struggled with poverty knows how extremely expensive it is to be poor."

—***James Baldwin,*** "Fifth Avenue Uptown: A Letter from Harlem," *Nobody Knows My Name,* 1961

"Any ordinary city is in fact two cities, one the city of the poor, the other of the rich, each at war with each other."

—***Plato,*** *The Republic*

"But when you doest alms, let not thy left hand know what thy right hand doeth."

—***Matthew 6:3***

"Half the world knows not how the other half lives."

—***George Herbert,*** *Jacula Prudentum,* 1640

"Has every defense contractor yielded a perfect product, at minimal cost? Has every cancer project brought a cure? Has every space launching succeeded? Has every diplomatic initiative brought peace? Why should a less-than-perfect record for social programs be less tolerable to society than failed economic, military, or diplomatic policies?"

—***Hyman Bookbinder,*** *New York Times,* 1989

"The honest poor can sometimes forget poverty. The honest rich can never forget it."

—***G. K. Chesterton,*** "Cockneys and Their Jokes," *All Things Considered,* 1908

"A hungry man is not a free man."

—***Adlai Stevenson,*** campaign speech, Kasson, Minnesota, September 6, 1952

"If a free society cannot help the many who are poor, it cannot save the few who are rich."

—***John F. Kennedy,*** Inaugural Address, January 20, 1961

"In the final analysis, the rich must not ignore the poor because both rich and poor are tied in a single garment of destiny. All life is interrelated, and all men are interdependent. The agony of the poor diminishes the rich, and the salvation of the poor enlarges the rich. We are inevitably our brother's keeper because of the interrelated structure of reality."

—***Martin Luther King, Jr.,*** speech, December 10, 1964

"Let not him who is houseless pull down the house of another, but let him work diligently and build one for himself, thus by example assuring that his own shall be safe from violence when built."

—***Abraham Lincoln,*** reply to the New York Workingman's Association, March 21, 1864

"Let us, above all, open wide the exits from poverty to the children of the poor."

—***Lyndon B. Johnson,*** Economic Report to Congress, 1964

"Love and business and family and religion and art and patriotism are nothing but shadows of words when a man's starving."

—***O. Henry,*** "Cupid à la Carte," *Heart of the West,* 1907

"Must hunger become anger and anger fury before anything will be done?"

—***John Steinbeck***

"No man can be wise on an empty stomach."

—***George Eliot,*** *Adam Bede,* 1859

"No men living are more worthy to be trusted than those who toil up from poverty."

—***Abraham Lincoln,*** First Annual Message to Congress, 1861

"People don't eat in the long run. They eat every day."

—***Harry L. Hopkins***

"People who are much too sensitive to demand of cripples that they run races ask of the poor that they get up and act just like everyone else in the society."

—***Michael Harrington,*** *The Other America,* 1962

"Political sovereignty is but a mockery without the means of meeting poverty and illiteracy and disease. Self-determination is but a slogan if the future holds no hope."

—***John F. Kennedy,*** address to United Nations General Assembly, September 25, 1961

"The poor are our brothers and sisters—people in the world who need love, who need care, who have to be wanted."

—***Mother Teresa,*** "Saints among Us," quoted in *Time,* 1975

"The poor can't lift themselves up by their own bootstraps because they have no boots."

—***Horace McKenna***

"The poor is hated even of his own neighbor: but the rich hath many friends."

—***Proverbs 14:20***

"A poor man with nothing in his belly needs hope, illusion, more than bread."

—***Georges Bernanos,*** *The Diary of a Country Priest,* 1936

"Poverty has many roots, but the taproot is ignorance."

—***Lyndon B. Johnson,*** message to Congress, January 12, 1965

"Poverty is an anomaly to rich people. It is very difficult to make out why people who want dinner do not ring the bell."

—***Walter Bagehot***

"Poverty is the mother of crime."

—***Cassiodorus,*** *Variae*

"Poverty makes you sad as well as wise."

—***Bertolt Brecht,*** *The Threepenny Opera,* 1928

"The rich man may never get into heaven, but the pauper is already serving his term in hell."

—***Alexander Chase,*** *Perspectives,* 1966

"A rich man shall hardly enter into the kingdom of heaven. And again I say unto you, it is easier for a camel to go through the eye of a needle than for a rich man to enter into the kingdom of heaven."

—***Matthew 20:23–24***

"Seeing so much poverty everywhere makes me think that God is not rich. He gives the appearance of it, but I suspect some financial difficulties."

—***Victor Hugo,*** *Les Misérables,* 1862

"Stand not too near the rich man lest he destroy thee—and not too far away lest he forget thee."

—***Aneurin Bevan***

"The test of our progress is not whether we add more to the abundance of those who have too much . . . it is whether we provide enough for those who have too little."

—***Franklin Delano Roosevelt***

"There is inherited wealth in this country and also inherited poverty."

—***John F. Kennedy,*** remarks at Amherst College, Amherst, Massachusetts, October 26, 1963

"There were times my pants were so thin I could sit on a dime and tell if it was heads or tails."

—***Spencer Tracy***

"This administration today, here and now, declares unconditional war on poverty."

—***Lyndon B. Johnson,*** Annual Message to Congress, 1964

"To be poor and independent is very nearly an impossibility."

—***William Cobbett,*** *Advice to Young Men,* 1829

"To recommend thrift to the poor is both grotesque and insulting. It is like advising a man who is starving to eat less."

—***Oscar Wilde,*** *The Soul of Man under Socialism,* 1881

"We cultivate refinement without extravagance and knowledge without effeminacy; wealth we employ more for use than for show, and place the real disgrace of poverty not in owning to the fact but in declining the struggle against it."

—***Thucydides,*** describing Athenians,
History of the Peloponnesian War, 403 B.C.

"We will win in the end. We learned many years ago that the rich may have the money, but the poor have the time."

—***César Chávez,*** quoted in *Newsweek,* September 22, 1975

"What you call crime is nothing: a murder here and theft there. What do they matter? They are only the accidents and illnesses of life: there are not fifty genuine profession criminals in London. But there are millions of poor people, abject people, dirty people, ill-fed, ill-clothed people. They poison us morally and physically: they kill the happiness of society: they force us to do away with our own liberties and to organize unnatural cruelties for fear they should rise against us and drag us down into their abyss. Only fools fear crime: we all fear poverty."

—***George Bernard Shaw,*** *Major Barbara,* 1905

"While the sun was said to never set on the British empire, there were city slums over which it had never risen."

—***Robert Blatchford***

"You can't talk to a person about his or her soul if that person has no food."

—***Horace McKenna***

40 PROGRESS AND CHANGE

"Adapt or perish, now as ever, is Nature's inexorable imperative."

—*H. G. Wells, Mind at the End of Its Tether,* 1946

"Behold, I make all things new."

—***Revelation 21:5***

"Beware of all enterprises that require new clothes."

—***Henry David Thoreau,*** *Walden,* 1854

"Both tears and sweat are salty, but they render a different result. Tears will get you sympathy; sweat will get you change."

—***Jesse Jackson***

"Cautious, careful people, always casting about to preserve their reputations and social standing, never can bring about a reform."

—***Susan B. Anthony,*** on the campaign for divorce law reform, 1860

"A conservative is a man who just sits and thinks, mostly sits."

—***Woodrow Wilson***

"A conservative is someone who believes in reform. But not now."

—***Mort Sahl***

"Conservatism is the worship of dead revolutions."

—***Clinton Rossiter***

"The Constitution makes us not rivals for power but partners for progress."

—***John F. Kennedy,*** State of the Union Address, Washington, D.C., January 11, 1962

"Every generation laughs at the old fashions, but follows religiously the new."

—***Henry David Thoreau,*** *Walden,* 1854

"Give me a lever and a place to stand, and I will move the world."

—***Archimedes***

"The great French marshal [Louis Hubert Gonzalve] Lyautey once asked his gardener to plant a tree. The gardener objected that the tree was slow growing and would not reach maturity for one hundred years. The marshal replied, 'In that case, there's no time to lose. Plant it this afternoon.'"

—***Robert F. Kennedy,*** address to the National Insurance Association, Los Angeles, California, July 26, 1962

"Greatness is a road leading toward the unknown."

—***Charles de Gaulle***

"Grief is felt not so much for the want of what we have never known, as for the loss of that to which we have been long accustomed."

—***Thucydides,*** *History of the Peloponnesian War,* 403 B.C.

"History is a relentless master. It has no present, only the past rushing toward the future. To try to hold fast is to be swept aside."

—***John F. Kennedy***

"I find the great thing in this world is not so much where we stand, as in what direction we are moving. To reach the port of heaven, we must sail sometimes with the wind and sometimes against it, but we must sail, and not drift, nor lie at anchor."

—***Oliver Wendell Holmes, Jr.***

"If I have seen further it is by standing on the shoulders of giants."

—***Isaac Newton,*** letter to Robert Hooke, February 5, 1676

"'If men do not build,' asks the poet, 'how shall they live?'"

—***Robert F. Kennedy,*** launching the Bedford-Stuyvesant Restoration Effort, Brooklyn, New York, December 10, 1966

"If one does not know to which port one is sailing, no wind is favorable."

—***Seneca,*** *Epistulae Morales*

"If you wait for tomorrow, tomorrow comes. If you don't wait for tomorrow, tomorrow comes."

—***African proverb***

"I hold it, that a little rebellion, now and then, is a good thing, and as necessary in the political world as storms in the physical."

—***Thomas Jefferson,*** letter to James Madison, January 30, 1787

"It is not strange . . . to mistake change for progress."

—***Millard Fillmore***

"It must be remembered that there is nothing more difficult to plan, more doubtful of success, nor more dangerous to manage than the creation of a new system. For the initiator has the enmity of all who profit by the preservation of the old institution and merely lukewarm defenders in those who would gain by the new one."

—***Niccolò Machiavelli,*** *The Prince,* 1532

"The journey of a thousand miles begins with a single step."

—***Lao-tzu,*** *Tao-te-ching*

"A love of tradition has never weakened a nation, indeed it has strengthened nations in their hour of peril; but the new view must come, the world must roll forward."

—***Winston Churchill,*** speech in the House of Commons, November 29, 1944

"Make no little plans: they have no magic to stir men's blood and probably themselves will never be realized. Make big plans."

—***Daniel H. Burnham***

"A man who is not a liberal at sixteen has no heart; a man who is not a conservative by sixty has no head."

—***Benjamin Disraeli***

"Men without hope, resigned to despair and oppression, do not make revolutions. It is when expectation replaces submission, when despair is touched with the awareness of possibility, that the forces of human desire and the passion for justice are unloosed."

—***Robert F. Kennedy,*** speech at the University of California at Berkeley, October 22, 1966

Most of the change we think we see in life
Is due to truths being in and out of favor.

—***Robert Frost,*** "The Black Cottage," 1914

"My mama always said life is like a box of chocolates. You never know what you're gonna get."

—***Tom Hanks as Forrest Gump*** in the movie version of Winston Groom's *Forrest Gump,* 1994

"Nothing can be created out of nothing."

—***Lucretius,*** *De Rerum Natura*

The old order changeth, yielding place to new;
And God fulfils himself in many ways,
Lest one good custom should corrupt the world.

—***Alfred, Lord Tennyson,*** "Idylls of the King," 1899

"One must wait until the evening to see how splendid the day has been."

—***Sophocles***

"The potential for loss when gambling on a certainty is infinite."

—***Winston Churchill***

"The public is a thick-skinned beast and you have to keep whacking away on its hide to let it know you're there."

—***Walt Whitman***

"Restlessness is discontent—and discontent is the first necessity of progress. Show me a thoroughly satisfied man and I will show you a failure."

—***Thomas Alva Edison***

"A revolution is coming—a revolution which will be peaceful if we are wise enough; compassionate if we care enough; successful if we are fortunate enough—but a revolution which is coming whether we will it or not. We can affect its character; we cannot alter its inevitability."

—***Robert F. Kennedy,*** "Redirecting United States Policy in Latin America," U.S. Senate, Washington, D.C., May 9, 1966

"The rung of a ladder was never meant to rest upon, but only to hold a man's foot long enough to enable him to put the other somewhat higher."

—***Thomas Henry Huxley,*** *Life and Letters of Thomas Henry Huxley,* 1913

"A state without the means of some change is without the means of its conservation."

—***Edmund Burke,*** *Reflections on the Revolution in France,* 1790

There is a tide in the affairs of men,
Which, taken at the flood, leads on to fortune;
Omitted, all the voyage of their life
Is bound in shallows and in miseries.
On such a full sea are we now afloat,
And we must take the current when it serves,
Or lose our ventures.

—***William Shakespeare,*** *Julius Caesar,* act 4, scene 3

"There is mighty little good in a mere spasm of reform. The reform that counts is that which comes through steady, continuous growth."

—***Theodore Roosevelt,*** speech decrying "muck-rakers," April 14, 1906

"There is nothing like returning to a place that remains unchanged to find the ways in which you yourself have altered."

—***Nelson Mandela***

"There is nothing permanent except change."

—***Heraclitus***

They paved paradise
And put up a parking lot.

—***Joni Mitchell,*** "Big Yellow Taxi," 1969

"This is not the end. It is not even the beginning of the end. But it is, perhaps, the end of the beginning."

—***Winston Churchill,*** on the Battle of Egypt, speech at the Lord Mayor's Day Luncheon, London, November 10, 1942

"Time and tide wait for no man."

—***John Heywood,*** *Proverbs,* 1546

"To destroy is always the first step in any creation."

—***E. E. Cummings,*** *Selected Letters,* 1955

"We are sailing with a corpse in the cargo."

—***Henrik Ibsen,*** on Europe's entering the twentieth century, 1897

"We can master change not through force or fear, but only through the free work of an understanding mind, through an openness to new knowledge and fresh outlooks, which can only strengthen the most fragile and the most powerful of human gifts: the gift of reason."

—***Robert F. Kennedy,*** "A Final Message to White South Africa," University of Witwatersrand, Johannesburg, South Africa, June 8, 1966

"We stand today on the edge of a new frontier. The new frontier of which I speak is not a set of promises—it is a set of challenges. It sums up not what I intend to offer the American people, but what I intend to ask of them. . . . It appeals to our pride, not our security—it holds the promise of more sacrifice instead of more security."

—***John F. Kennedy,*** acceptance speech, Democratic National Convention, July 15, 1960

"What has violence ever accomplished? What has it ever created? No martyr's cause has ever been stilled by his assassin's bullet."

—***Robert F. Kennedy,*** speech delivered the morning after the assassination of Martin Luther King, Jr., to the City Club, Cleveland, Ohio, April 5, 1968

"When great changes occur in history, when great principles are involved, as a rule the majority are wrong."

—***Eugene V. Debs,*** defending himself in court on charges stemming from his opposition to World War I, September 1, 1918

"Wise and prudent men—intelligent conservatives—have long known that in a changing world, worthy institutions can be conserved only by adjusting them to the changing time."

—***Franklin Delano Roosevelt***

"You cannot step twice into the same river; for other waters are continually flowing on. It is in changing that things find repose."

—***Heraclitus***

"You don't need a weatherman to know which way the wind blows."

—***Bob Dylan,*** "Subterranean Homesick Blues," 1965

41 RACE AND ETHNICITY

"The biggest lie is that, if you're American, it doesn't matter what race, creed, nationality you are—the color of your skin doesn't matter, it's the person that you are, and if you do a good job, you can succeed. Bullshit! Race has everything to do with everything."

—***Spike Lee***

"Color is not a human or a personal reality; it is a political reality."

—***James Baldwin,*** *The Fire Next Time,* 1962

"The danger of race prejudice always is that it tends to lump people together and ignore the individual."

—***Pearl S. Buck,*** commencement address at Harvard University, June 5, 1942

"For racism to die, a totally different America must be born."

—***Stokely Carmichael,*** "Power and Racism," 1966

"The glorification of one race and the consequent debasement of another—or others—always has been and always will be recipe for murder."

—***James Baldwin,*** *The Fire Next Time,* 1962

"The Golden Rule is not sentimentality but the deepest practical wisdom. For the teaching of our time is that cruelty is contagious, and its disease knows no bounds of race or nation. Where men can be deprived because their skin is black, in the fullness of time others will be deprived because their skin is white."

—***Albert Camus***

"Hath not a Jew eyes? . . . If you prick us, do we not bleed? If you tickle us, do we not laugh? If you poison us, do we not die? And if you wrong us, shall we not revenge? If we are like you in the rest, we will resemble you in that."

—***William Shakespeare,*** *Merchant of Venice,* act 3, scene 1. Spoken by Shylock, a Jewish merchant.

"Hatred is the coward's revenge for being intimidated."

—***George Bernard Shaw***

"The Hebrews have done more to civilize men than any other nation. If I were an atheist, and believed in blind eternal fate, I should still believe that fate had ordained the Jews to be the most essential instrument for civilizing the nations."

—***John Adams,*** letter to F. A. Vanderkemp, 1815

"The highest test of the civilization of any race is in its willingness to extend a helping hand to the less fortunate. A race, like an individual, lifts itself up by lifting others up."

—***Booker T. Washington,*** Fifth Tuskegee Conference, 1896

"I am invisible, understand, simply because people refuse to see me."

—***Ralph Ellison,*** *Invisible Man,* 1952

"In Basel I founded the Jewish state. If I said this aloud today; I would be answered by universal laughter. Perhaps in five years, and certainly in fifty, everyone will agree."

—***Theodor Herzl,*** in his diary, during the First Zionist Congress in Basel, Switzerland, September 1897

"Ireland has the honor of being the only country which never persecuted the Jews . . . Because she never let them in."

—***James Joyce,*** *Ulysses,* 1914

"I sent the [Friar's] club a wire stating, 'Please accept my resignation. I don't want to belong to any club that will accept me as a member.'"

—***Groucho Marx,*** reacting to the Friar's Club's policy of excluding Jews, *Groucho and Me,* 1959

"It was a happy day in America when the first unhappy slave was landed on its shores. There, in our tortured induction into this 'land of liberty,' we built its most graceful civilization. Its wealth, its flowering fields, its handsome homes, its pretty traditions, its guarded leisure, and its music were all our creations.

"We stirred in our shackles, and our unrest awakened justice in the hearts of a courageous few, and we re-created in America the desire for true democracy."

—***Duke Ellington,*** speaking at a Los Angeles church, February 12, 1941

"I will permit no man to narrow and degrade my soul by making me hate him."

—*Booker T. Washington*

"Let me tell you something we have against Moses. He took us forty years through the desert in order to bring us to the one spot in the Middle East that has no oil."

—*Golda Meir*

"A man who takes away another man's freedom is a prisoner of hatred; he is locked behind the bars of prejudice and narrow-mindedness. I am not truly free if I am taking away someone else's freedom, just as surely as I am not free when my freedom is taken from me. The oppressed and the oppressor alike are robbed of their humanity."

—*Nelson Mandela, Long Walk to Freedom,* 1995

"The most certain test by which we judge whether a country is really free is the amount of security enjoyed by minorities."

—*Lord Acton*

"Once I thought to write a history of immigrants in America. Then I discovered that immigrants are American history."

—*Oscar Handlin, The Uprooted,* 1951

"Prejudice is a raft onto which the shipwrecked mind clambers and paddles to safety."

—*Ben Hecht*

"The problem of the Twentieth Century is the problem of the color-line."

—*W.E.B. Du Bois,* "To the Nations of the World,"
Pan-African Congress, London, 1900

"Racism is man's gravest threat to man—the maximum of hatred for a minimum of reason."

—*Abraham Joshua Heschel*

"Racism is not an excuse to not do the best you can."

—*Arthur Ashe*

"Sad to say, Jefferson is not the only American statesman who has spoken high-sounding words in favor of freedom, and then left his own children to die slaves."

—*William Wells Brown,* letter to his former master,
Enoch Price, *The Liberator,* December 14, 1849

"Sitting at the table doesn't make you a diner. You must be eating some of what's on the plate. Being here in America doesn't make you an American. Being born here in America doesn't make you an American."

—***Malcolm X,*** "The Ballot or the Bullet" speech, April 3, 1964

"There is no news to report about Auschwitz. There is compulsion to write something about it, a compulsion that grows out of a restless feeling that to have visited Auschwitz and then be turned away without having said or written anything would somehow be a most grievous act of discourtesy to those who died here."

—***A. M. Rosenthal,*** "There Is No News from Auschwitz," *New York Times,* August 31, 1958

"They came to us speaking many tongues—but a single language, the universal language of human aspiration."

—***Franklin Delano Roosevelt,*** address commemorating the fiftieth anniversary of the Statue of Liberty, New York, October 28, 1936

"The twentieth-century ideals of America have been the ideals of the Jew for more than twenty centuries."

—***Louis D. Brandeis,*** "A Call to the Educated Jew," 1914

"We are an ancient people, and though we have often, on the long hard road which we have traveled, been disillusioned, we have never been disheartened. We have never lost faith in the sovereignty and the ultimate triumph of great moral principles."

—***Abba Hillel Silver,*** addressing the United Nations General Assembly, May 8, 1947

"We can never get civil rights in America until our human rights are first restored. We will never be recognized as citizens there until we are first recognized as humans."

—***Malcolm X,*** "Racism: The Cancer That Is Destroying America," August 25, 1964

"We didn't land on Plymouth Rock, my brothers and sisters—Plymouth Rock landed on *us!*"

—***Malcolm X,*** *The Autobiography of Malcolm X,* 1965

"We Negro writers, just by being black, have been on the blacklist all our lives. . . . Censorship for us begins at the color line."

—***Langston Hughes,*** address to the National Assembly of Authors and Dramatists Symposium, May 7, 1957

"We shall be free only together, black and white. We shall survive only together, black and white. We can be human only together, black and white."

—***Desmond Tutu***

"When I say, 'Don't think of me as Black or White,' all I'm saying is, view me as a person. I know my race."

—***Michael Jordan***

"The white man saves the whooping crane, he saves the goose in Hawaii, but he is not saving the way of life of the Indian."

—***Anonymous,*** attributed to a Blackfoot Indian

"Yes, I am a Jew, and when the ancestors of the right honorable gentlemen were brutal savages in an unknown island, mine were priests in the temple of Solomon."

—***Benjamin Disraeli,*** reply to a racial slur
by Daniel O'Connell, 1835

42 RELIGION AND FAITH

"And God said, 'Let there be light'; and there was light."

—*Genesis 1:3*

"And in that day shall the deaf hear the words of the book, and the eyes of the blind shall see out of obscurity and out of darkness."

—*Isaiah 29:18*

"Basically, I'm for anything that gets you through the night—be it prayer, tranquilizers, or a bottle of Jack Daniel's."

—***Frank Sinatra***

"Conscience is God's presence in man."

—***Emanuel Swedenborg,*** *Arcana Coelestia,* 1749–1756

"Don't wait for the last judgment—it takes place every day."

—***Albert Camus,*** *The Fall,* 1957

"Faith is believing in things when common sense tells you not to."

—***Maureen O'Hara as Doris Walker*** to her daughter, Susan, in *Miracle on 34th Street,* screenplay by Valentine Davies and George Seaton, 1947

"Faith is not taught by arguments. It is taught by lives."

—***Archibald MacLeish***

"The fear of the Lord is the beginning of wisdom."

—***Psalm 111:10***

"For the believer there are no questions and for the unbeliever there are no answers."

—***Menachem Mendel***

Forgive, O Lord, my little jokes on Thee
And I'll forgive Thy great big one on me.

—***Robert Frost,*** "Cluster of Faith," 1962

"God creates the cure before He sends the malady."

—***The Talmud***

"God sends us nothing but riddles."

—***Feodor Dostoyevsky,*** *The Brothers Karamazov,* 1879

God's in His Heaven—
All's right with the world!

—***Robert Browning,*** "Pippa Passes," 1841

"God wills man to be creator—his first job is to create himself as a complete being. Man, the mute being, must search for speech and find it, all by himself. Man comes into our world as a hylic, amorphous being. He is created in the image of God, but this image is a challenge to be met, not a gratuitous gift."

—***Joseph B. Soloveitchik***

"Have we not all one Father? Did not one God create us all? Why then do we deal unkindly with one another?"

—***Malachi 2:10***

"An honest man's the noblest work of God."

—***Alexander Pope,*** *Essay on Man,* 1734

"How many things which served us yesterday as articles of faith are fables for us today?"

—***Michel de Montaigne,*** *Essays,* 1580–1595

"I am Alpha and Omega, the beginning and the end, the first and the last."

—***Revelation 21:6***

"I believe that our Heavenly Father invented man because he was disappointed in the monkey."

—***Mark Twain***

"I fear that Christians who stand with only one leg upon earth, also stand with only one leg in heaven."

—***Dietrich Bonhoeffer,*** letter to his fiancée, 1943

"If one does not speak, not even God can hear."

—***Patricio Flores***

"If we will not be governed by God, we must be governed by tyrants."

—***William Penn***

I see Thee in the starry field,
I see Thee in the harvest's yield,
In every breath, in every sound,
An echo of Thy name is found.
The blade of grass, the simple flower,
Bear witness to Thy matchless power.

—***Abraham Ibn Ezra***

"I will lift up mine eyes unto the hills, from whence cometh my help. My help cometh from the Lord, which made heaven and earth."

—***Psalm 121:1–2***

"I would like to live a long life. Longevity has its place. But I'm not concerned about that now. I just want to do God's will. And He's allowed me to go up to the mountain. And I've looked over, and I've seen the Promised Land. I may not get there with you, but I want you to know tonight that we as a people will get to the Promised Land."

—***Martin Luther King, Jr.,*** speech at Mason Temple Church, Memphis, Tennessee, April 3, 1968. He was assassinated the next day.

"I would no more quarrel with a man because of his religion than I would because of his art."

—***Mary Baker Eddy,*** "Harvest," 1906

"Let us hope that a kind of Providence will put a speedy end to the acts of God under which we have been laboring."

—***Peter De Vries***

"A little philosophy inclines a man to atheism, but depth in philosophy brings men's minds to religion."

—***Francis Bacon,*** "Of Atheism," 1625

"Man doth not live by bread only, but by every word that proceedeth out of the mouth of the Lord doth man live."

—*Deuteronomy 8:3*

"A man of great faith can afford a little skepticism."

—*Friedrich Nietzsche*

"Naked I came out of my mother's womb, and naked I shall return thither; the Lord gave and the Lord hath taken away; blessed be the name of the Lord."

—*Job 1:21*

"Nothing that is worth doing can be achieved in a lifetime; therefore, we must be saved by hope. Nothing which is true or beautiful or good makes complete sense in any immediate context of history; therefore, we must be saved by faith. Nothing we do, however virtuous, can be accomplished alone; therefore, we are saved by love."

—***Reinhold Niebuhr,*** *The Irony of American History,* 1952

"One of the proofs of the immortality of the soul is that myriads have believed in it. They have also believed the world was flat."

—*Mark Twain*

"Pride goeth before destruction, and an haughty spirit before a fall."

—*Proverbs 16:18*

"A prophet is not without honor, save in his own country."

—*Matthew 13:57*

"Puritanism. The haunting fear that someone, somewhere, may be happy."

—***H. L. Mencken,*** *A Mencken Chrestomathy,* 1949

"Religion consists in a set of things which the average man thinks he believes and wishes he were certain."

—*Mark Twain*

"Religions are born and may die, but superstition is immortal."

—***Will and Ariel Durant,*** *The Age of Reason Begins,* 1950

"There are many scapegoats for our blunders, but the most popular one is Providence."

—*Mark Twain*

"There is no argument in the world that carries the hatred that a religious belief does. The more learned a man is the less consideration he has for another man's belief."

—***Will Rogers***

There's a divinity that shapes our ends,
Rough-hew them how we will.

—***William Shakespeare,*** *Hamlet,* act 5, scene 2

"They that wait upon the Lord shall renew their strength; they shall mount up with wings as eagles; they shall run, and not weary; they shall walk, and not faint."

—***Isaiah 40:31***

"To everything there is a season, and a time to every purpose under the heaven."

—***Ecclesiastes 3:1***

"We have just enough religion to make us hate, but not enough to make us love one another."

—***Jonathan Swift,*** *Thoughts on Various Subjects,* 1711

"We were good Presbyterian boys when the weather was doubtful; when it was fair we did wander a little from the fold."

—***Mark Twain,*** "Sixty-seventh Birthday" speech at the Metropolitan Club, New York, November 28, 1902

"What hath God wrought!"

—***Numbers 23:23.*** Quoted by Samuel F. B. Morse in the first electric telegraph message on May 24, 1844

"What we are is God's gift to us. What we become is our gift to God."

—***Proverb***

"The world is very different now . . . and yet the same revolutionary beliefs for which our forebears fought are still at issue around the globe—the belief that the rights of man come not from the generosity of the state but from the hand of God."

—***John F. Kennedy,*** Inaugural Address, January 20, 1961

"You can preach a better sermon with your life than with your lips."

—***Oliver Goldsmith***

"You say that your husband is a religious man; tell him when you meet him, that I say that I am not much of a judge of religion, but that, in my opinion, the religion that sets men to rebel and fight against their government, because, as they think, that government does not sufficiently help *some* men to eat their bread on the sweat of *other* men's faces, is not the sort of religion upon which people can get to heaven."

—***Abraham Lincoln,*** reply to two women from Tennessee petitioning for the release of their husbands from prison, 1864

43 RESPONSIBILITY

> Accuse not Nature! she hath done her part;
> Do thou but thine.

—***John Milton,*** *Paradise Lost,* 1667. Adam is speaking to Eve.

"The best years of your life are the ones in which you decide your problems are your own. You do not blame them on your mother, the ecology, or the president. You realize that you control your own destiny."

—***Albert Ellis***

"Blessed is he who expects nothing, for he shall never be disappointed."

—***Alexander Pope,*** letter to John Gay, 1735

"The difference between insanity and genius is success."

—***Jonathan Pryce as Elliot Carver,*** in the James Bond film *Tomorrow Never Dies,* screenplay by Bruce Feirstein, 1994

> The fault, dear Brutus, is not in our stars,
> But in ourselves, that we are underlings.

—***William Shakespeare,*** *Julius Caesar,* act 1, scene 2

"The harder the conflict, the more glorious the triumph. What we obtain too cheap, we esteem too lightly; it is dearness only that gives everything its value. . . . I love the man that can smile in trouble, that can gather strength from distress and grow brave by reflection. 'Tis the business of little minds to shrink; but he whose heart is firm, and whose conscience approves his conduct, will pursue his principles unto death."

—***Thomas Paine,*** *The American Crisis,* December 23, 1776

"He that would govern others, first should be the master of himself."

—***Philip Massinger,*** *The Bondman,* 1624

"Honor is a harder master than the law."

—***Mark Twain,*** "Mark Twain to Pay All,"
San Francisco Examiner, April 17, 1895

"I believe that every right implies a responsibility; every opportunity, an obligation; every possession, a duty."

—***John D. Rockefeller, Jr.,*** personal credo

"I do not promise you ease. I do not promise you comfort. But I do promise you these: hardship, weariness, and suffering. And with them, I promise you victory."

—***Giuseppe Garibaldi***

"If I am not for myself, then who will be? But if I am for myself alone, who am I?"

—***Hillel the Elder***

"If I get to Paris, I won't need any more. If I don't—well, I won't need any more either."

—***Charles Lindbergh,*** reply when he was asked upon his departure for Paris in the *Spirit of St. Louis* if he required more than the five sandwiches he had aboard to sustain him, Roosevelt Field, Long Island, May 20, 1927

"If there ever could be a proper time for mere catch arguments, that time surely is not now. In times like the present, men should utter nothing for which they would not be personally responsible through time and in eternity."

—***Abraham Lincoln,*** Annual Message to Congress,
December 1, 1862

"I have not become the king's first minister in order to preside over the liquidation of the British Empire."

—***Winston Churchill,*** referring to the demands by Gandhi and the Congress Party of India for complete independence

"In the long run, we shape our lives, and we shape ourselves. The process never ends until we die. And the choices we make are ultimately our own responsibility."

—***Eleanor Roosevelt***

"It doesn't matter. We know where to go."

—***Russell P. ("Red") Reeder,*** remark made on D-Day upon discovering that his regiment had landed two miles south of its designated target

Neither a borrower nor a lender be;
For loan oft loses both itself and friend,
And borrowing dulls the edge of husbandry.
This above all: to thine own self be true,
And it must follow, as the night the day,
Thou canst not then be false to any man.

—***William Shakespeare,*** *Hamlet,* act 1, scene 3

"No man can terrorize a whole nation unless we are all his accomplices."

—***Edward R. Murrow,*** on Senator Joseph McCarthy, *See It Now,* March 7, 1954

"The only gift is a portion of thyself."

—***Ralph Waldo Emerson,*** "Gifts," *Essays,* 1844

"Patience is bitter, but its fruit is sweet."

—***Aristotle***

"The price of greatness is responsibility."

—***Winston Churchill,*** address at Harvard University, September 6, 1943

"The reward of a thing well done is to have done it."

—***Ralph Waldo Emerson,*** "New England Reformers," *Essays,* 1844

"Service is the rent we pay for being. It is the very purpose of life, and not something you do in your spare time."

—***Marian Wright Edelman,*** speech at Howard University, Washington, D.C., May 12, 1990

"There is no greater glory than to work for the public's good."

—***Edmund Burke***

"These men destroyed free government in Germany and now plead to be excused from responsibility because they became slaves. They are in the position of the fictional boy who murdered his father and mother and then pleaded for leniency because he was an orphan."

—***Robert H. Jackson,*** presiding at the Nazi war crimes tribunal in Nuremberg, Germany, November 1945

"The things I never say never get me into trouble."

—***Calvin Coolidge***

"The world goes on only because of those who disregard their own existence."

—***The Talmud***

"The world is a fine place and worth fighting for."

—***Ernest Hemingway,*** *For Whom the Bell Tolls,* 1940

"You are not only responsible for what you say, but also for what you do not say."

—***Martin Luther***

"You took the good things for granted. Now you must earn them again. . . . For every right that you cherish, you have a duty which you must fulfill. For every hope that you entertain, you have a task you must perform. For every good that you wish could happen . . . you will have to sacrifice your comfort and your ease. There is nothing for nothing any longer."

—***Walter Lippmann,*** speech to the Harvard Class of 1910 at their thirtieth reunion, June 18, 1940

44 SCIENCE AND TECHNOLOGY

"The actual building of roads devoted to motor cars is not for the near future, in spite of many rumors to that effect."

—***Harper's Weekly,*** 1902

"All the world's a laboratory to the inquiring mind."

—***Martin Fischer***

"America, supremely the land of liberty, is also supremely the land of science. Freedom is the oxygen without which science cannot breathe."

—***David Sarnoff,*** "Electronics—Today and Tomorrow," 1954

"Any sufficiently advanced technology is indistinguishable from magic."

—***Arthur C. Clarke,*** *Profiles of the Future,* 1962

"Archaeology sounds like dull sport in five syllables. It isn't. It's the Peeping Tom of the sciences. It is the sand-box of men who care not where they are going; they merely want to know where everybody else has been."

—***Jim Bishop,*** "Sifting the Sea for Time's Treasures," *New York Journal-American,* March 14, 1961

"The art of our era is not art, but technology. Today Rembrandt is painting automobiles; Shakespeare is writing research reports; Michelangelo is designing more efficient bank lobbies."

—***Howard Sparks,*** *The Petrified Truth,* 1969

"The Con Ed system is in the best shape in fifteen years, and there's no problem about the summer."

—***Charles Franklin Luce,*** chairman of Consolidated Edison, hours before the New York City blackout, July 1977

"A customer can have a car painted any color as long as it's black."

—***Henry Ford,*** on the options offered on the Model T

"The difference between machines and human beings is that human beings can be reproduced by unskilled labor."

—***Arthur C. Clarke***

"Discovery consists of seeing what everybody has seen and thinking what nobody has thought."

—***Albert von Szent-Györgyi***

"Do not worry about your problems with mathematics. I assure you mine are still greater."

—***Albert Einstein,*** to a high school student, January 7, 1943

"Equipped with his five senses, man explores the universe around him and calls the adventure Science."

—***Edwin Powell Hubble,*** *The Nature of Science,* 1954

"Every science begins as philosophy and ends as art."

—***Will Durant,*** *The Story of Philosophy,* 1926

"Every science has been an outcast."

—***Robert G. Ingersoll,*** *The Liberty of Man, Woman, and Child,* 1877

"If there is technological advance without social advance, there is, almost automatically, an increase in human misery."

—***Michael Harrington,*** *The Other America,* 1962

"In science the credit goes to the man who convinces the world, not to the man to whom the idea first occurs."

—***Francis Darwin,*** *Eugenics Review,* 1914

"The Internet will not tell us what to do about individuals and societies that cannot afford to be on the Net. It will not tell us how to pay attention to those who are left out of the race. It will not show us—any more than our libraries full of books will show us—how to create a humane and just society."

—***Neil Rudenstine,*** commencement address at Harvard University, June 6, 1996

"I think there is a world market for maybe five computers."

—***Thomas Watson,*** chairman of IBM, 1943

"Landing and moving about the moon offers so many serious problems for human beings that it will take science another 200 years to lick them."

—***Science Digest,*** 1948

"Man has mounted science, and is now run away . . . science will be the master of man. . . . Some day, science may have the existence of man in its power, and the human race may commit suicide by blowing up the world."

—***Henry Adams,*** *Letters of Henry Adams,* 1862

"Man has wrested from nature the power to make the world a desert and to make the desert bloom."

—***Adlai Stevenson***

"The most incomprehensible thing about the world is that it is comprehensible."

—***Albert Einstein,*** "Physics and Reality," March 1936

"Mute though it is, the bridge sounds your call to freedom, a call that to you is the voice of opportunity, of new leisure, new prosperity, new hopes, new ideals, new aspirations, new outlooks, a finer and a better life."

—***Joseph Baermann Strauss,*** groundbreaking ceremony for the Golden Gate Bridge, February 1933

"My publisher told me that the number of readers of this book will be inversely proportional to the number of equations it contains."

—***Stephen Hawking,*** *A Brief History of Time,* 1988

"One machine can do the work of fifty ordinary men. No machine can do the work of one extraordinary man."

—***Elbert Hubbard,*** *The Roycroft Dictionary and Book of Epigrams,* 1923

"One never notices what has been done; one can only see what remains to be done."

—***Marie Curie,*** letter to her brother, March 18, 1894

"One test result is worth one thousand expert opinions."

—***Wernher von Braun***

"The ordinary 'horseless carriage' is at present a luxury for the wealthy; and although its price will probably fall in the future, it will never, of course, come into as common use as the bicycle."

—***Literary Digest,*** 1899

"Ours is a world of nuclear giants and ethical infants. If we continue to develop our technology without wisdom or prudence, our servant may prove to be our executioner."

—***Omar Bradley***

"Science can only ascertain what *is,* but not what *should be,* and outside of its domain value judgments of all kinds remain necessary."

—***Albert Einstein,*** *Out of My Later Years,* 1950

"Science has torn from nature a secret so vast in its potentialities that our minds cower from the terror it creates. Yet terror is not enough to inhibit the use of the atomic bomb. The terror created by weapons has never stopped man from employing them. For each new weapon a defense has been produced, in time. But now we face a condition in which adequate defense does not exist."

—***Bernard Baruch,*** speech to the United Nations Atomic Energy Commission on Atomic Control, 1946

"Science without religion is lame; religion without science is blind."

—***Albert Einstein,*** *Out of My Later Years,* 1950

"The simplest schoolboy is now familiar with truths for which Archimedes would have sacrificed his life."

—***Ernest Renan,*** *Recollections of My Youth,* 1883

"That is the essence of science: ask an impertinent question, and you are on the way to the pertinent answer."

—***Jacob Bronowski,*** *The Ascent of Man,* 1973

"There are no such things as incurable, there are only things for which man has not found a cure."

—***Bernard Baruch,*** quoting his father, Simon Baruch, a pioneer surgeon, in a speech to the President's Committee on Employment of the Physically Handicapped, April 30, 1954

"True science teaches, above all, to doubt, and to be ignorant."

—***Miguel de Unamuno,*** *The Tragic Sense of Life,* 1912

"The universe is full of magical things patiently waiting for our wits to grow sharper."

—***Eden Phillpotts***

"We do not want to live in a world where the machine has mastered the man; we want to live in a world where man has mastered the machine."

—***Frank Lloyd Wright,*** interpretation of "An Organic Architecture," May 1939

"We have grasped the mystery of the atom and rejected the Sermon on the Mount."

—***Omar Bradley,*** speech on Armistice Day, 1948

"We live in a society exquisitely dependent on science and technology, in which hardly anyone knows anything about science and technology."

—***Carl Sagan***

"When you are courting a nice girl an hour seems like a second. When you sit on a red-hot cinder a second seems like an hour. That's relativity."

—***Albert Einstein***

"While theoretically and technically television may be feasible, commercially and financially I consider it an impossibility, a development of which we need waste little time dreaming."

—***Lee De Forest,*** 1926

"The Wright Brothers flew right through the smokescreen of impossibility."

—***Charles Franklin Kettering***

45 SOCIETY

"[Another great task] is to confront the poverty of satisfaction—a lack of purpose and dignity—that afflicts us all. Too much and too long, we seem to have surrendered community excellence and community values in the mere accumulation of material things."

—***Robert F. Kennedy,*** "Recapturing America's Moral Vision," University of Kansas, Lawrence, March 18, 1968

"As man increases his knowledge of the heavens, why should he fear the unknown on earth? As man draws nearer to the stars, why should he not also draw nearer to his neighbor?"

—***Lyndon B. Johnson,*** news conference in Johnson City, Texas, August 29, 1965

"A celebrity is a person who works hard all his life to become well known, then wears dark glasses to avoid being recognized."

—***Fred Allen,*** *Treadmill to Oblivion,* 1954

"Civilization: A limitless multiplication of unnecessary necessities."

—***Mark Twain***

"Fame sometimes hath created something out of nothing."

—***Thomas Fuller,*** "Of Fame," 1642

"The good neighbor looks beyond the external accidents and discerns those inner qualities that make all men human and, therefore, brothers."

—***Martin Luther King, Jr.,*** *Strength to Love,* 1963

"The Great Society is not a safe harbor. The Great Society is a place where men are more concerned with the quality of their goals than the quantity of their goods."

—***Lyndon B. Johnson,*** address at the University of Michigan, Ann Arbor, May 22, 1964

"The happiness of every age is chained in mutual dependence upon that of every other."

—***John Quincy Adams,*** Plymouth, Massachusetts, December 22, 1802

"The highest and best form of efficiency is the spontaneous cooperation of a free people."

—***Woodrow Wilson***

"It is not always the same thing to be a good man and a good citizen."

—***Aristotle,*** *Nicomachean Ethics*

"It is not from top to bottom that societies die; it is from bottom to top."

—***Henry George,*** *Progress and Poverty,* 1879

"I wish the wets would become so soused they would be speechless, and that the drys would become so perfect that the Lord would come down and take them away from here—and that would leave the country to the rest of us who are tired of listening to both of them."

—***Will Rogers,*** commenting on Prohibition

"Laws are sand, customs are rock. Laws can be evaded and punishment escaped, but an openly transgressed custom brings sure punishment."

—***Mark Twain***

"The main advantage of being famous is that when you bore people at dinner parties they think it is their fault."

—***Henry Kissinger***

"Make money and the whole world will conspire to call you a gentleman."

—***Mark Twain***

"The most important office [is] that of private citizen."

—***Louis D. Brandeis,*** letter, *Boston Record,* April 14, 1903

"Never speak disrespectfully of society. Only people who can't get into it do that."

—***Oscar Wilde,*** *The Importance of Being Earnest,* 1895

"Nothing makes you more tolerant of a neighbor's noisy party than being there."

—***Franklin P. Adams***

"The only way to solve the traffic problem of this country is to pass a law that only paid-for cars are allowed to use the highways."

—***Will Rogers***

"Rock is strong, but iron shatters it. Fire melts iron; water extinguishes fire; clouds carry away water, and wind drives away clouds. Man can withstand the wind, but fear conquers man; wine dispels fear, but sleep overcomes wine. And death rules over sleep. But more powerful than all ten are sweet acts of charity and lovingness."

—***Judah bar Ila'i***

"A society grows great when old men plant trees whose shade they know they shall never sit in."

—***Greek proverb***

"Society is indeed a contract . . . it becomes a partnership not only between those who are living, but between those who are living, those who are dead, and those who are to be born."

—***Edmund Burke,*** *Reflections on the Revolution in France,* 1790

"Society is like the air, necessary to breathe, but insufficient to live on."

—***George Santayana,*** *Little Essays,* 1920

"Society is no comfort to one not sociable."

—***William Shakespeare,*** *Cymbeline,* act 4, scene 2

"Society was invented for a remedy against injustice."

—***William Warburton,*** *The Divine Legation of Moses,* 1737

"A society whose principal conception of community is small, insular groups clinging to traditional bonds is a society on the road to profound conflict and division."

—***Alan Brinkley,*** "Liberty and Community," 1997

"The state has no place in the nation's bedroom."

—***Pierre Trudeau,*** interview, Ottawa, December 22, 1967

"Strange, isn't it? Each man's life touches so many other lives, and when he isn't around he leaves an awful hole, doesn't he?"

—***Henry Travers as Clarence Odbody, Angel Second Class,*** to George Bailey, in *It's a Wonderful Life,* screenplay by Frances Goodrich and Albert Hackett, 1946

"Those who corrupt the public mind are just as evil as those whose steal from the public purse."

—***Adlai Stevenson,*** speech in Albuquerque, New Mexico, 1952

"The thoughts of the best minds always become the last opinion of society."

—***Ralph Waldo Emerson,*** letter to Thomas Carlyle

"Toots Shor's restaurant is so crowded nobody goes there anymore."

—***Yogi Berra***

"Tradition is not something you inherit. If you want it, you must obtain it with great labor, sacrifice, toil, engagement."

—***T. S. Eliot,*** *Tradition and the Individual Talent,* 1919

"The true test of civilization is not the census, nor the size of cities, nor the crops—no, but the kind of man the country turns out."

—***Ralph Waldo Emerson,*** "Civilization,"
Society and Solitude, 1870

"The Union has become not merely a physical union of states, but rather a spiritual union in common ideals of our people. Within it is room for every variety of opinion, every possible experiment in social progress. Out of such variety comes growth, but only if we preserve and maintain our spiritual solidarity."

—***Herbert Hoover,*** Memorial Day address, Gettysburg
National Cemetery, Pennsylvania, 1929

"We have to face the fact that either all of us are going to die together or we are going to learn to live together and if we are to live together we have to talk."

—***Eleanor Roosevelt***

"We want a society where people are free to make choices, to make mistakes, to be generous and compassionate. This is what we mean by a moral society; not a society where the state is responsible for everything, and no one is responsible for the state."

—***Margaret Thatcher***

"What is hateful unto you, do not do to your neighbor. That is the whole Torah and the rest of it is commentary. Now go forth and learn it."

—***Hillel the Elder,*** responding to a heathen who wanted
to be taught the whole Torah while standing on one foot,
Talmudic Tractate Shabbat

"When you make a world tolerable for yourself you make a world tolerable for others."

—***Anaïs Nin,*** *The Diary of Anaïs Nin,* 1974

"Without society, and a society to our taste, men are never contented."

—***Thomas Jefferson***

46 U.S. GOVERNMENT

"The American eagle on the Presidential seal holds in his talons both the olive branch of peace and the arrows of military might. On the ceiling in the Presidential office, constructed many years ago, that eagle is facing the arrows of war on its left. But on the newer carpet on the floor, reflecting a change initiated by President Roosevelt and implemented by President Truman immediately after the war, that eagle is now facing the olive branch of peace. And it is in that spirit, the spirit of both preparedness and peace, that this Nation today is stronger than ever before."

—***John F. Kennedy,*** speech at the University of Maine, October 19, 1963

"Encoded in Americans' civic chromosomes, in their political DNA, is a deep—literally, congenital—suspicion of all government, and especially of that government that is most distant from them."

—***George Will,*** *Restoration*, 1992

"Honest conviction is my courage; the Constitution is my guide."

—***Andrew Johnson***

"The House has more sense than anyone in it."

—***Thomas B. Reed***

"If there is any fixed star in our constitutional constellation, it is that no official, high or petty, can prescribe what shall be orthodox in politics, nationalism, religion, or other matters of opinion or force citizens to confess by word or act their faith therein."

—***Robert H. Jackson,*** Supreme Court decision in *West Virginia State Board of Education v. Barnette,* 1943

"I honestly believe there are people so excited over this election that they think the President has something to do with running this country."

—***Will Rogers,*** October 30, 1932

"I should like to be known as a former President who minded his own business."

—***Calvin Coolidge***

"I sit here all day trying to persuade people to do the things they ought to have sense enough to do without my persuading them. That's all the powers of the President amount to."

—***Harry S. Truman***

"It could probably be shown by facts and figures that there is no distinctly native American criminal class except Congress."

—***Mark Twain,*** *Following the Equator,* 1898

"It has recently been suggested that whether I serve one or two terms in the Presidency, I will find myself at the end of that period at what might be called the awkward age, too old to begin a new career and too young to write my memoirs."

—***John F. Kennedy,*** speech at the National Industrial Conference Board, Washington, D.C., February 13, 1961

"I think this is the most extraordinary collection of talent, of human knowledge, that has ever been gathered together at the White House—with the possible exception of when Thomas Jefferson dined alone."

—***John F. Kennedy,*** at a White House dinner honoring Nobel Prize winners, April 29, 1962

"It is one of the happy incidents of the federal system that a single courageous State may, if its citizens choose, serve as a laboratory; and try novel social and economic experiments without risk to the rest of the country."

—***Louis D. Brandeis,*** dissenting opinion in the Supreme Court decision *New State Ice Co. v. Liebmann,* 285 U.S. 311, 1932

"John Kennedy set free the spirit of America. The honest optimism was released. Quiet courage and civility became the mark of American government."

—***Eugene McCarthy,*** speech to the Conference of Concerned Democrats, a group organized to oppose the Vietnam War, Chicago, Illinois, December 2, 1967

"Liberty and Union, now and forever, one and inseparable!"

—***Daniel Webster,*** reply to Senator Robert Y. Hayne of South Carolina during a debate regarding the control of state lands by the federal government, *Second Speech on Foote's Resolution,* January 27, 1830

"Lincoln. . . . Every politician always talks about him, but none of them ever imitate him."

—*Will Rogers*

"A little group of willful men, representative of no opinion but their own, have rendered the great government of the United States helpless and contemptible."

—***Woodrow Wilson,*** response to a Senate filibuster on a bill to arm American merchant vessels endangered by German U-boats prior to U.S. entry into World War I, 1917

"Most governments have been based, practically, on the denial of equal rights of men; . . . *ours* began by *affirming* those rights."

—***Abraham Lincoln,*** 1854

"Mr. Lincoln is already beaten. He cannot be re-elected."

—***Horace Greeley,*** August 14, 1864

"My country has in its wisdom contrived for me the most insignificant office that ever the invention of man contrived or his imagination conceived."

—***John Adams,*** letter written upon his selection as vice president, 1789

"My policy is to have no policy."

—***Abraham Lincoln***

"No man who ever held the office of President would congratulate a friend on obtaining it."

—***John Adams***

"No man will ever bring out of the presidency the reputation which carries him into it."

—***Thomas Jefferson***

"On the side of the Union, it is a struggle for maintaining in the world that form and substance of government whose leading object is to elevate the condition of men—to lift artificial weights from all shoulders—to clear the paths of laudable pursuit for all—to afford all an unfettered start, and a fair chance, in the race of life."

—***Abraham Lincoln,*** July 4, 1861

"The presidency is not just a place to protect the present. It is a focus for the possibilities of the future."

—***Lyndon B. Johnson***

"[The President] is the personal embodiment and representative of [the American people's] dignity and majesty."

—***William Howard Taft.*** Senator Joseph Lieberman used this quotation in a speech criticizing President Bill Clinton, September 3, 1998.

"Senators who go down in defeat in vain defense of a single principle will not be on hand to fight for that or another principle in the future."

—***John F. Kennedy***

"Statistics have proven that the surest way to get anything out of the public mind and never hear of it again is to have a Senate Committee appointed to look into it."

—***Will Rogers***

"Suppose you were an idiot, and suppose you were a member of Congress—but I repeat myself."

—***Mark Twain***

"This home of legislative debate represents human liberty in the purest form yet devised."

—***Douglas MacArthur,*** addressing a Joint Session of Congress, April 19, 1951

"This is a Senate, a Senate of equals, of men of individual honor and personal character, and of absolute independence. We know no masters, we acknowledge no dictator. This is a hall for mutual consultation and discussion, not an arena for the exhibition of champions."

—***Daniel Webster,*** speech in the U.S. Senate, January 26, 1830

"The United States is a peaceful nation. And where our strength and determination are clear, our words need merely to convey conviction, not belligerence. If we are strong, our strength will speak for itself. If we are weak, words will be of no help."

—***John F. Kennedy***

"The vice-presidency isn't worth a pitcher of warm piss."

—***John Nance Garner,*** quoted in *Cactus Jack,* 1978

"We can maintain military power without militarism; political power without oppression; and moral power without compulsion or complacency."

—***Adlai Stevenson***

"We give the President more work than a man can do, more responsibility than a man should take, more pressure than a man can bear. We abuse him often and rarely praise him. We wear him out, use him up, eat him up. And with all this, Americans have a love for the President that goes beyond party loyalty or nationality; he is ours and we exercise the right to destroy him."

—***John Steinbeck,*** *America and the Americans,* 1966

"We should resolve now that the health of this Nation is a national concern; that financial barriers in the way of attaining health shall be removed; that the health of all its citizens deserves the help of all the Nation."

—***Harry S. Truman***

"Winning the presidency is condemning yourself to four years of drinking Californian wine."

—***Theodore Roosevelt***

47 UNITY

"All for one, one for all."

—***Alexandre Dumas,*** *The Three Musketeers,* 1844

"All of the links in the chain pulled together, and the chain became unbreakable."

—***George S. Patton,*** on the success of the U.S. Army in North Africa, June 1944

All your strength is in your union.
All your danger is in discord;
Therefore be at peace henceforward,
And as brothers live together.

—***Henry Wadsworth Longfellow,*** *The Song of Hiawatha,* part 1, 1855

"The best and most successful commanders of all grades are those who win the respect, confidence, and affection of their subordinates by justice and firmness, tempered by kindness. The discipline which makes the soldiers of a free country reliable in battle is not to be gained by harsh or tyrannical treatment. On the contrary, such treatment is far more likely to destroy than to make an army."

—***U.S. Army Manual***

"A common danger unites even the bitterest enemies."

—***Aristotle,*** *Politics*

"Death and sorrow will be the companions of our journey; hardship our garment; constancy and valor our only shield. We must be united; we must be undaunted; we must be inflexible."

—***Winston Churchill,*** report on the war to the House of Commons, October 8, 1940

"For the strength of the Pack is the Wolf, and the strength of the Wolf is the Pack."

—***Rudyard Kipling,*** "The Law of the Jungle,"
The Second Jungle Book, 1895

"A house divided against itself cannot stand."

—***Abraham Lincoln,*** address to the Republican
State Convention, Springfield, Illinois, June 16, 1858

"I believe it is the dove of peace, which, taking its aerial flight from the dome of the Capitol, carries the glad tidings of assured peace and restored harmony to all the remotest extremities of this distracted land."

—***Henry Clay,*** expressing hope for the efficacy
of the Compromise of 1850

"I want unity but above everything else, I want a party that will fight for the things that we know to be right at home and abroad."

—***Eleanor Roosevelt,*** speech to the Democratic National
Advisory Committee, New York City, 1959

"Let North and South—let all Americans—let all lovers of liberty everywhere—join in the great and good work. If we do this, we shall not only have saved the Union; but we shall have so saved it, as to make, and to keep it, forever worthy of the saving. We shall have saved it, that the succeeding millions of free happy people, the world over, shall rise up, and call us blessed, to the latest generations."

—***Abraham Lincoln,*** speech on the Kansas-Nebraska Act,
Peoria, Illinois, October 16, 1854

"Let us then, fellow-citizens, unite with one heart and one mind; let us restore to social intercourse that harmony and affection without which liberty and even life itself are but dreary things. And let us reflect, that having banished from our land that religious intolerance under which mankind so long bled and suffered, we have yet gained little, if we countenance a political intolerance."

—***Thomas Jefferson,*** First Inaugural Address, March 4, 1801

"Many people with different backgrounds, cultures, languages, and creeds combine to make a nation. But that nation is greater than the sum total of the individual skills and talents of its people. Something more grows out of their unity than can be calculated by adding the assets of individual contributions. That intangible quantity is often due to the differences which make the texture of the nation rich. Therefore, we must never wipe out or deride the differences amongst us—for where there is no difference, there is only indifference."

—***Louis Nizer***

"Men, I now know, do not fight for flag or country, for the Marine Corps or glory or any other abstraction. They fight for one another. Any man in combat who lacks comrades who will die for him, or for whom he is willing to die, is not a man at all. He is truly damned."

—***William Manchester,*** *Goodbye, Darkness: A Memoir of the Pacific War,* 1980

"Must we go on in many groping, disorganized, separate units to defeat or shall we move as one great team to victory?"

—***Franklin Delano Roosevelt,*** urging passage of the National Recovery Act, 1933

"A nation united can never be conquered."

—***Thomas Jefferson,*** letter to John Adams, 1816

"One country, one constitution, one destiny."

—***Daniel Webster,*** speech, March 15, 1837

"Only peril can bring the French together. One can't impose unity out of the blue on a country that has 265 different kinds of cheese."

—***Charles de Gaulle,*** 1951

"Political unity should be given great weight, but it also should be related to some sensible program."

—***Henry Kissinger***

"The realization that we are all bound together by hope of a common future rather than by reverence for a common past has helped us to build upon this continent a unity unapproached in any similar area or population in the whole world."

—***Franklin Delano Roosevelt,*** address commemorating the fiftieth anniversary of the Statue of Liberty, New York, 1936

"That which unites us is, must be, stronger than that which divides us. We can concentrate on what unites us, and secure the future for all our children; or we can concentrate on what divides us, and fail our duty through argument and resentment and waste."

—***Robert F. Kennedy***

Then join hand in hand, brave Americans all!
By uniting we stand, by dividing we fall.

—***John Dickinson,*** *The Liberty Song,* 1768

"There are no problems we cannot solve together, and very few we can solve by ourselves."

—***Lyndon B. Johnson,*** at a news conference, referring to the NATO alliance, 1964

"There are only two forces that unite men—fear and interest."

—***Napoleon Bonaparte,*** *Maxims,* 1804–1815

"There is no more sure tie between friends than when they are united in their objects and wishes."

—***Marcus Tullius Cicero,*** *Oratio Pro Cnaeo Plancio*

. . . thou canst not stir a flower
Without troubling of a star.

—***Francis Thompson,*** *The Mistress of Vision,* 1897

"Through our scientific genius we have made of the world a neighborhood; now through our moral and spiritual genius we must make of it a brotherhood."

—***Martin Luther King, Jr.,*** "Facing the Challenge of a New Age," address to the First Annual Institute on Non-Violence and Social Change, Montgomery, Alabama, December 1956

"Union gives strength."

—***Aesop,*** "The Bundle of Sticks"

"We come to reason, not to dominate. We do not seek to have our way, but to find a common way."

—***Lyndon B. Johnson,*** speech at Georgetown University discussing the American relationship with NATO, 1964

"We must all hang together, or, most assuredly, we shall all hang separately."

—***Benjamin Franklin,*** remark made at the signing of the Declaration of Independence, July 4, 1776

"We must begin the great task that is before us by abandoning once and for all the illusion that we can ever again isolate ourselves from the rest of humanity."

—***Franklin Delano Roosevelt,*** statement released shortly after the attack on Pearl Harbor, December 1941

"When a country is at war we want Congressmen, regardless of party, to back up the government of the United States."

—***Franklin Delano Roosevelt,*** 1942

"When spider webs unite, they can tie up a lion."

—*African proverb*

"When wealth is centralized, the people are dispersed. When wealth is distributed, the people are united."

—*Confucius, The Analects*

"With malice toward none; with charity for all; with firmness in the right, as God gives us to see the right, let us strive on to finish the work we are in: to bind up the nation's wounds, to care for him who shall have borne the battle, and for his widow and his orphan, to do all which may achieve and cherish a just and lasting peace among ourselves, and with all nations."

—*Abraham Lincoln,* Second Inaugural Address, March 4, 1865

"You don't compromise principles, but you harmonize tactics to preserve unity."

—*John W. McCormack*

48 URBAN AFFAIRS

"The American city should be a collection of communities where every member has a right to belong. It should be a place where every man feels safe on his streets and in the house of his friends. It should be a place where each individual's dignity and self-respect is strengthened by the respect and affection of his neighbors. It should be a place where each of us can find the satisfaction and warmth which comes from being a member of the community of man. This is what man sought at the dawn of civilization. It is what we seek today."

—***Lyndon B. Johnson,*** special message to the Congress on the nation's cities, 1965

"As a remedy to life in society, I would suggest the big city. Nowadays, it is the only desert within our means."

—***Albert Camus,*** *Notebooks 1935–1942*

"The axis of the earth sticks out visibly through the center of each and every town or city."

—***Oliver Wendell Holmes,*** *The Autocrat of the Breakfast-Table,* 1858

"Cities are, by definition, full of strangers."

—***Jane Jacobs,*** *The Death and Life of Great American Cities,* 1961

"The cities are not the problem. They are the solution. The city is not the creator of social problems, and it doesn't spread them. It solves them; for the city is the machine of social change."

—***John Lindsay,*** *Plainview Texas Herald,* 1972

"The city is not a concrete jungle, it is a human zoo."

—***Desmond Morris,*** Introduction to *The Human Zoo,* 1969

"A city, too, like an individual, has a work to do; and that city which is best adapted to the fulfillment of its work is to be deemed greatest."

—***Aristotle,*** *Poetics*

"The city was, is, and always will be the single most important source of economic, social, educational, cultural and political innovation and vitality. With all the difficulties we have today, we are this country's heartbeat, and it strangles us at its own peril."

—***Kenneth Gibson,*** commencement speech
at Jersey City State College, 1971

"Commuters give the city its title restlessness, nature gives it solidity and continuity; but the settlers give it passion."

—***E. B. White,*** *Here Is New York,* 1949

"For [Europeans] a city is, above all, a past; to [Americans] it is mainly a future; what they like in the city is everything it has not yet become and everything it can be."

—***Jean-Paul Sartre***

For students of the troubled heart
Cities are perfect works of art.

—***Christopher Morley,*** *John Mistletoe,* 1931

A great city is that which has the greatest men and women,
If it be a few ragged huts it is still the greatest city in the whole world.

—***Walt Whitman,*** "Song of the Broad-Axe,"
Leaves of Grass, 1855

"If you would be known, and not know, vegetate in a village; if you would know, and not be known, live in a city."

—***Charles Caleb Colton,*** *Lacon,* 1820

"I have observed, that in a great city even the poorest, the lowest can be himself, whereas in a small community even the richest does not feel he really lives, that he can breathe."

—***Johann Wolfgang von Goethe***

"It was divine nature which gave us the country, and man's skill that built the cities."

—***Varro,*** *De Re Rustica*

"I view great cities as pestilential to the morals, the health, and the liberties of man."

—***Thomas Jefferson,*** letter to Benjamin Rush, September 23, 1800

"Men come together in cities for security; they stay together for the good life."

—***Aristotle***

"[New York] is the place where all the aspirations of the Western World meet to form one vast master aspiration, as powerful as the suction of a steam dredge. It is the icing on the pie called Christian civilization."

—***H. L. Mencken,*** *Prejudices, Sixth Series,* 1927

"New York is to the nation what the church spire is to the village—the visible sign of aspiration and faith."

—***E. B. White***

"Peace and freedom walk together. In too many of our cities today, the peace is not secure because freedom is incomplete."

—***John F. Kennedy,*** commencement address at American University, Washington, D.C., June 10, 1963

"The plight of the cities—their physical decay and human despair that pervades them—is the great internal problem of the American nation, a challenge which must be met."

—***Robert F. Kennedy,*** Modern City Conference, Buffalo, New York, January 20, 1967

"The real illness of the American city today, and especially of the deprived groups within it, is voicelessness."

—***Harvey Cox,*** *The Secular City,* 1966

"A strong America depends on its cities—America's glory and sometimes America's shame."

—***John F. Kennedy,*** State of the Union Address, 1962

"There is and has long been . . . a special bond between New York and me. . . . How often, at difficult moments, I looked to New York, I listened to New York, to find out what you were thinking and feeling here, and always I found a comforting echo."

—***Charles de Gaulle,*** 1960

"We Europeans change within changeless cities, and our houses and neighborhoods outlive us; American cities change faster than their inhabitants do, and it is the inhabitants who outlive the cities."

—***Jean-Paul Sartre***

"We will neglect our cities to our peril, for in neglecting them we neglect the nation."

—***John F. Kennedy,*** message to Congress, January 30, 1962

"What is the city but the people?"

—***William Shakespeare,*** *Coriolanus,* act 2, scene 1

"When you look at a city, it's like reading the hopes, aspirations, and pride of everyone who built it."

—***Hugh Newell Jacobsen,*** 1984

49 WAR

"The advice 'bomb them back to the Stone Age' may show that the speaker is already there himself, but it could, if followed, force all of us to join him."

—*Robert F. Kennedy*

"After a victory there are no enemies, but only men!"

—***Napoleon Bonaparte,*** reprimanding a soldier showing disrespect for the enemy dead

"All diplomacy is a continuation of war by other means."

—***Zhou Enlai,*** *Saturday Evening Post,* March 27, 1954

"An appeaser is one who feeds a crocodile, hoping it will eat him last."

—***Winston Churchill,*** *Reader's Digest,* December 1954

And when he goes to heaven,
To God he will tell,
Another Marine reporting, Sir—
I've served my time in Hell.

—***Anonymous.*** Inscription on the grave of a U.S. Marine killed in World War II

"An army marches on its stomach."

—***Napoleon Bonaparte***

"As men do not live on bread alone, they do not fight by armaments alone. Those who man our defenses and those behind them who build our defense must have the stamina and the courage which come from an unshakable belief in the manner of life which they are defending."

—***Franklin Delano Roosevelt,*** speaking on the necessity of the Lend-Lease Act, January 6, 1941

"Battle is the most magnificent competition in which a human being can indulge. It brings out all that is best and it removes all that is base."

—***George S. Patton,*** rallying American troops in Britain, June 1944

"The battle, sir, is not to the strong alone; it is to the vigilant, the active, the brave."

—***Patrick Henry,*** speech to the Virginia Convention, Richmond, Virginia, March 23, 1775

"Better one bad general than two good ones."

—***Napoleon Bonaparte***

"Both read the same Bible, and pray to the same God; and each invokes His aid against each other. It may seem strange that any men should dare to ask a just God's assistance in wringing their bread from the sweat of other men's faces, but let us judge not, that we be judged. The prayers of both could not be answered. That of neither has been answered fully. The Almighty has His own purposes."

—***Abraham Lincoln,*** speaking of soldiers of both the North and the South, Second Inaugural Address, March 4, 1864

Cannon to right of them,
Cannon to left of them,
Cannon in front of them,
Volley'd and thunder'd;
Storm'd at with shot and shell,
Boldly they rode and well,
Into the jaws of Death,
Into the mouth of hell,
Rode the six hundred.

—***Alfred, Lord Tennyson,*** "The Charge of the Light Brigade," 1854

"Contrary to what we sometimes used to think, the spirit is of no avail against the sword, but the spirit together with the sword will always win out over the sword alone."

—***Albert Camus,*** *Resistance, Rebellion, and Death,* 1960

"Dictators ride to and fro upon tigers which they dare not dismount. And the tigers are getting hungry."

—***Winston Churchill,*** *While England Slept,* 1936

"Don't worry; Barbados is with you."

—*James Lawrence,* legendary cable from the West Indies to "confirm" the support of Barbados for the British declaration of war on Germany in 1939

The enemy advances: we retreat.
The enemy halts: we harass.
The enemy tires: we attack.
The enemy retreats: we pursue.

—*Mao Tse-tung,* Party Report, 1928

"Every single man in this Army plays a vital role. Don't ever let up. Don't ever think that your job is unimportant. Every man has a job to do and he must do it. Every man is a vital link in the great chain."

—*George S. Patton,* rallying American troops in Britain, June 1944

"The fate of unborn millions will now depend, under God, on the courage and conduct of this army. . . . We have, therefore, to resolve to conquer or die."

—*George Washington,* address to his troops, August 27, 1776

"General, you must look to your Division."
"General Lee, I have no Division."

—*Robert E. Lee,* exchange with *George Pickett* after his unsuccessful assault on the Union line known as "Pickett's Charge," Battle of Gettysburg, Pennsylvania, 1863

"Gentlemen, examine this ground carefully, it is going to be a battlefield."

—*Napoleon Bonaparte,* selecting positions before an engagement with Russo-Austrian armies near Brunn, November 19, 1805

"Hear me, my chiefs! I am tired; my heart is sick and sad. From where the sun now stands I will fight no more forever."

—*Chief Joseph,* statement of surrender to the U.S. Army of the Nez Percé Indians

"He who does not advance retreats."

—*Chinese proverb*

"History is littered with the wars which everybody knew would never happen."

—*Enoch Powell,* speech, October 19, 1967

"The history of failure in war can be summed up in two words: Too late. Too late in comprehending the deadly purpose of a potential enemy; too late in realizing the mortal danger; too late in preparedness; too late in uniting all possible forces for resistance; too late in standing with one's friends."

—***Douglas MacArthur***

"I feel all we have done is to awaken a sleeping giant and fill him with a terrible resolve."

—***Isoroku Yamamoto,*** reacting to the Japanese attack on Pearl Harbor in the movie *Tora! Tora! Tora!* 1970

"If General McClellan does not want to use the army, I would like to borrow it."

—***Abraham Lincoln,*** remarking on the slowness of George McClellan to attack the Confederacy

"If my countrymen should catch you, I believe they would first cut off that lame leg which was wounded in the cause of freedom and virtue, and bury it with the honors of war; and afterwards hang the remainder of your body in gibbets, high."

—***George Washington,*** response to Benedict Arnold's question regarding his expected treatment by the Americans if captured and tried for treason. Arnold's leg had been wounded while he was serving with the Continental Army at the Battle of Saratoga before his betrayal of the Revolution.

"If we were base enough to retire it is now too late to retire from the contest. There is no retreat but in submission to slavery! Our chains are forged! Their clanking may be heard on the plains of Boston! The war is inevitable—and let it come! I repeat it, sir, let it come!"

—***Patrick Henry,*** speech to the Virginia Convention, September 23, 1775

"I have nothing to offer but blood, toil, tears, and sweat. . . . You ask, what is our aim? I can answer in one word. It is victory. Victory at all costs—victory in spite of all terrors—victory, however long and hard the road may be, for without victory there is no survival."

—***Winston Churchill,*** address to Parliament, May 13, 1940

"I know not with what weapons World War III will be fought, but World War IV will be fought with sticks and stones."

—***Albert Einstein***

"Indomitable in retreat; invincible in advance; insufferable in victory."

—***Winston Churchill*** on Field Marshall Bernard Law Montgomery

"In fact, every war has been preceded by a peace conference. That's what always starts the next war."

—*Will Rogers*

"In war before the battle is joined, plans are everything, but once the shooting begins, plans are worthless."

—*Dwight D. Eisenhower*

"It [the American Navy] does not have the strength to fight or the speed to run away."

—***William C. Whitney,*** secretary of the navy, questioning America's ability to enforce the Monroe Doctrine

"I tell you Wellington is a bad general, the English are bad soldiers; we will settle this matter by lunchtime."

—***Napoleon Bonaparte,*** at breakfast with his generals prior to the Battle of Waterloo, June 18, 1815

"It is better to suffer certain injustices than to commit them even to win wars; such deeds do us more harm than a hundred underground forces on the enemy's side."

—***Albert Camus,*** *Resistance, Rebellion and Death,* 1960

"It is to the interest of mankind that there should be someone who is unconquered, someone against whom fortune has no power."

—***Seneca***

"It is well that war is so terrible. We should grow too fond of it."

—***Robert E. Lee,*** after the Battle of Fredericksburg, December 13, 1862

"I will not take by sacrifice what I can achieve by strategy."

—***Douglas MacArthur***

"I would rather die a thousand deaths."

—***Robert E. Lee,*** on his impending surrender to Ulysses S. Grant at Appomattox

". . . the Kentucky father whose two sons died in battle, one in Union blue, the other in Confederate gray, the father inscribing on the stone over their double grave, 'God knows which was right'? We do not know."

—***Carl Sandburg,*** speech before a Joint Session of Congress marking the 150th anniversary of the birth of Abraham Lincoln, February 12, 1959

"The lamps are going out all over Europe; we shall not see them lit again in our lifetime."

—***Edward Grey,*** on the eve of World War I, August 3, 1914, as quoted by Barbara Tuchman in *The Guns of August,* 1962

"The more you sweat in peacetime, the less you bleed during war."

—***Chinese proverb***

"The most difficult task I have had since the war began, in dealing with foreign nations, has been to convince them that we do not want any material advantage out of this war. They cannot understand it."

—***Anna Howard Shaw,*** rallying support for Woodrow Wilson's Fourteen Points, May 1919

"My center is giving way, my right is retreating, situation excellent. I shall attack."

—***Ferdinand Foch,*** message sent during the first Battle of the Marne, September 1914

"Never in the field of human conflict was so much owed by so many to so few."

—***Winston Churchill,*** tribute to the Royal Air Force, House of Commons, August 20, 1940

"No matter what happens, the U.S. Navy is not going to be caught napping."

—***Frank Knox,*** uttered prior to the Japanese surprise attack on Pearl Harbor, December 7, 1941

"No one would take seriously the equally illogical plan of disbanding our fire department, or disbanding our police department to stop crime."

—***Douglas MacArthur,*** speech warning against disarmament as a means to peace

"The object of war is not to die for your country, but to make the other bastard die for his."

—***George S. Patton***

"Old soldiers never die; they just fade away."

—***Douglas MacArthur,*** farewell speech before a Joint Session of Congress, April 19, 1951

"Once war is forced upon us, there is no other alternative than to apply every available means to bring it to a swift end. War's very object is victory, not prolonged indecision. In war, indeed, there can be no substitute for victory."

—***Douglas MacArthur,*** farewell speech before a Joint Session of Congress, April 19, 1951

"Only when our arms are sufficient, without doubt, can we be certain, without doubt, that they will never have to be employed."

—***John F. Kennedy,*** Inaugural Address, January 20, 1961

"Outside, the storms of war may blow and the lands may be lashed with the fury of its gales, but in our own hearts this Sunday morning there is peace. . . . Our consciences are at rest."

—***Winston Churchill,*** address to Parliament delivered shortly after Britain declared war on Germany, September 3, 1939

"Political power grows out of the barrel of a gun."

—***Mao Tse-tung,*** "Problems of War and Strategy," November 6, 1938

"The problem in defense spending is to figure out how far you should go without destroying from within what you are trying to defend from without."

—***Dwight D. Eisenhower***

"Punishment is not prevention. History offers cold comfort to those who think grievance and despair can be subdued by force."

—***Robert F. Kennedy,*** *To Seek a Newer World,* 1967

"Put your trust in God; but keep your powder dry."

—***Oliver Cromwell***

"The quickest way of ending a war is to lose it."

—***George Orwell,*** *Polemic,* May 1946

"A revolution is not a dinner party."

—***Mao Tse-tung,*** "Report on an Investigation of the Peasant Movement in Hunan," March 1927

"The right is more precious than peace."

—***Woodrow Wilson,*** address to Congress in support of U.S. entry into World War I, April 2, 1917

"Shall it be said of us, that we know how to conquer but not to profit by our victories?"

—***Napoleon Bonaparte,*** rallying his troops in the Italian campaign, 1796

"A single British soldier—and we will see to it that he is killed.'"

—***Ferdinand Foch,*** reply to Woodrow Wilson, when asked what would be the smallest British military force useful to him at the front

"Stand your ground. Don't fire unless fired upon, but if they mean to have a war, let it begin here!"

—***John Parker,*** at the Battle of Lexington, April 19, 1775

"The sword is the axis of the world and its power is absolute."

—***Charles de Gaulle,*** *Vers l'armée de métier,* 1934

"There are no atheists in foxholes."

—***William T. Cummings,*** "Sermons on Bataan," 1942

"There is no such thing as inevitable war. If war comes it will be from failure of human wisdom."

—***Bonar Law***

"There is nothing more exhilarating than to be shot at without result."

—***Winston Churchill,*** recalling his military service in the Boer War

"There is only one decisive victory: the last."

—***Karl von Clausewitz,*** *Arming the Nations,* 1831

"They also serve who only stand and wait."

—***John Milton,*** "When I Consider How My Light Is Spent," 1652

"This is why the war is not an ordinary war. It is not a conflict for markets or territories. It is a desperate struggle for the possession of the souls of men."

—***Harold L. Ickes,*** "I Am an American Day" speech, Central Park, New York, May 18, 1941

To save the world, you asked this man to die:
Would this man, could he see you now, ask why?

—***W. H. Auden,*** "Epitaph for an Unknown Soldier," *The Shield of Achilles,* 1954

"War hath no fury like a non-combatant."

—***C. E. Montague,*** *Disenchantment,* 1922

"War is evil, but it is often the lesser evil."

—***George Orwell,*** *Looking Back on the Spanish Civil War,* 1945

"War is merely the extension of state policy by other means."

—***Karl von Clausewitz,*** *On War,* 1831

"War! It is too serious a matter to leave to the military."

—***Georges Clemenceau,*** quoted in *Clemenceau,* 1886

"Water shapes its course according to the nature of the ground over which it flows. . . . Therefore, just as water retains no constant shape, so in warfare there are no constant conditions."

—***Sun Tzu,*** *The Art of War*

"We are advocates of the abolition of war, we do not want war; but war can only be abolished through war, and in order to get rid of the gun it is necessary to take up the gun."

—***Mao Tse-tung,*** "Problems of War and Strategy," November 6, 1938

"We have met the enemy, and they are ours."

—***Oliver Hazard Perry,*** letter to General William Henry Harrison after the Battle of Lake Erie, September 10, 1813

"We have one motto, 'Audacious, audacious, always audacious.' Remember that. From here on out, until we win or die in the attempt, we will always be audacious."

—***George S. Patton,*** rallying the troops, France, July 31, 1944

"West Point taught us not the skill to unravel conflicting political creeds . . . but rather to illustrate by our lives manly courage and loyalty to our convictions."

—***Edward Porter Alexander***

"When war comes, you must draw the sword and throw away the scabbard."

—***Thomas "Stonewall" Jackson***

"You can't make war upon rebellion."

—***T. E. Lawrence ("Lawrence of Arabia"),*** on the struggle for Irish independence

"You do your worst—and we will do our best."

—***Winston Churchill,*** speech, County Hall, London, July 14, 1941

"You just tell me the brand of whiskey Grant drinks—I would like to send a barrel of it to my other generals."

—***Abraham Lincoln,*** reply to advisors who complained of Ulysses Grant's drinking habits, November 26, 1863

50 YOUTH

"Adolescents turn on you—that's their job."

—***Ron Howard***

Ah, what shall I be at fifty,
Should nature keep me alive,
If I find the world so bitter
When I am but twenty-five?

—***Alfred, Lord Tennyson,*** "Maud; a Monodrama," 1855

"Almost everything that is great has been done by youth."

—***Benjamin Disraeli,*** *Coningsby,* 1844

"Americans began by loving youth, and now, out of adult self-pity, they worship it."

—***Jacques Barzun,*** *The House of Intellect,* 1959

"Childhood is the kingdom where nobody dies."

—***Edna St. Vincent Millay,*** *Wine from These Grapes,* 1934

"The children are always the chief victims of social chaos."

—***Agnes E. Meyer,*** *Out of These Roots,* 1953

Children know the grace of God
Better than most of us. They see the world
The way the morning brings it back to them.
New and born and fresh and wonderful.

—***Archibald MacLeish***

"Children's talent to endure stems from their ignorance of alternatives."

—***Maya Angelou,*** *I Know Why the Caged Bird Sings,* 1970

"Each child is an adventure into a better life—an opportunity to change the old pattern and make it new."

—***Hubert H. Humphrey***

"Every child comes with the message that God is not yet discouraged of man."

—***Rabindranath Tagore***

"Familiarity breeds contempt—and children."

—***Mark Twain***

"Give me a child for the first seven years, and you may do what you like with him afterwards."

—***Anonymous,*** maxim attributed to the Jesuits

"He that spareth his rod hates his son."

—***Proverbs 12:24***

"I believe the child should be taught from the very first that the whole world is his world, that adult and child share one world, that all generations are needed."

—***Pearl S. Buck,*** *To My Daughters, with Love,* 1967

"If our American way of life fails the child, it fails us all."

—***Pearl S. Buck,*** *Children for Adoption,* 1964

"The illusions of childhood are necessary experiences: a child should not be denied a balloon just because an adult knows that sooner or later it will burst."

—***Marcelene Cox,*** *Ladies' Home Journal,* 1948

"In every child who is born, under no matter what circumstances, and of no matter what parents, the potentiality of the human race is born again."

—***James Agee***

"Instead of implying that the ideals we cherish are safely embalmed in the memory of old battles, we should tell them that each generation re-fights the crucial battles and either brings new vitality to the ideals or allows them to decay."

—***John W. Gardner***

"In the last analysis civilization itself is measured by the way in which children will live and what chance they will have in the world."

—***Mary Heaton Vorse,*** *A Footnote to Folly,* 1935

"I remember my youth and the feeling that will never come back anymore—the feeling that I could last for ever, outlast the sea, the earth, and all men; the deceitful feeling that lures us on to perils, to love, to vain effort—to death."

—***Joseph Conrad,*** *Youth,* 1902

"It is an illusion that youth is happy, an illusion of those who have lost it."

—***W. Somerset Maugham,*** *Of Human Bondage,* 1915

"It is not possible for civilization to flow backward while there is youth in the world."

—***Helen Keller,*** *Midstream,* 1930

"It is the malady of our age that the young are so busy teaching us that they have no time left to learn."

—***Eric Hoffer***

"Live as long as you may, the first twenty years are the longest half of your life."

—***Robert Southey,*** *The Doctor,* 1834–1847

"My clients are the children; my clients are the next generation."

—***Woodrow Wilson,*** pleading the cause of the League of Nations

"My views on birth control are somewhat distorted by the fact that I was seventh of nine children."

—***Robert F. Kennedy***

"No man can possibly know what life means, what the world means, until he has a child and loves it. And then the whole universe changes, and nothing will ever seem exactly as it seemed before."

—***Lafcadio Hearn***

"No one has yet fully realized the wealth of sympathy, kindness, and generosity hidden in the soul of a child. The effort of every true educator should be to unlock that treasure."

—***Emma Goldman,*** *Living My Life,* 1931

"No wise man ever wished to be younger."

—***Jonathan Swift***

"One starts to get young at the age of sixty and then it's too late."

—***Pablo Picasso***

"Our answer is the world's hope; it is to rely on youth. The cruelties and obstacles of this swiftly changing planet will not yield to obsolete dogmas and outworn slogans. It cannot be moved by those who cling to a present which is already dying, who prefer the illusion of security to the excitement of danger. It demands the qualities of youth: not a time of life but a state of mind, a temper of the will, a quality of the imagination, a predominance of courage over timidity, of the appetite for adventure over the love of ease."

—***Robert F. Kennedy,*** "Day of Affirmation" address, University of Cape Town, South Africa, June 6, 1966

"Perhaps we cannot prevent this from being a world in which children suffer, but we can lessen the number of suffering children."

—***Albert Camus***

So much of adolescence is an ill-defined dying,
An intolerable waiting,
A longing for another place and time,
Another condition.

—***Theodore Roethke,*** "I'm Here," *The Collected Verse of Theodore Roethke,* 1961

So nigh is grandeur to our dust,
So near is God to man,
When duty whispers low, *Thou must,*
The youth replies *I can.*

—***Ralph Waldo Emerson,*** "Voluntaries," 1863

"Those whom the gods love grow young."

—***Oscar Wilde***

"Through our great good fortune, in our youth our hearts were touched with fire. It was given to us to learn at the outset that life is a profound and passionate thing."

—***Oliver Wendell Holmes, Jr.,*** speech to John Sedgwick Post No. 4, Grand Army of the Republic, Keene, New Hampshire, 1884

"Too much indulgence has ruined thousands of children; too much *Love* not one."

—***Fanny Fern,*** *Caper Sauce,* 1872

Was there ever a cause too lost,
Ever a cause that was lost too long,
Or that showed with the lapse of time too vain
For the generous tears of youth and song?

—***Robert Frost,*** "Hannibal," *West-Running Brook,* 1928

"We cannot always build the future for our youth, but we can build our youth for the future."

—***Franklin Delano Roosevelt,*** speech at the University of Pennsylvania, Philadelphia, 1940

"We live in an age when to be young and to be indifferent can be no longer synonymous. We must prepare for the coming hour. The claims of the future are represented by suffering millions; and the youth of a nation are the trustees of posterity."

—***Benjamin Disraeli,*** *Sybil,* 1845

"What its children become, that will the community become."

—***Suzanne La Follette,*** "Woman and Marriage," *Concerning Women,* 1926

"When I was younger I could remember anything, whcther it happened or not."

—***Mark Twain***

"When we want to infuse new ideas, to modify or better the habits and customs of a people, to breathe new vigor into its national traits, we must use the child as our vehicle; for little can be accomplished with adults."

—***Maria Montessori,*** *The Absorbent Mind,* 1949

"You must know that there is nothing higher and stronger and more wholesome and good for life in the future than some good memory, especially of childhood, of home. People talk to you a great deal about your education, but some good, sacred memory, preserved from childhood, is perhaps the best education. If a man carries many such memories with him into life, he is safe to the end of his days."

—***Feodor Dostoyevsky,*** *Brothers Karamazov,* 1879

"The young are inclined to measure yesterday's ways by tomorrow's standards."

—***Madeleine Brent,*** *Moonraker's Bride,* 1973

"The young do not know enough to be prudent, and therefore they attempt the impossible, and achieve it, generation after generation."

—***Pearl S. Buck***

"Youth is, after all, just a moment, but it is the moment, the spark that you always carry in your heart."

—***Raisa M. Gorbachev,*** *I Hope,* 1991

"Youth is a wonderful thing. What a crime to waste it on children."

—***George Bernard Shaw***

"Youth is not a time of life—it is a state of mind. It is a temper of the will; a quality of the imagination; a vigor of the emotions; it is a freshness of the deep springs of life. Youth means a temperamental predominance of courage over timidity, of the appetite for adventure over a life of ease. . . . Nobody grows old by merely living a number of years; people grow old by deserting their ideals."

—***Samuel Ullman,*** "Youth," 1922

"Youth is stranger than fiction."

—***Marcelene Cox,*** *Ladies' Home Journal,* 1951

"Youth lives in an atmosphere of energy waiting to make contact."

—***Hallie Flanagan,*** *Dynamo,* 1943

"Youth, which is forgiven everything, forgives itself nothing: age, which forgives itself everything, is forgiven nothing."

—***George Bernard Shaw,*** "Maxims for Revolutionists,"
Man and Superman, 1903

Bibliography

Adler, Bill, ed. *The Kennedy Wit.* New York: Bantam Books, 1965.
Alternbernd, Lynn. *Anthology: An Introduction to Literature.* New York: Macmillan, 1977.
Ambrose, Stephen. *Undaunted Courage.* New York: Touchstone, 1996.
America the Beautiful: In the Words of RFK. New York: G. P. Putnam's Sons, 1968.
Andrews, Robert, ed. *The Columbia Dictionary of Quotations.* New York: Columbia University Press, 1993.
———. *Famous Lines.* New York: Columbia University Press, 1997.
Angle, Paul M., and Earl Schenck Miers, eds. *The Living Lincoln: The Man and His Times, In His Own Words.* New York: Barnes & Noble, 1955.
Apple, R. W., Jr. "A First Step with No End in Sight." *New York Times,* October 6, 1998.
Applewhite, Ashton, William R. Evans III, and Andrew Frothingham, eds. *"And I Quote."* New York: St. Martin's Press, 1992.
Baker, Daniel B., ed. *Political Quotations.* Detroit: Gale Research, Inc., 1996.
———. *Power Quotes.* Detroit: Visible Ink Press, 1992.
Bartlett, John. *Familiar Quotations.* 13th ed. Boston: Little, Brown, 1955.
———. *Familiar Quotations.* 16th ed. Boston: Little, Brown, 1992.
Basler, Roy P., ed., *The Collected Works of Abraham Lincoln.* Second Supplement, 1848–1865. New Brunswick, N.J.: Rutgers University Press, 1990.
Beilenson, Peter L., ed. *The Spirit of '76.* Mount Vernon: Peter Pauper Press, 1974.
Bishop, Jim. *FDR's Last Year: April 1944–April 1945.* London: Hart-Davis MacGibbon, 1975.
Blair, Hugh. *Lectures on Rhetoric.* Carbondale: Southern Illinois University Press, 1965.
Bobrick, Benson. *Angel in the Whirlwind.* New York: Simon and Schuster, 1997.
Bohle, Bruce, ed. *The Home Book of American Quotations.* New York: Dodd, Mead, 1967.
Bollen, Peter, ed. *A Handbook of Great Labor Quotations.* Lynnfield, Mass.: Hillside Books, 1983.
Bradley, John P., Leo F. Daniels, and Thomas C. Jones, eds. *The International Dictionary of Thoughts.* Chicago: J. F. Ferguson Publishers, 1969.
Brain, Richard, ed. *Oxford Dictionary of Quotations.* Oxford: Oxford University Press, 1980.
Brinkley, Alan, et al. *The New Federalist Papers.* New York: W. W. Norton, 1997.
Broder, David. "Jerry Ford's Sense." *Washington Post,* June 6, 1999, A 37.
Bruccoli, Matthew, ed. *The Notebooks of F. Scott Fitzgerald.* New York: Harcourt Brace Jovanovich/Bruccoli Clark, 1978.
Buber, Martin. *Tales of the Hasidim.* New York: Schocken Books, 1991.
Bunim, Irving M. *Ethics from Sinai.* New York: Philipp Feldheim, 1964.

Byrne, Robert, ed. *1,911 Best Things Anybody Ever Said.* New York: Random House, 1988.
Camp, Wesley, ed. *Camp's Unfamiliar Quotations from 2000 BC to the Present.* Englewood Cliffs, N.J.: Prentice-Hall, 1990.
Carpenter, Francis B., *The Inner Life of Abraham Lincoln: Six Months at the White House.* Lincoln: University of Nebraska Press, 1995.
Carroll, Andrew, ed. *Letters of a Nation: A Collection of Extraordinary American Letters.* New York: Kodansha, 1997.
Carruth, Gorton, and Eugene Ehrlich, eds. *The Harper Book of American Quotations.* New York: Harper & Row, 1988.
Cerf, Christopher, and Victor Navasky, eds. *The Experts Speak.* New York: Pantheon Books, 1984.
Chandwani, Ashok. "Forced to Look in the Mirror." *Montreal Gazeteer,* February 1, 1999.
Clapp, James A., ed. *The City: A Dictionary of Quotable Thoughts on Cities and Urban Life.* New Brunswick, N.J.: Center for Urban Policy Research, 1984.
Collins, Reba, ed. *Will Rogers Says . . .* Oklahoma City: Neighbors and Quaid, 1993.
Corey, Melinda, and George Ochon, eds. *The Dictionary of Film Quotations.* New York: Random House, 1998.
Crawley, Tom, ed. *The Wordsworth Dictionary of Film Quotations.* New York: Wordsworth Editions Ltd., 1998.
Crofton, Ian, ed. *A Dictionary of Art Quotations.* London: Routledge, 1988.
Daintith, John, ed. *The Macmillan Dictionary of Quotations.* New York: Macmillan, 1989.
Davis, Kenneth S. *The Politics of Honor: A Biography of Adlai E. Stevenson.* New York: Putnam, 1967.
Dillard, Irving, ed. *The Spirit of Liberty: Papers and Addresses of Learned Hand.* New York: Alfred A. Knopf, 1960.
Donadio, Stephen, et al., eds. *The New York Public Library Book of Twentieth Century American Quotations.* New York: Warner Books, 1992.
Dulaney, H. G., and Edward Hake Phillips, eds. *Speak, Mister Speaker.* Bonham, Tex.: Sam Rayburn Foundation, 1978.
Editors of Reader's Digest. *The Reader's Digest Treasury of Modern Quotations.* New York: Reader's Digest Press, 1975.
Eigen, Lewis D., and Jonathan P. Siegel, eds. *The Macmillan Dictionary of Political Quotations.* New York: Macmillan, 1993.
Elon, Amos. *Herzl.* Tel Aviv: 'Am 'Oved, 1977.
Evans, Bergen, ed. *Dictionary of Quotations.* New York: Delacorte Press, 1968.
Farber, Bernard E., ed. *A Teacher's Treasury of Quotations.* Jefferson, N.C.: McFarland & Company, 1985.
Fitzhenry, Robert. *Barnes and Noble Book of Quotations.* New York: Barnes and Noble, 1987.
Frank, Leonard Roy, ed. *Influencing Minds.* Portland: Feral House, 1995.
Friedman, Gil, ed. *Dictionary of Love.* Arcata, Calif.: Yara Press, 1990.
Gale's Quotations. New York: Gale Research, Inc., 1995.
Gardner, Gerald C., ed. *The Quotable Mr. Kennedy.* New York: Abelard-Schuman, 1962.
Gibran, Kahlil. *The Prophet.* New York: Alfred A. Knopf, 1968.
Gilbert, Felix. *To the Farewell Address.* Princeton, N.J.: Princeton University Press, 1961.
Giles, Lionel, ed. *The Art of War.* London: Luzac & Co., 1910.
Gonzalez, Rosie. *The Fire in Our Souls.* New York: Plume, 1996.
Goodwin, Doris Kearns. *Lyndon Johnson and the American Dream.* Norwalk, Conn.: Easton Press, 1987.
Green, Jonathan, ed. *Says Who?* Avon: The Bath Press, 1988.
Guterman, Norbert. *A Book of Latin Quotations.* Garden City, N.Y.: Doubleday, 1966.

Guthman, Edwin O., and C. Richard Allen, eds. *RFK: Collected Speeches.* New York: Viking Press, 1993.
Harrison, Maureen, and Steve Gilbert, eds. *Abraham Lincoln: Word for Word.* San Diego: Excellent Books, 1994.
———. *John F. Kennedy: In His Own Words.* New York: Barnes and Noble, 1993.
———. *Thomas Jefferson: In His Own Words.* New York: Barnes and Noble, 1993.
Hawking, Stephen. *A Brief History of Time.* Garden City, N.Y.: Bantam Books/Doubleday, 1998.
Hayes, Sara H., ed. *The Quotable Lyndon B. Johnson.* New York: Grosset & Dunlap, 1968.
Haythornthwaite, Philip J., et al., eds., *Napoleon: The Final Verdict.* London: Arms and Armour, 1996.
Heinl, Robert Debs, ed. *Dictionary of Military and Naval Quotations.* Annapolis: Naval Institute Press, 1966.
Hentoff, Nat. *Speaking Freely.* New York: Alfred A. Knopf, 1997.
Hofstader, Richard, ed. *Great Issues in American History.* Vol. 2. New York: Vintage, 1958.
Hofstader, Richard, and B. K. Hofstader, eds. *Great Issues in American History.* Vol. 3. New York: Vintage, 1982.
Hohenberg, John. *The New Front Page.* New York: Columbia University Press, 1966.
Holms, John, and Karin Baji, eds. *Bite-Size Twain.* New York: St. Martin's Press, 1998.
Hotchner, A. E. *Papa Hemingway.* London: Mayflower, 1968.
Hovey, E. Paul, ed. *The Treasury of Inspirational Anecdotes, Quotations, and Illustrations.* Grand Rapids, Mich.: Fleming H. Revell Company, 1959.
Humes, James C., ed. *The Wit and Wisdom of Benjamin Franklin.* New York: HarperCollins, 1995.
———. *The Wit and Wisdom of Winston Churchill.* New York: HarperCollins, 1994.
Hurd, Charles, ed. *A Treasury of Great American Speeches,* New York: Hawthorn Books, 1959.
James, Lawrence. *The Rise and Fall of the British Empire.* London: Little, Brown, 1994.
James, Robert Rhodes, ed. *Winston S. Churchill: His Complete Speeches.* Vol. 7. New York: Chelsea House Publishers, 1974.
James, Simon, ed. *A Dictionary of Economic Quotations.* Totowa, N.J.: Roman and Allanheld, 1984.
James, William. *Writings 1902–1910.* New York: Viking Press, 1987.
Jay, Antony, ed. *The Oxford Dictionary of Political Quotations.* Oxford: Oxford University Press, 1996.
Johnson, Paul. *A History of the American People.* New York: HarperCollins, 1997.
Jones, High Percy, ed. *Dictionary of Foreign Phrases and Classical Quotations.* Boston: Milford House, 1972.
Kaplan, Justin, ed. *Bartlett's Familiar Quotations.* Boston: Little, Brown, 1992.
Keats, John. *The Poetical Works of John Keats.* London: Macmillan, 1898.
Kenin, Richard, and Justin Wintle, eds. *The Dictionary of Biographical Quotations.* New York: Alfred A. Knopf, 1978.
Kennedy, John F. *Why England Slept.* Garden City, N.Y.: Doubleday, 1961.
Kennedy, Maxwell Taylor, ed., *Make Gentle the Life of This Good World: The Vision of Robert F. Kennedy.* New York: Harcourt Brace, 1998.
King, Anita, ed. *Quotations in Black.* Westport, Conn.: Greenwood Press, 1981.
King, Martin Luther, Jr. *Where Do We Go from Here: Chaos or Community?* New York: Harper Books, 1967.
Kissinger, Henry. *Diplomacy.* New York: Touchstone Press, 1996.
Knowles, Elizabeth, ed. *The Oxford Dictionary of Phrase, Saying, and Quotation.* Oxford: Oxford University Press, 1997.
Kolatch, Alfred, ed. *Great Jewish Quotations.* New York: Jonathan David Publishers, 1996.

Kronenberger, Louis, and W. H. Auden, eds. *The Viking Book of Amorphisms*. New York: Penguin Books, 1981.
Lau, D. C., ed. *Mencius*. London: Penguin Classics, 1970.
Lieberman, Gerald F., ed. *3,500 Good Quotes for Speakers*. Garden City, N.Y. : Doubleday, 1983.
Lipscomb, Andrew Adgate, Albert Ellery Bergh, and Richard Holland Johnston, eds. *The Writings of Thomas Jefferson (Memorial Edition)*. Washington, D.C.: Thomas Jefferson Memorial Foundation, 1903–1904.
Loeb, Aaron John, ed. *The Wit and Wisdom of Mark Twain*. New York: Barnes and Noble, 1996.
MacHale, Des, ed. *Humorous Quotations*. Cork, Ireland: Mercier Press. 1994.
The Macmillan Dictionary of Quotations. New York: Macmillan, 1989.
Maggio, Rosalie, ed. *The New Beacon Book of Quotations by Women*. Boston: Beacon Press, 1996.
Magill, Frank N., ed. *Magill's Quotations in Context*. New York: Harper & Row, 1969.
Manchester, William. *American Caesar: Douglas MacArthur, 1880–1964*. Boston: Little, Brown, 1978.
Mao Tse-tung. *Quotations of Mao Tse-tung*. N.p., n.d.
Mariniss, David. *First in His Class: A Biography of Bill Clinton*. New York: Simon and Schuster, 1995.
Marx, Karl. *Communist Manifesto*. London: Allen and Unwin, 1961.
Mencken, H. L., ed. *A New Dictionary of Quotations*. New York: Alfred A. Knopf, 1982.
Mullane, Deirdre, ed. *Words to Make My Dream Children Live*. Garden City, N.Y.: Doubleday, 1995.
Nixon, Richard. *Beyond Peace*. New York: Random House, 1994.
Oldroyd, Osborn, ed. *Words of Lincoln*. Rahway, N.J.: The Mershon Company Press, 1895.
Partington, Angela, ed. *The Oxford Dictionary of Quotations*. New York: Oxford University Press, 1992.
Paterson, Thomas G., J. Garry Clifford, and Kenneth I. Hagan, eds. *American Foreign Policy: A History Since 1900*. Lexington, Mass.: D. C. Heath, 1991.
Pepper, Frank S., ed. *The Wit and Wisdom of the 20th Century*. New York: Peter Bedrick Books, 1987.
Peter, Laurence J., ed. *Peter's Quotations*. New York: Bantam Books, 1977.
Petras, Kathryn, and Ross Petras, eds. *The Whole World Book of Quotations*. Reading, Mass.: Addison-Wesley, 1994.
Peyrifite, Alain. *The Immobile Empire*. New York: Alfred A. Knopf, 1992.
Platt, Suzy, ed. *Respectfully Quoted*. Washington, D.C.: Library of Congress, 1989.
Platz, Mabel, ed. *Anthology of Speeches*. New York: W. H. Wilson, 1940.
Prochnow, Herbert V., and Herbert V. Prochnow, Jr., eds. *The Public Speaker's Treasure Chest*. New York: Harper & Row, 1986.
Public Papers of the Presidents. Washington, D.C.: National Archives and Records Service, 1961.
Quotations from Our Presidents. Mount Vernon, Va.: Peter Pauper Press, 1969.
Radice, Betty, ed. *Confucius: The Analects*. London: Penguin Classics, 1979.
Ramage, Craufurd, ed. *Beautiful Thoughts from Latin Authors*. Liverpool: Edward Howell, 1877.
Rasmussen, R. Kent, ed. *The Quotable Mark Twain*. Chicago: Contemporary Books, 1997.
Ratcliffe, Susan, ed. *Oxford Love Quotations*. New York: Oxford University Press, 1999.
Ringo, Miriam, ed. *Nobody Said It Better!* Chicago: Rand McNally, 1980.
Roberts, Kate Louise, ed. *Hoyt's New Encyclopedia of Practical Quotations*. New York: Funk & Wagnall, 1922.

Rosenman, Samuel I., ed. *Public Papers and Addresses of Franklin Delano Roosevelt.* New York: Random House, 1938.

Safire, William. "Impeachment Election," *New York Times,* September 21, 1998.

———, ed. *Lend Me Your Ears.* New York: W. W. Norton, 1997.

Schlesinger, Arthur M. *Robert Kennedy and His Times.* New York: Ballantine Books, 1978.

Seldes, George, ed. *The Great Quotations: A Unique Anthology of the Wisdom of the Centuries.* New York: Citadel Press, 1993.

———. *The Great Thoughts.* New York: Ballantine Books, 1985.

Settel, T. S. *The Wisdom of JFK.* New York: Dutton, 1965.

Shaara, Michael. *The Killer Angels: A Novel.* New York: McKay, 1974.

Shafritz, Jay M., ed. *Words on War.* Englewood Cliffs, N.J.: Prentice-Hall, 1990.

Sherrin, Ned, ed. *The Oxford Dictionary of Humorous Quotations.* Oxford: Oxford University Press, 1995.

Simon, James, ed. *A Dictionary of Economic Quotations.* Totowa, N.J.: Roman and Allanheld, 1984.

Simpson, James B., ed. *Contemporary Quotations.* New York: Thomas Y. Crowell, 1964.

Smallwood, James M. *Will Rogers' Weekly Articles.* Vol. 1. Tulsa: Oklahoma State University Press, 1982.

Sorenson, Theodore C., ed. *Let the Word Go Forth: The Speeches, Statements, and Writings of John F. Kennedy.* New York: Delacorte Press, 1988.

Stevenson, Burton, ed. *The Home Book of Quotations.* New York: Dodd, Mead, 1967.

Swinton, William. *Campaigns of the Army of the Potomac: A Critical History of Operations in Virginia, Maryland, and Pennsylvania from the Commencement to the Close of the War, 1861–1865.* New York: Scribner's, 1882.

Theroux, Phyllis. *The Book of Eulogies.* New York: New Scribner Books, 1997.

Thomsett, Jean, and Michael Thomsett, eds. *Sex and Love Quotations.* Jefferson, N.C.: McFarland, 1995.

Thoreau, Henry David. *Thoreau.* Philadelphia: Courage Books, 1990.

Thucydides. *The History of the Peloponnesian War.* Boston: Everyman's Classic Library, 1995.

Titelman, Gregory, ed. *Random House Dictionary of Popular Proverbs and Sayings.* New York: Random House, 1996.

Tomlinson, Gerald, ed. *Treasury of Religious Quotations.* Englewood Cliffs, N.J.: Prentice-Hall, 1991.

Torrey, Bradford, and Francis H. Allen, eds. *The Journal of Henry D. Thoreau.* New York: Dover, 1962.

Torricelli, Robert, ed. *In Our Own Words.* New York: Kodansha International, 1999.

Tripp, Rhoda Thomas, ed. *The International Thesaurus of Quotations.* New York: Thomas Y. Crowell, 1970.

Tuchman, Barbara. *The Guns of August.* New York: Macmillan, 1962.

———. *The Proud Tower.* New York: Macmillan, 1966.

United Auto Workers Education Dept. *Quotations of Social Significance to Union Leaders.* Publication No. 415. Detroit: UAW Education Dept., 1968.

Van Ekeren, Glenn, ed. *The Speaker's Sourcebook: Quotes, Stories, and Anecdotes for Every Occasion.* Englewood Cliffs, N.J.: Prentice-Hall, 1988.

Viereck, George Sylvester. "What Life Means to Einstein." *Saturday Evening Post,* October 26, 1929.

Ward La Cour, Donna, ed. *Artists in Quotation: A Dictionary of the Creative Thoughts of Printers, Sculptors, Designers, Writers, Educators, and Others.* Jefferson, N.C.: McFarland, 1989.

Washington, James, ed. *I Have a Dream: Writings and Speeches That Changed the World.* New York: HarperCollins, 1992.

Watson, Burton, ed. *The Basic Writings of Mo Tzu, Xun Tzu, and Han Fei Tzu.* New York: Columbia University Press, 1967.
Waxman, Meyer. *A History of Jewish Literature.* New York: T. Yoseloff, 1960.
Weeks, Albert, ed. *Brassey's Soviet and Communist Quotations.* Washington, D.C.: Pergamon-Brassey's International Defense Publishers, 1987.
Whipple, Edwin P., ed. *The Speeches and Orations of Daniel Webster.* Boston: Little, Brown, 1910.
Will, George. *Restoration: Congress, Term Limits, and the Recovery of Deliberative Democracy.* New York: Maxwell Macmillan International, 1992.
Wills, Gary. *Certain Trumpets.* New York: Simon and Schuster, 1984.
The Wisdom of Karl Marx. New York: Philosophical Library Inc., 1967.
Wit and Wisdom of Woodrow Wilson. Garden City, N.Y.: Doubleday, 1916.
Woods, Ralph L., ed. *The Modern Handbook of Humor.* New York: McGraw-Hill, 1967.

Web Sources

Art-bin.com
Busboy.sped.ukans.edu/~adams.sciquot.html
Cid.unomaha.edu/~wwwengl/translations/kara12.htm
Historyplace.com
Home.earthlink.net/~ccblack/shabazz/quotes.html
Home.sol.no/~ewing/
Jrobell.home.mindspring.com/
Latin.about.com/education/latin/library/blphrase.htm
Life.bio.sunysb.edu/ee/msr/quotes1.html#Art
Members.tripod.com/nclassen/winston_churchil_quotes.htm
Members.tripod.com/~Smiley963/sports.html
Members.tripod.com/~TechBabe
Philosophy.about.com/education/philosophy/library/blqdescartes.htm
Priovich.com/quotes.html
Quotes.sterlingtechnology.com
Ubernova.home.mondspring.com/quotes.htm
www.afriprov.org
www.al-islam.org/masoom/sayings/prophsayings.html
www.anet-chi.com/~jdonohue.texts.latquots.txt
www.athenet.net/~jlindsay/SkepticQuotes.html
www.biography.com
www.chambers.com.au
www.chesco.com
www.corsinet.com/braincandy/proverb.html
www.cp-tel.net/miller/BilLee/quotes/
www.cyber-nation.com/victory/quotations/
www.duke.edu/~thp2/camus/quotes
www.fn.net/~degood/poor.html
www.geocities.com/Athens/academy/9054/Proverbs.html
www.geocities.com/Athens/Delphi/4360
www.geocities.com/Athens/Oracle/6517

www.geocities.com/heartland/valley/1561/quotes.html
www.geocities.com/SoHo/1469/flwquote.html
www.geocities.com/SoHo/Museum/2852/poetqtsf.html
www.geocities.com/SouthBeach/3797/quotes.html
www.geocities.com/~spanoudi/quote–09c.html
www.greatbasin.net/~doconnor/index.html
www.gunnar.cc.com
www.haven.boston.ma/us/~julian/mquotes.html
www.hickoksports.com/quotes/
www.highpower.net/alexis.htm
www.igc.org/laborquotes/attitude.html
www.inforum.net
www.io.com/~rga/saying193.html
www.itsnet.com/home/getlost/quotes.html
www.jimpoz.com/quotes/aging.html
www.jokes2go.com
www.kinderart.com/
www.metro2000.net/~stabbot/trquotes.htm
www.miracosta.cc.ca.us
www.obs-us.com/obs/english/books/Mandela/Mandela.html
www.parks.sonoma.net/JLStory.html
www.pcisys.net/~ronkrob/frost.html
www.premiumhealth.com
www.quotablequotes.com
www.quotelady.com
www.quoteland.com
www.sba.oakland/faculty/vansell/
www.sharedparenting.net/thoughts_to_ponder/quotes.html
www.skygod.com/quotes
www.stripe.colorado.edu/%7Ejudy/einstein.html
www.tamu.edu/scom/pres/speeches/
www.theodoreroosevelt.org/life/quotes.htm
www.undergrad.math.uwaterloo.ca/~cewood/quoteclassic.htm
www.us-israel.org
www.whitehouse.gov/WH/glimpse/presidents/html/ww28.html
www.winstonchurchill.org/captain.htm
www.wsu.edu:8080/~wldciv/world_civ_reader_2/african_proverbs.html

Permissions

Maya Angelou, excerpt from *I Know Why the Caged Bird Sings,* 1970, reprinted by permission of Random House, Inc.

W. H. Auden, "Epitaph for an Unknown Soldier," from *The Shield of Achilles,* 1954.

Bob Dylan, excerpt from "Subterranean Homesick Blues," 1965.

T. S. Eliot, excerpt from *Murder in the Cathedral,* 1935, reprinted by kind permission of Valerie Eliot.

Robert Frost, excerpts from "Forgive, O Lord," and "Precaution," in *The Poetry of Robert Frost,* edited by Edward Connery Lathem. Copyright © 1936, 1962 by Robert Frost, 1964 by Lesley Frost Ballantine, 1969 by Henry Holt and Co. Reprinted by permission of Henry Holt and Company, LLC.

Alan Jay Lerner, lyrics, and Frederick Loewe, music, excerpt from "Camelot," © 1960 by Alan Jay Lerner and Frederick Loewe (renewed) Chappell & Co. (ASCAP), publisher and owner of allied rights throughout the world. All rights reserved. Reprinted by permission of Warner Bros. Publications, Miami, Florida 33014.

Archibald MacLeish, excerpt from "The Young Dead Soldiers," *Collected Poems 1917–1982.* Copyright © 1985 by the estate of Archibald MacLeish. Reprinted by permission of Houghton Mifflin Company. All rights reserved.

Edna St. Vincent Millay, excerpt from "Childhood Is the Kingdom Where Nobody Dies," in *Collected Poems* (HarperCollins). Copyright © 1934, 1962 by Edna St. Vincent Millay and Norma Millay Ellis. All rights reserved. Reprinted by permission of Elizabeth Barnett, literary executor.

Joni Mitchell, excerpt from "Big Yellow Taxi," 1969, reprinted by permission of S. L. Feldman & Associates.

Ogden Nash's poems reprinted by kind permission of Linell Nash Smith and Isabel Nash Eberstadt.

Theodore Roethke, excerpt from "I'm Here," in *Collected Poems of Theodore Roethke.* Copyright © 1956 by Theodore Roethke. All rights reserved. Reprinted by permission of Doubleday, a division of Random House, Inc.

Dylan Thomas, excerpts from "And Death Shall Have No Dominion," "Do Not Go Gentle into That Good Night," and "A Refusal to Mourn the Death, by Fire, of a Child in London," in *The Poems of Dylan Thomas.* Copyright © 1943 by New Directions Publishing Corp. Reprinted by permission of New Directions Publishing Group.

Index

About the Editor

Robert G. Torricelli began his work in Washington, D.C., during the Carter Administration as Assistant Counsel to Vice President Walter Mondale. In 1982 he was elected to the House of Representatives for the Ninety-eighth Congress and for each successive Congress until 1996, when the people of New Jersey elected him to the United States Senate. He is the editor of *In Our Own Words: Extraordinary Speeches of the American Century* (1999).